IMAGES
of America

MICHIGAN HUMANE SOCIETY

ANIMAL WELFARE IN DETROIT

1877–2002

This book is dedicated to all who fought the battle before us,
those who fight the fight today, and those who will carry on after we have gone.

IMAGES of America

MICHIGAN HUMANE SOCIETY

ANIMAL WELFARE IN DETROIT

1877–2002

Michigan Humane Society

ARCADIA PUBLISHING

ISBN 978-0-7385-2028-5

Published by Arcadia Publishing
Charleston, South Carolina

Printed in the United States of America

Library of Congress Catalog Card Number: 2002111550

For all general information contact Arcadia Publishing at:
Telephone 843-853-2070
Fax 843-853-0044
E-Mail sales@arcadiapublishing.com
For customer service and orders:
Toll-Free 1-888-313-2665

Visit us on the Internet at www.arcadiapublishing.com

CONTENTS

ACKNOWLEDGMENTS

This book was a joint effort between the Michigan Humane Society and the Burton Historical Collection of the Detroit Public Library. The archives of the Michigan Humane Society provided much of the foundation for this book, but we would not have been able to fill in the gaps, so to speak, without the direct assistance of David Poremba, Manager of the Burton Historical Collection, and the research and writing of Marta Diffen, Michigan Humane Society.

INTRODUCTION

Pressure for humane treatment of animals was building as early as 1789 in England. Known as "the hell of dumb animals," England was notorious for barbaric amusements such as dog fighting and horse beating. In 1822, Britain's Parliament passed several ordinances concerned with "prevention of cruel and improper treatment of cattle," "overloading of cab horses," and "stopping organized animal fighting." In addition, in 1824, the Royal Society for the Prevention of Cruelty to Animals (RSPCA) was founded to aid the fight for humane treatment for animals.

The humane movement in the United States was gaining ground in the 1870s through the efforts of a dedicated few who sought social change. Very early policy makers, officers, and board members of Detroit humane organizations were prominent, influential Detroiters such as Mr. and Mrs. Abner Larned, Henry Ford, Frank Cody, Mrs. Henry Ledyard, Mr. and Mrs. John Dodge, and Thomas W. Palmer, who went on to become a U.S. Senator. More important than who these people were was what they were doing. These Detroiters had a vision that set the course for today's Michigan Humane Society. Early Society efforts focused on improving conditions for and treatment of working horses, protecting women and children from abuse and neglect, and teaching humane values.

The first documented animal cruelty investigator was Arthur C. Curtis. During over 40 years of service to the Michigan Humane Society, Curtis often explained why he had taken the job: "When I was a cavalryman in the Boer War, both I and my horse were wounded behind enemy lines in Africa. But in spite of his pain, that horse carried me back to my own lines. He later had to be killed. I've never forgotten that and since have had a very deep feeling for animals." Curtis volunteered his services until funds were available to pay him. He was named Humane Marshall by then Governor Woodbridge N. Ferris. As Humane Marshall, Curtis had statewide authority to investigate charges of animal cruelty.

During the early years, most animal cruelty work involved the protection of horses and prosecution of abusers. With up to 68,000 horses toiling daily in the city, neglect, overwork, cruel treatment, and even intentional brutality to a rival's horses were common occurrences. In 1923, a teamster was arrested for starving a borrowed horse. The animal gnawed a hole in one side of the stable to feed its hunger. In January 1925, 17 horses were discovered in a tent, one frozen to death and the others suffering from extreme cold. A Detroit Judge fined the owner $100 or 60 days in jail. Prosecuted under a felony statute, a teamster was charged with "malicious injury to personal property" after tearing out a horse's tongue when its owner refused to give the man work.

Since 1925, Humane Education has been an organized, primary program of the Michigan Humane Society. In 1927, over 190 Detroit schools were visited. Junior Humane Society memberships were made available for school-age children in 1931, and several members of the Junior Humane Society raised funds for the Society through concerts, plays, and candy sales. By 1945, humane education was in effect in all Detroit Public Schools.

Originally established in the heart of the city, the Michigan Humane Society has expanded with Detroit. With shelter and clinic locations in the outlying communities of Rochester Hills and Westland, as well as the original permanent shelter facility set up in Detroit in 1931, Michigan Humane Society serves communities in two of Michigan's most populated counties. Providing shelter and protection through two world wars, suburban development, and civil disturbances, the Michigan Humane Society has proven to be an invaluable organization to the area.

Today, the Michigan Humane Society is a statewide leader in animal protection and is one of the largest sheltering societies in the United States, providing services for over 80,000 homeless, injured, and needy animals each year. In addition to rescuing, sheltering, and placing domestic animals, the Society operates rescue, rehabilitation, and relocation programs for wild and exotic animals. It also operates three full-service veterinary clinics, a Humane Education program, and a Pet Education Center and behavior help line.

Throughout its 125 years of service to the animals and people of Detroit, the Society's mission has never faltered:

The mission of the Michigan Humane Society is to provide the highest quality service and compassion to the animals entrusted to our care, to measurably reduce companion animal overpopulation, and take a leadership role in promoting humane values for the benefit of all animals.

One

Horse Power and the Building of Detroit

1870–1900

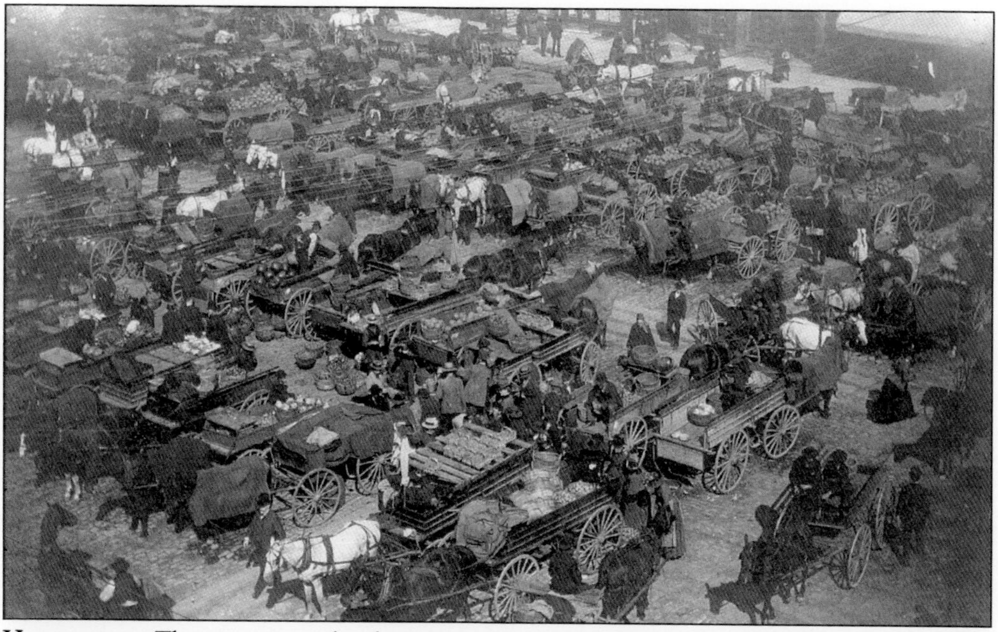

Horsepower. The primary mode of transportation for people in the city of Detroit during the 19th century was the horse, as this scene on market day in downtown Detroit attests. Upwards of 60,000 horses toiled daily in and around the city, mostly hauling materials from one point to another. By the end of the Civil War, the humane movement was gaining ground in the United States, supported by influential businessmen and fueled by anti-slavery sentiment and other social movements of the century. (Courtesy of Burton Historical Collection.)

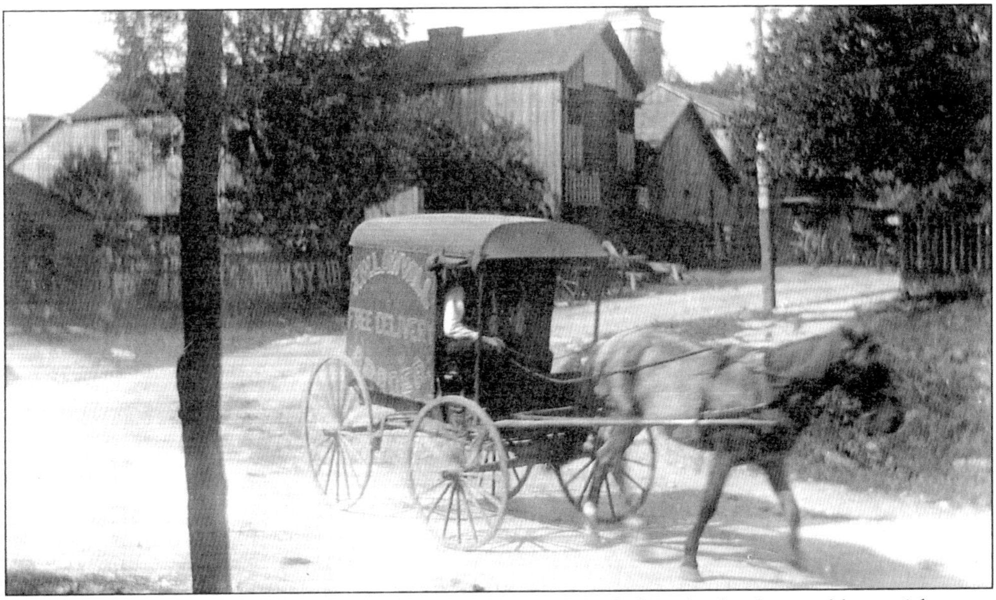

Free Delivery. The residential areas of the city resounded with the beat of horses' hooves as drivers made their rounds of deliveries—in this case, a free home grocery delivery by J.W. Hawhill company. While a well-cared-for animal was essential to the success of any business at the turn of the century, not all drivers of horses provided for their animals nor treated them well. (Courtesy of Burton Historical Collection.)

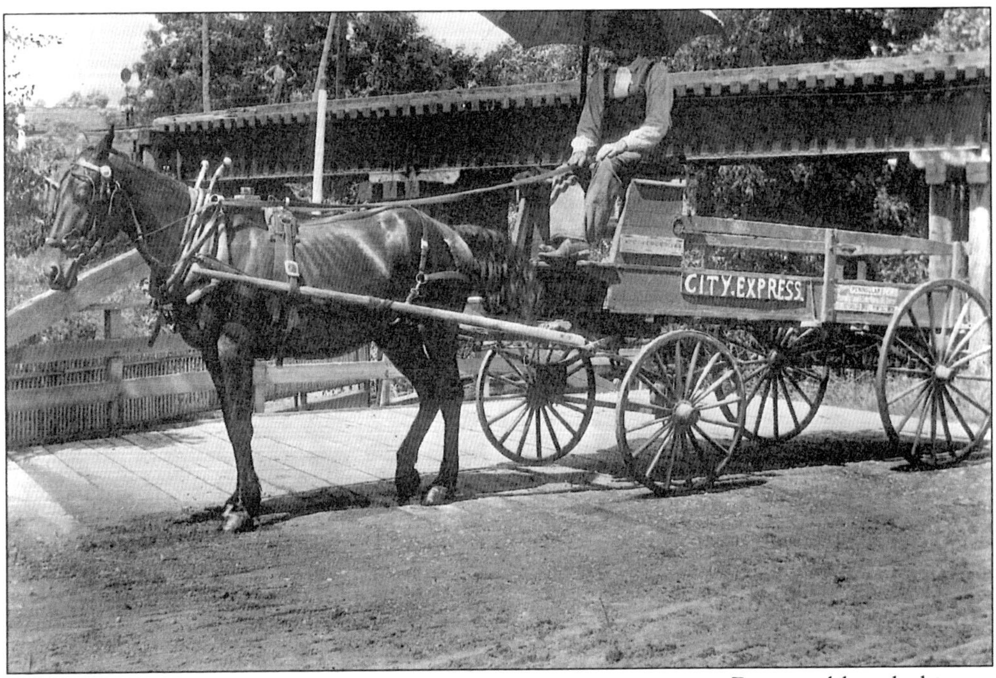

Have Horse, Will Haul. There were five major express companies in Detroit, although this one may have been an independent contractor judging from the variety of advertising on his wagon and umbrella. Ready to perform light to medium hauling, this horse appears to be properly cared for and properly outfitted for the job at hand. (Courtesy of Burton Historical Collection.)

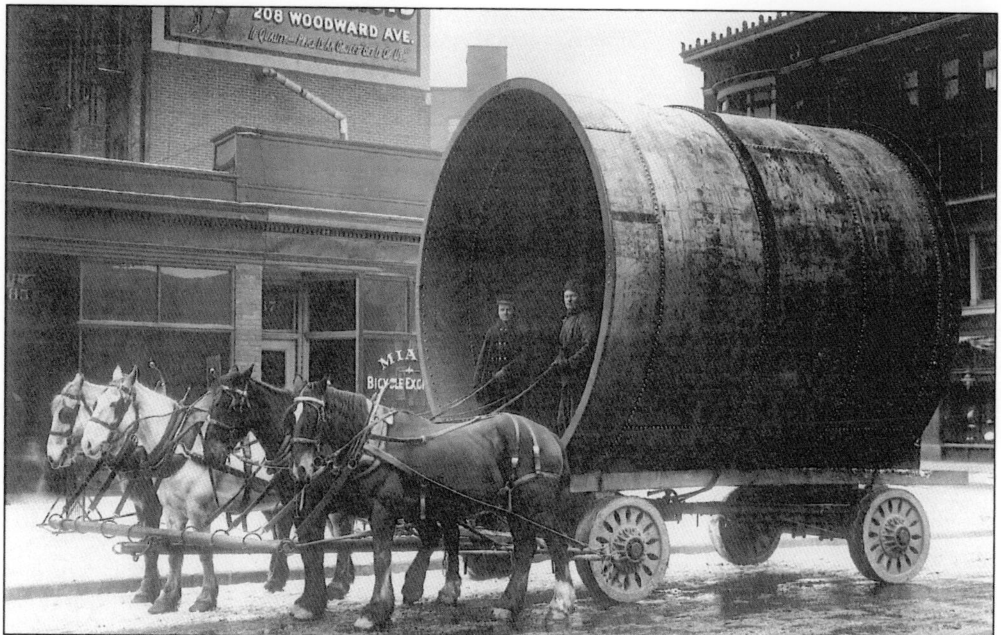

HEAVY HAULING. Two matched sets of horses haul a gigantic pipe along Woodward Avenue. Destined to become part of the city's sewer system, the pipe was produced by the Russell Wheel and Foundry Company, located at the foot of Walker Street on the Detroit River. (Courtesy of Burton Historical Collection.)

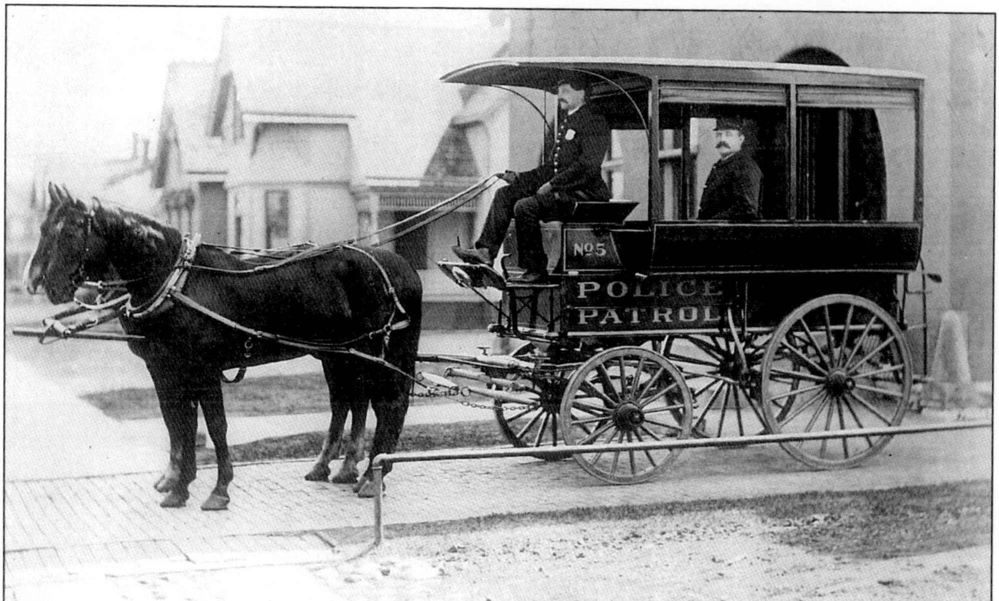

POLICE HORSES. Two matched black horses drew the Detroit Police Departments' paddy wagon, known as the Black Maria. Detroit was the second city in the United States to use a vehicle to transport its officers to their beats and prisoners to jail. The horses used by the police department were cared for appropriately. (Courtesy of Burton Historical Collection.)

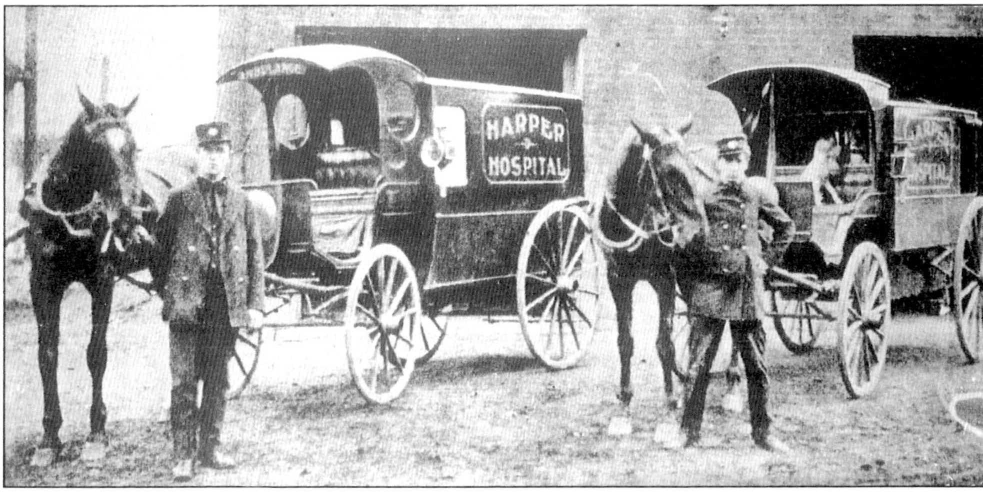

Harper Hospital Ambulances. Horses performed many services that had direct impact on citizens of the city. These horses performed services essential to the health and well-being of Detroiters by hauling the ambulances of Harper Hospital, opened in 1866. This emergency crew also had a dog mascot, seated in the ambulance on the right. (Courtesy of Burton Historical Collection.)

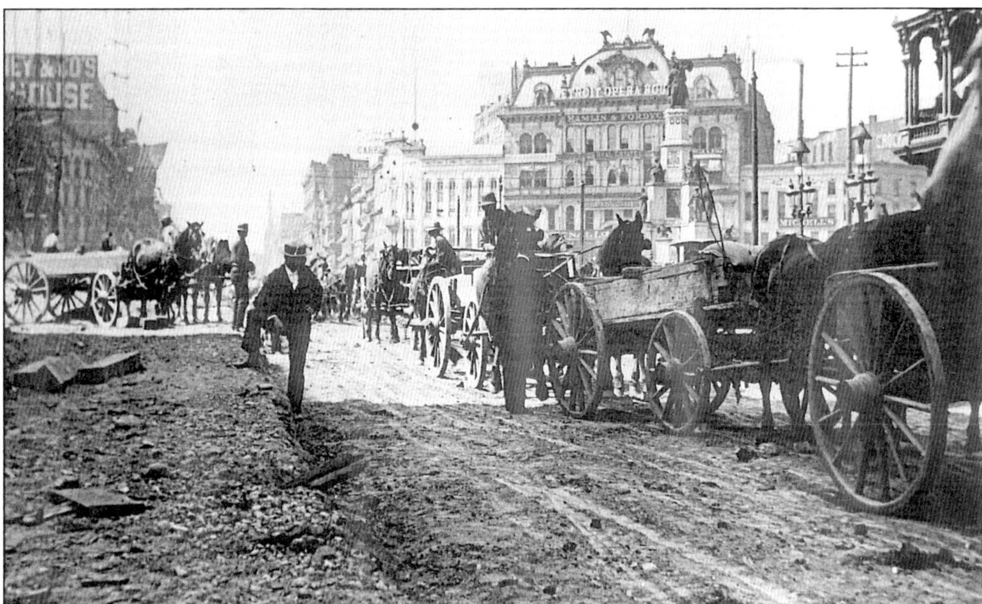

Woodward Avenue Near The Campus Martius. Teamsters and their teams line the east side of Woodward Avenue waiting to haul earth and rock from, as well as bring paving material to, this improvement project in the heart of the city. Hauling heavy loads was a burden to the draft horse and horses were often overloaded and overworked by teamsters trying to meet the needs of a growing community. (Courtesy of Burton Historical Collection.)

HUDSON'S DELIVERY SERVICE. J.L. Hudson opened his second store on Woodward Avenue in 1887 and used horses to deliver goods to customers around the city. His prospering department store business relied on providing dependable service to his customers, and provisions for delivery horses was crucial to his business development. (Courtesy of Burton Historical Collection.)

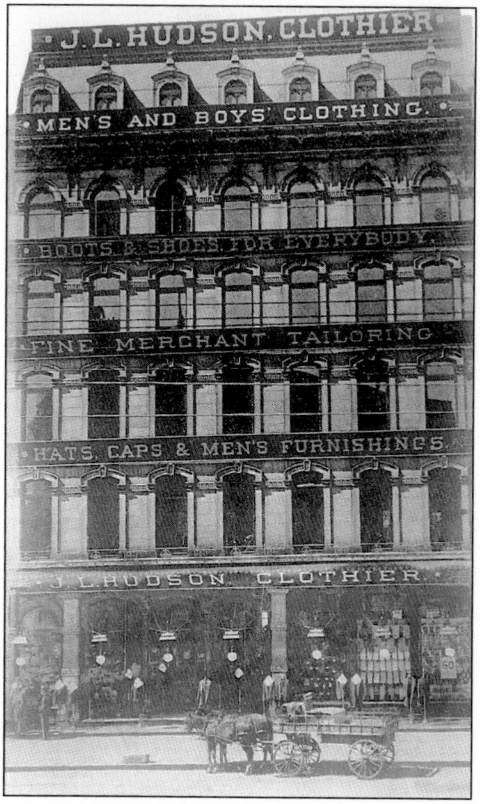

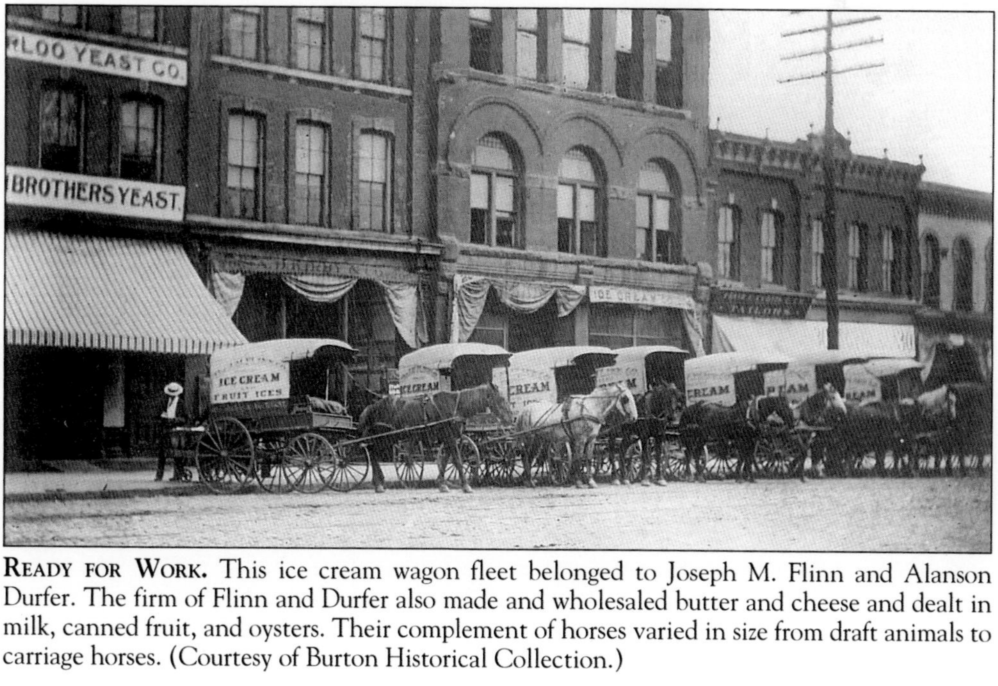

READY FOR WORK. This ice cream wagon fleet belonged to Joseph M. Flinn and Alanson Durfer. The firm of Flinn and Durfer also made and wholesaled butter and cheese and dealt in milk, canned fruit, and oysters. Their complement of horses varied in size from draft animals to carriage horses. (Courtesy of Burton Historical Collection.)

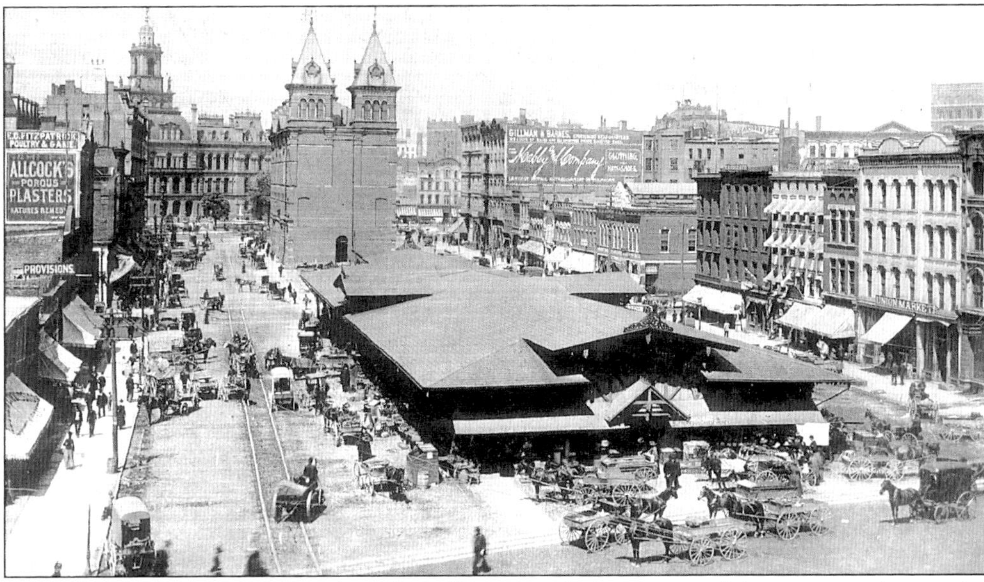

DETROIT'S CENTRAL MARKET. The value of horses to the prosperity of the city is evident in this photograph of Central Market taken during the 1880s. There are horses hitched to farmers' wagons, delivery wagons, teamsters' wagons, and carriages poised to haul goods and people wherever they need to go. (Courtesy of Burton Historical Collection.)

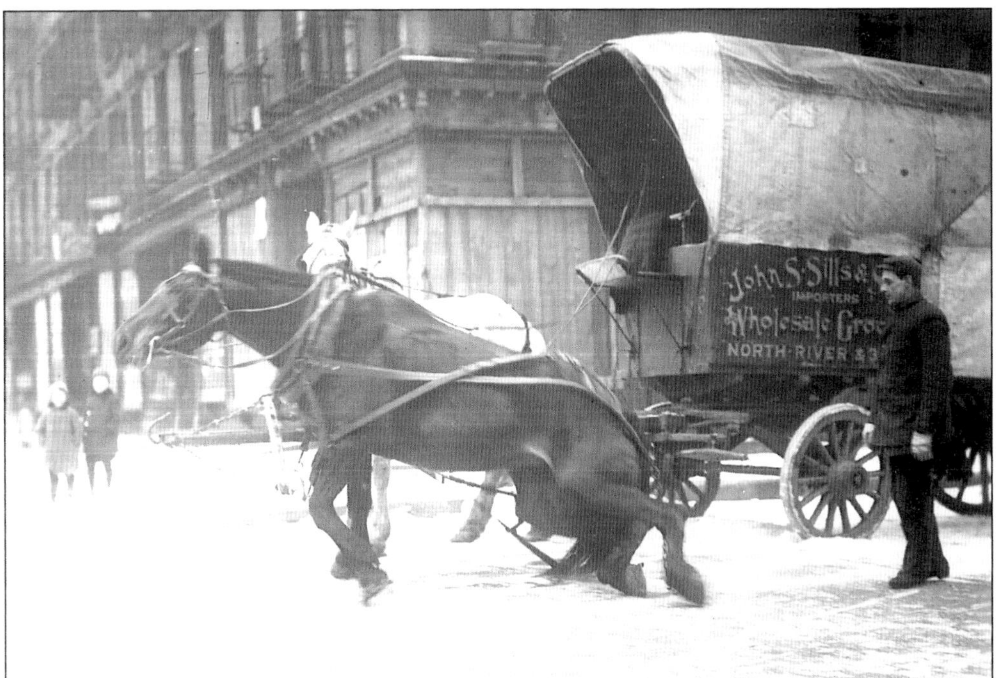

UNSAFE FOOTING ON SLICK WINTER STREETS. Sometimes, Mother Nature had a hand in the conditions endured by the workhorses in the city. Horses worked in all kinds of conditions and weather, often at great risk and peril. Slippery and icy streets often made for treacherous working conditions as illustrated by this photograph. (Courtesy of Burton Historical Collection.)

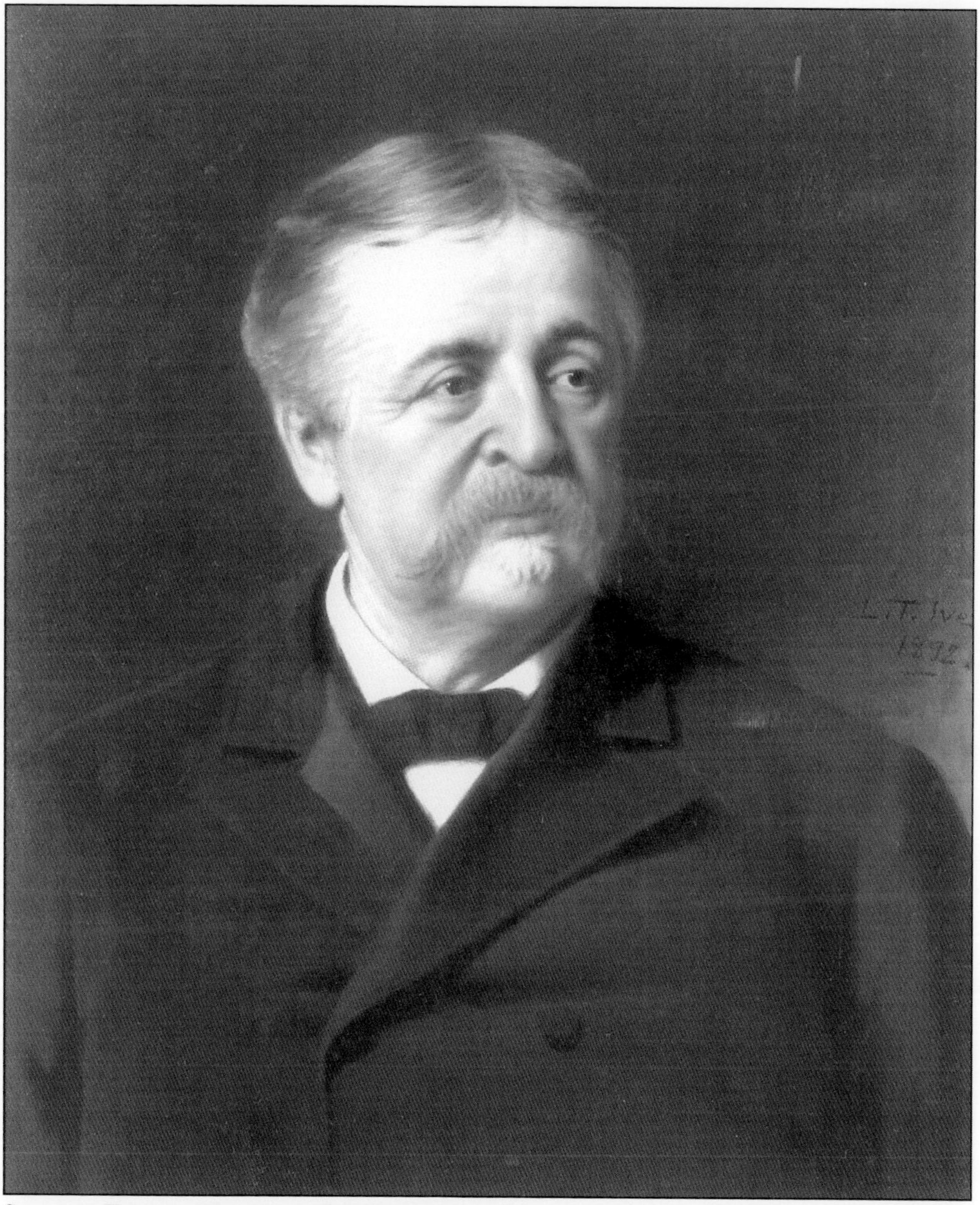

SENATOR THOMAS WITHERALL PALMER. Born in Detroit on January 25, 1830, and a resident of the city, Palmer attended public school in Detroit and graduated from the University of Michigan. He engaged himself in the lumbering business and amassed great wealth. In 1877, Palmer was instrumental in the formation of the Michigan Society for the Prevention of Cruelty to Animals, and he served as the Society's first president until he was elected to the United States Senate in 1883. The Michigan Society for the Prevention of Cruelty to Animals was the first organization of its kind in Michigan and was the predecessor of today's Michigan Humane Society. The need for animal protection in the city of Detroit was centered almost entirely on the workhorses and the MSPCA was a strong advocate for anti-cruelty laws. It was modeled after the American Society for the Prevention of Cruelty to Animals, founded in New York in 1866 by wealthy American businessman Henry Bergh. (Courtesy of Burton Historical Collection.)

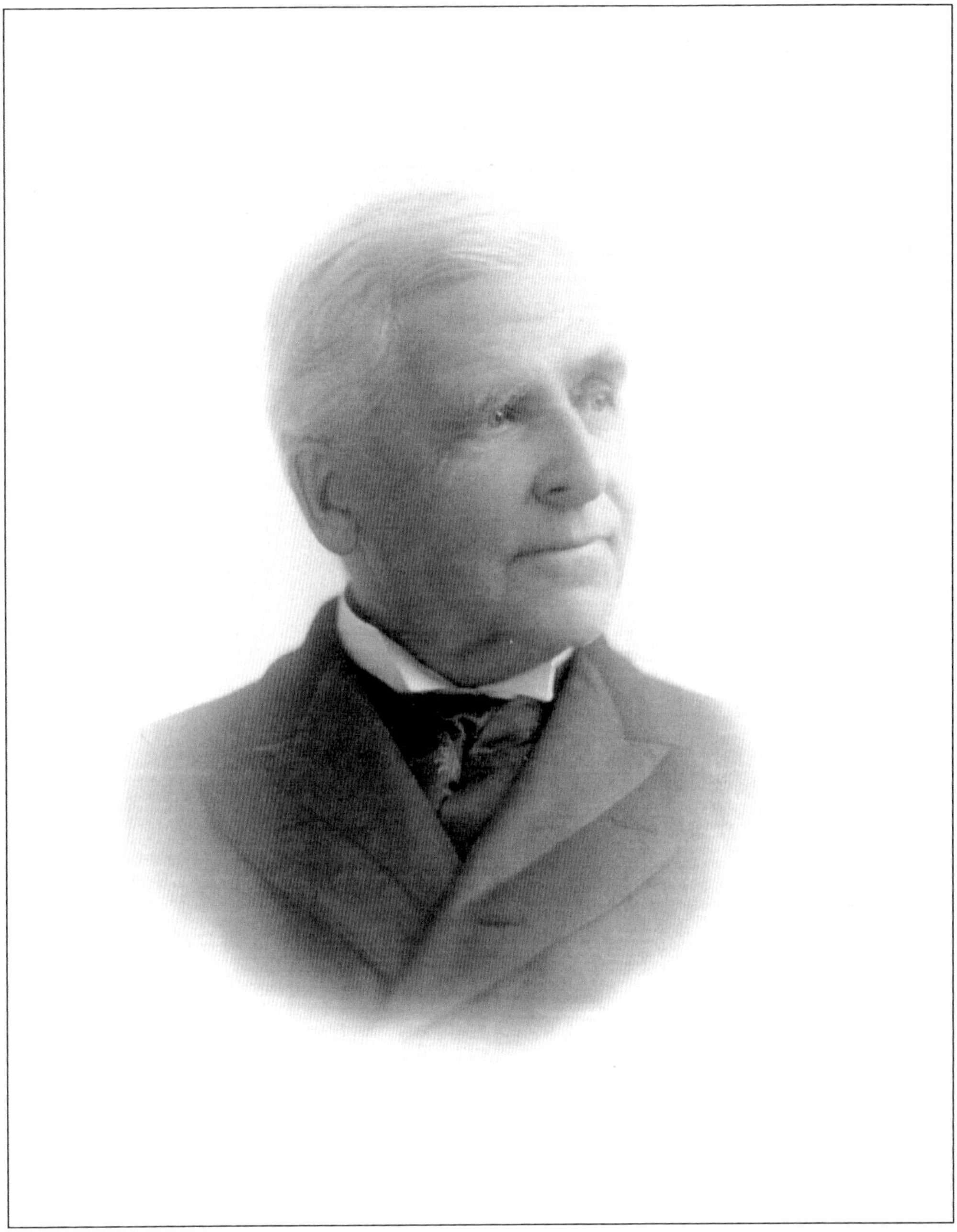

ALEXANDER LEWIS. Mayor of Detroit in 1876 and 1877, Alexander Lewis was born in Sandwich, Ontario, Canada. Lewis came to Detroit in 1837 and worked in a general store for $4 a month. In 1842, he formed his own freight and commission company, and in 1862, he opened a flour and grain business, from which he gained considerable wealth. His long association with draft animals in his various business ventures made him an able spokesman for the Michigan Society for the Prevention of Cruelty to Animals. Upon formation of the Society in 1877, Lewis served as vice president to Thomas W. Palmer. The two began laying the foundation for the animal protection movement in Detroit and garnered support from the citizens of the city as well as other influential Detroiters. (Courtesy of Burton Historical Collection.)

LAFAYETTE AVENUE. The Abstract Building on Lafayette Avenue, just west of Michigan Avenue, was the site of the first meeting of the Michigan Society for the Prevention of Cruelty to Animals. The Burton Title and Abstract Company maintained the first floor while other rooms on the upper floors were let out. (Courtesy of Burton Historical Collection.)

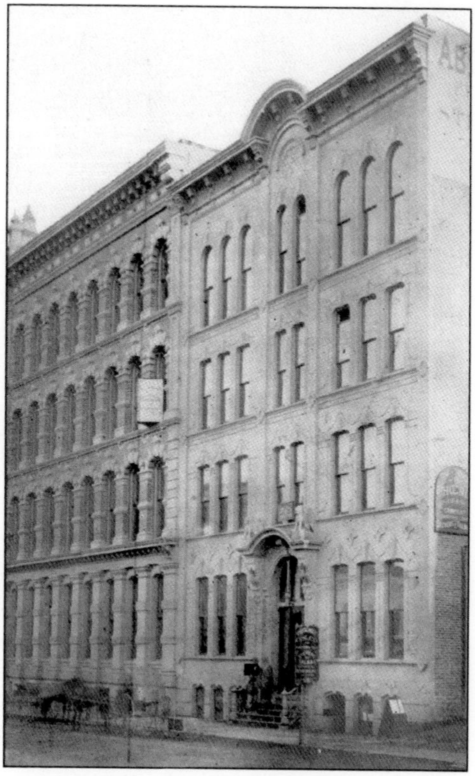

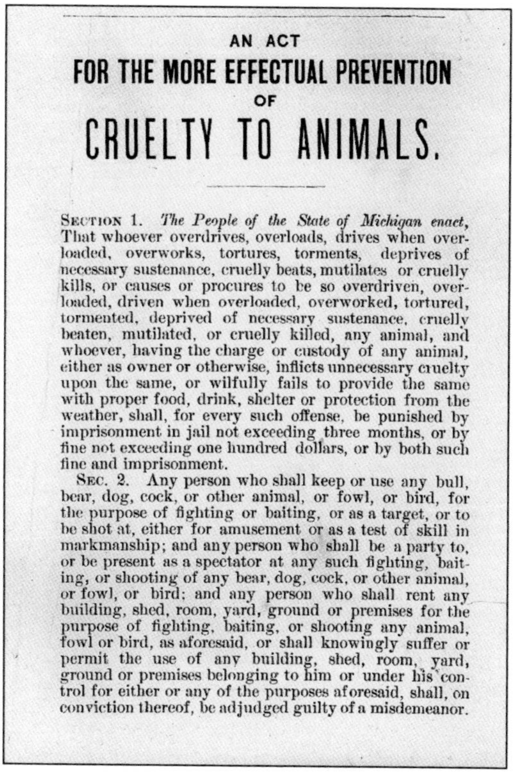

AN ACT

FOR THE MORE EFFECTUAL PREVENTION

OF

CRUELTY TO ANIMALS.

SECTION 1. *The People of the State of Michigan enact,* That whoever overdrives, overloads, drives when overloaded, overworks, tortures, torments, deprives of necessary sustenance, cruelly beats, mutilates or cruelly kills, or causes or procures to be so overdriven, overloaded, driven when overloaded, overworked, tortured, tormented, deprived of necessary sustenance, cruelly beaten, mutilated, or cruelly killed, any animal, and whoever, having the charge or custody of any animal, either as owner or otherwise, inflicts unnecessary cruelty upon the same, or wilfully fails to provide the same with proper food, drink, shelter or protection from the weather, shall, for every such offense, be punished by imprisonment in jail not exceeding three months, or by fine not exceeding one hundred dollars, or by both such fine and imprisonment.

SEC. 2. Any person who shall keep or use any bull, bear, dog, cock, or other animal, or fowl, or bird, for the purpose of fighting or baiting, or as a target, or to be shot at, either for amusement or as a test of skill in marksmanship; and any person who shall be a party to, or be present as a spectator at any such fighting, baiting, or shooting of any bear, dog, cock, or other animal, or fowl, or bird; and any person who shall rent any building, shed, room, yard, ground or premises for the purpose of fighting, baiting, or shooting any animal, fowl or bird, as aforesaid, or shall knowingly suffer or permit the use of any building, shed, room, yard, ground or premises belonging to him or under his control for either or any of the purposes aforesaid, shall, on conviction thereof, be adjudged guilty of a misdemeanor.

IT'S THE LAW. Approved on April 25, 1877, "An Act for the More Effectual Prevention of Cruelty to Animals" replaced two earlier acts with much stronger language and punishment for offenders. It also allowed for properly recognized societies to designate one or more persons in each county to uncover and prosecute all cases of cruelty. (Courtesy of Burton Historical Collection.)

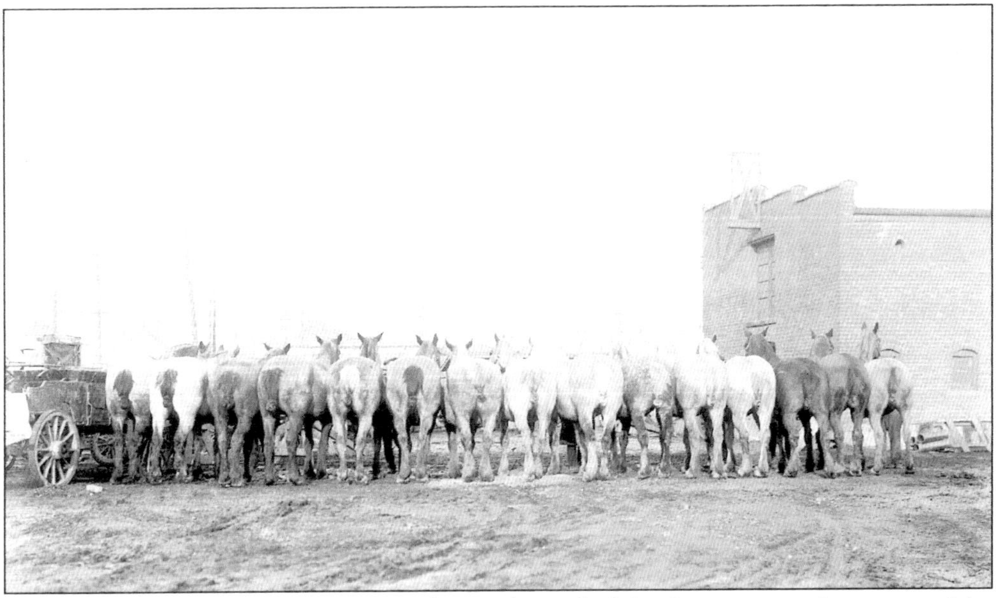

A Horses' Tale. Work horses get together at the end of the day to swap tales at one of the city's livery stables where they were fed, watered, and stabled for the night. The stables could be independently owned or part of a larger business operation. The conditions of some livery stables were deplorable, and the Michigan Humane Society was instrumental in the passing of an ordinance demanding improved conditions. (Courtesy of Burton Historical Collection.)

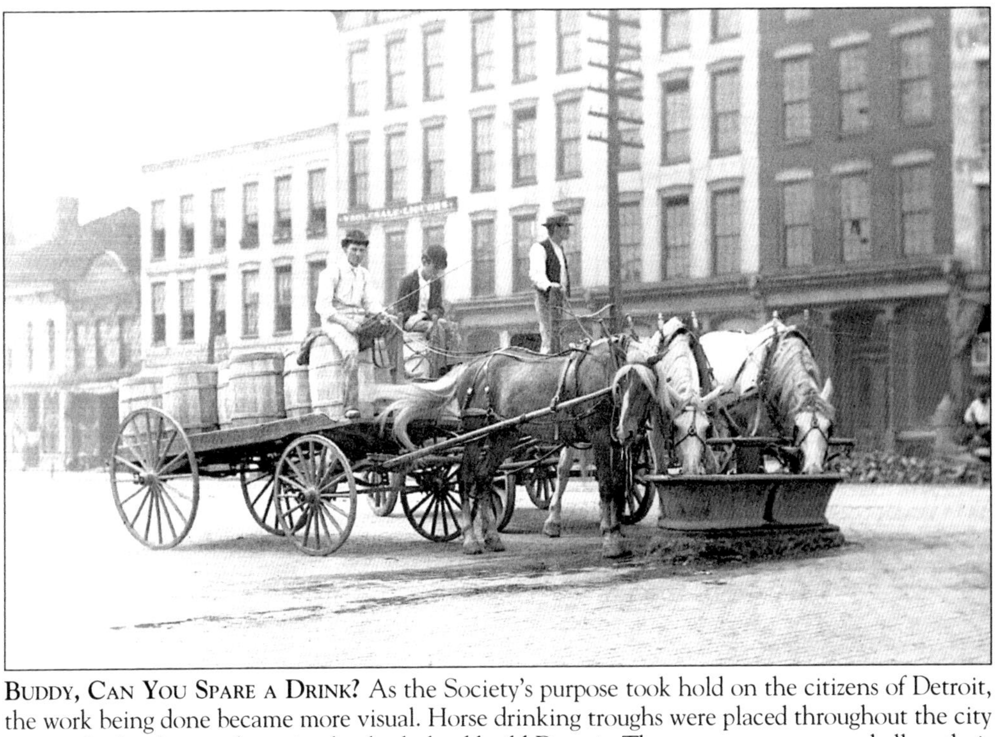

Buddy, Can You Spare a Drink? As the Society's purpose took hold on the citizens of Detroit, the work being done became more visual. Horse drinking troughs were placed throughout the city to ease the burden on the animals who helped build Detroit. These teamsters stop and allow their teams to drink sometime in the late 1880s. (Courtesy of Burton Historical Collection.)

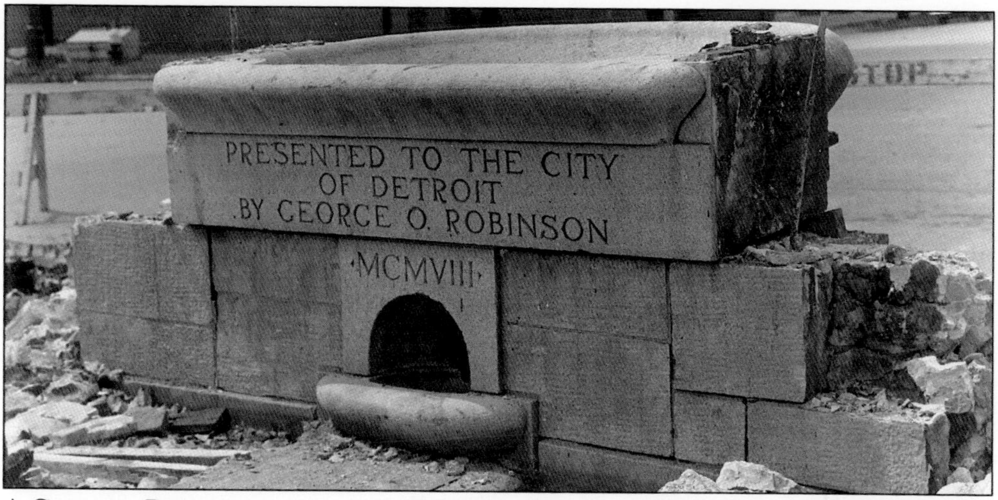

A GRATEFUL BENEFACTOR. George O. Robinson was a successful lawyer who also had dealings in the lumber and mining business. The lumber and mining business was dependent upon workhorses for its survival. In 1908, Robinson donated this trough to the city in honor of those hard-working animals. This trough was located on Cass Avenue near Ledyard and at the time of this photo, was being disassembled for storage. (Courtesy of Burton Historical Collection.)

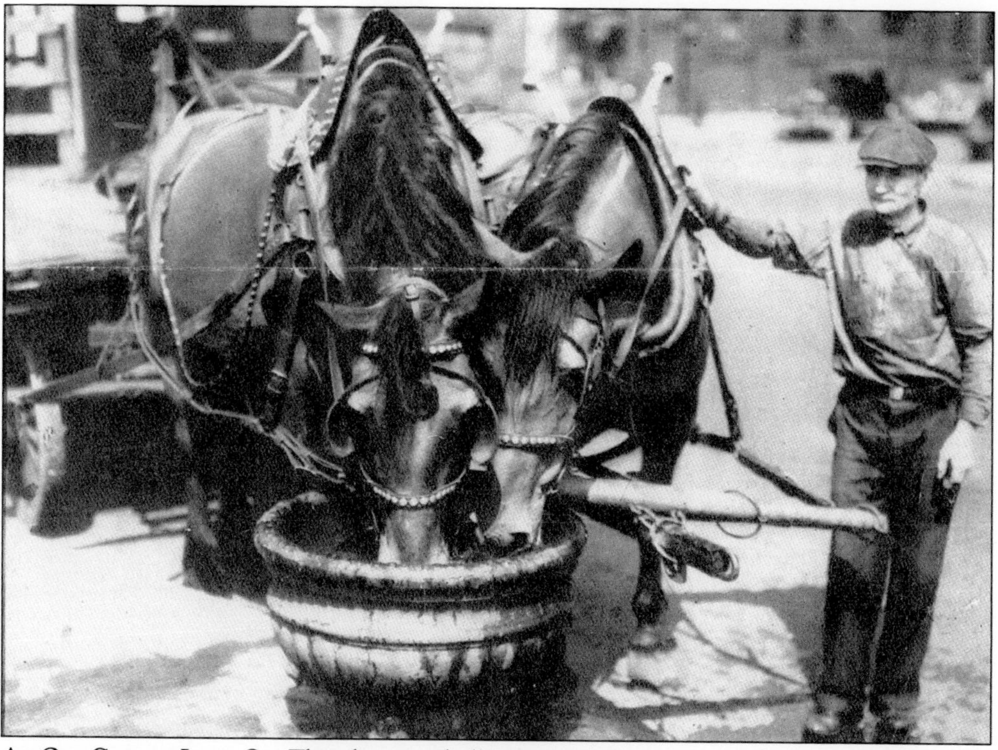

AN OLD CUSTOM LIVES ON. This photograph illustrates a different type of drinking trough supplied for the horses in the city. The driver, John Lindquist, was a driver for the same company for 42 years and still watered his horses at this trough at Eighth and Fort Streets. The Michigan Humane Society was a driving force behind placing drinking troughs in the city. As many as 106 troughs were constructed throughout the city by the 1920s. (Courtesy of *Detroit News*.)

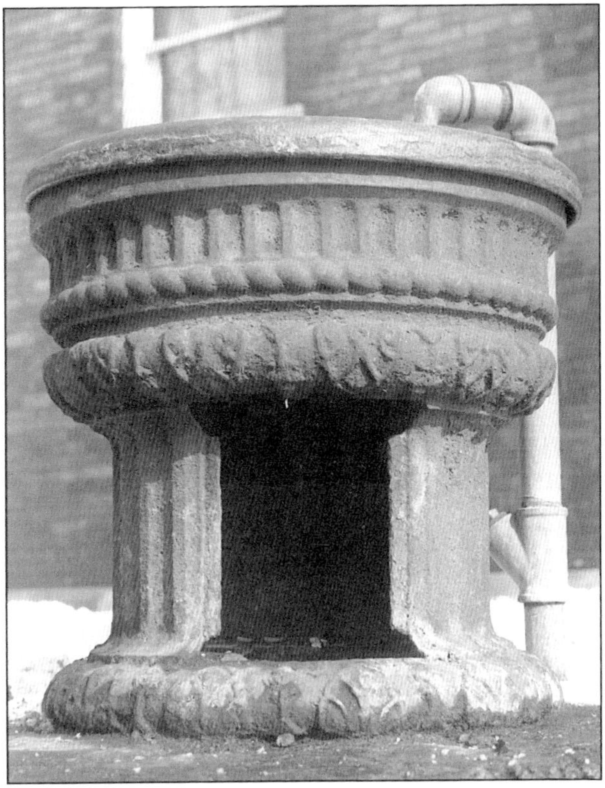

Sweet Fountain Treat. A close-up of this type of trough shows the efforts to ornament the piece while keeping it simple and functional. The pipes on the right side allowed the team driver to fill the bowl of the trough with fresh water and provide well-deserved refreshment. (Courtesy of Burton Historical Collection.)

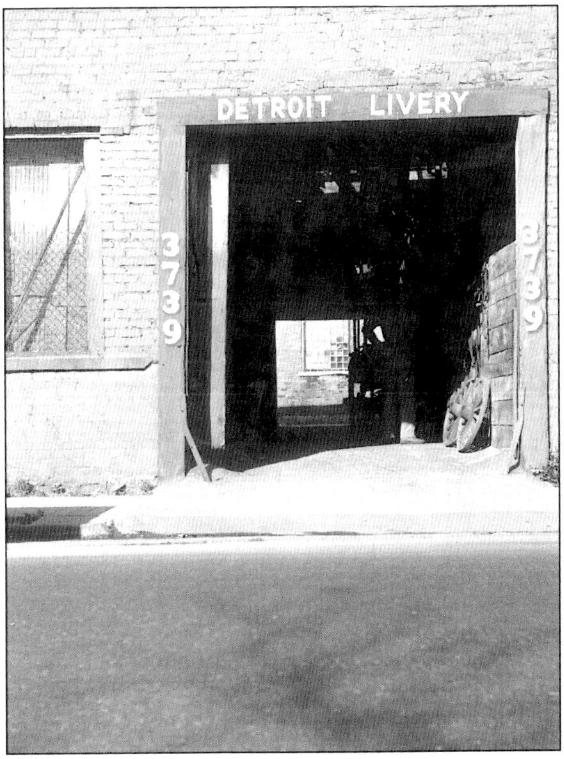

The Last Livery. The Detroit Livery was the last livery stable in the city that catered to the general public. It was located at 3739 Beaubien and had been in business for over 80 years. The Humane Marshall of the Michigan Humane Society frequently inspected livery stables and stockyards to check conditions. (Courtesy of Burton Historical Collection.)

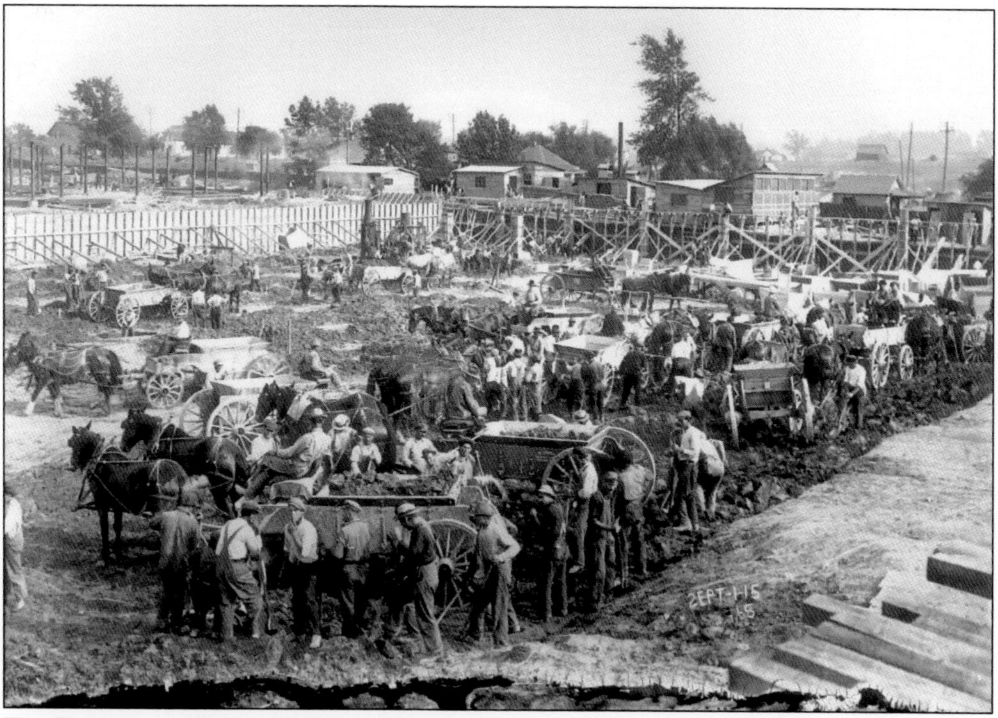

THE POWER THAT BUILT DETROIT. Construction sites such as this were located throughout the city during the late 1800s and early 1900s. This photo illustrates the methods used to transport building materials from the mills to the job site. It was not uncommon to see horses overloaded in the streets, and the Michigan Humane Society actively pursued those who mistreated their teams. (Courtesy of Burton Historical Collection.)

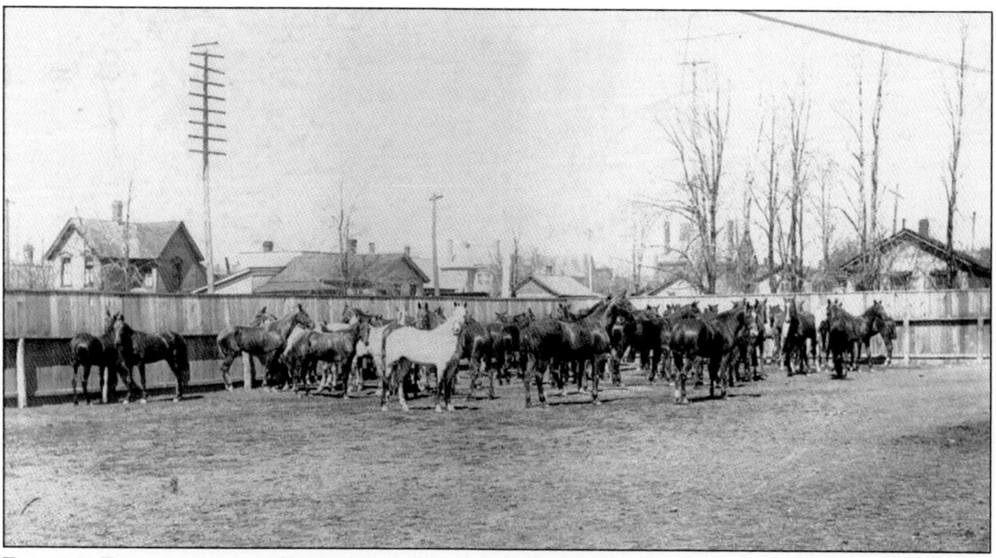

ROOM TO ROAM. A group of horses enjoy some rest and recuperation in an exercise paddock, which was often located next to the boarding stable. Time off work and out of harness was important to the well-being of the work horse. The paddocks and stables were regularly inspected by agents of the Michigan Humane Society. (Courtesy of Burton Historical Collection.)

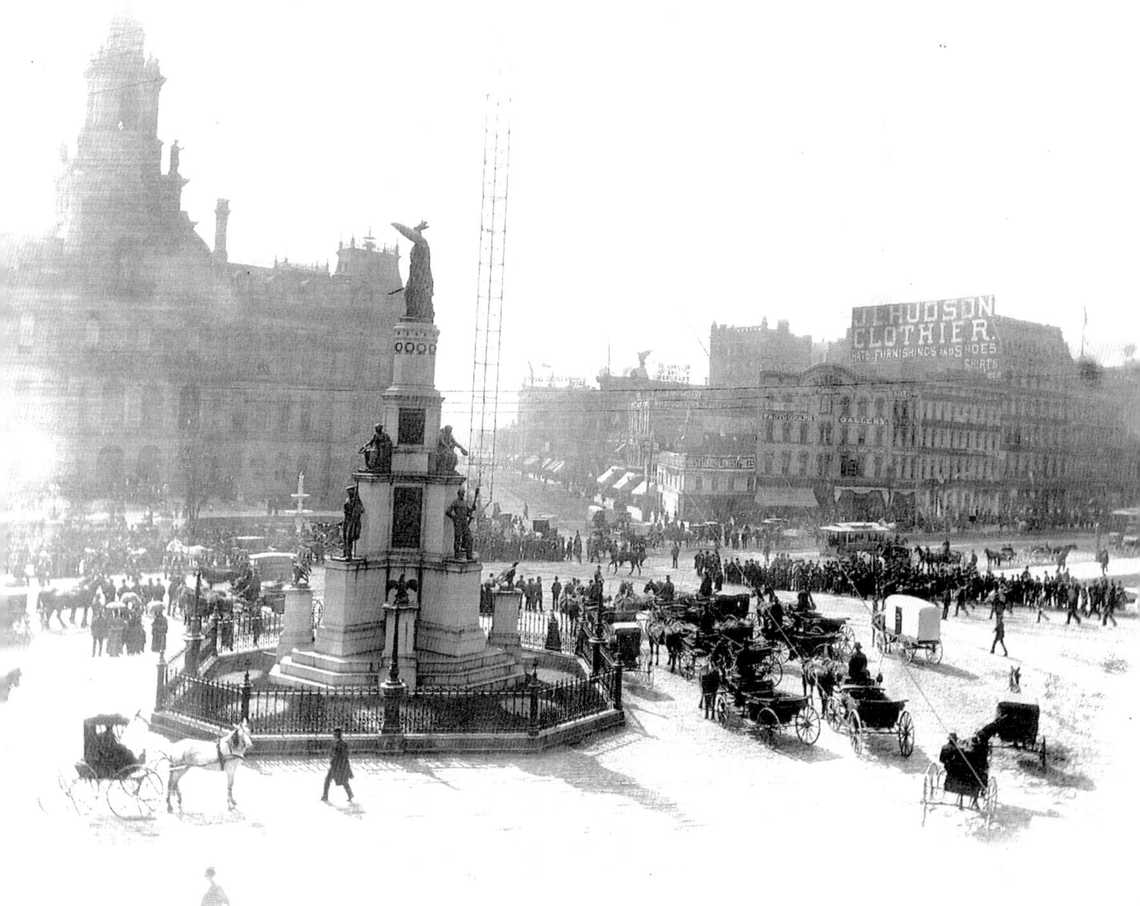

The Heart of the City. This panoramic view shows a crowded Campus Martius, which served the city for decades as a central meeting place, and illustrates the primary mode of transportation available to Detroiters—horse-drawn carts and carriages. The growth and prosperity of the city meant, among many other things, a proliferation of animals inhabiting the city, especially horses. Early records of the Society document hundreds of cases of cruelty to horses. Rivals would injure each other's horses in an effort to gain work for their own team. Some would prey upon those in dire need of a horse and sell an animal too old and worn out to be of any use to the buyer. Early attempts to pass a law making it illegal to do this failed in Michigan. When the Society wrote and backed a bill prohibiting this practice, it did, finally, become a law that Society agents stringently enforced. (Courtesy of Burton Historical Collection.)

Two

Establishing the Roots of Animal Welfare

1870–1900

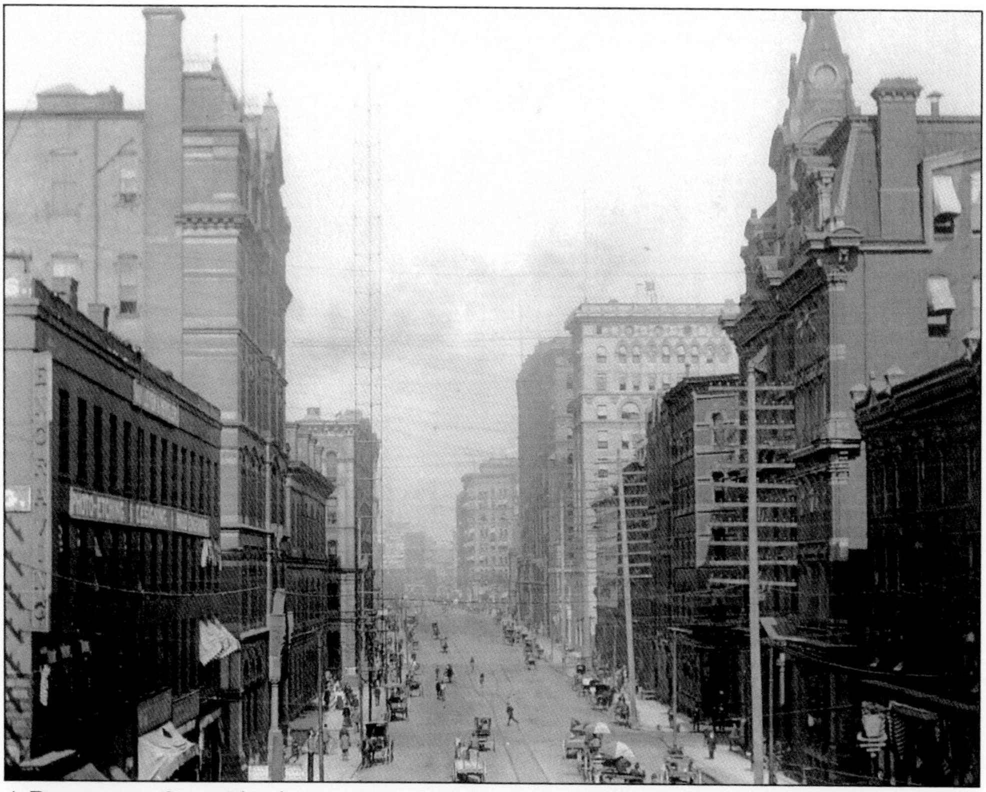

A Prospering City. The downtown area of the city has taken on a more recognizable shape by the end of the century, as this photograph of Griswold Street shows. The Buhl Block and the Telegraph Block still team with horse-drawn vehicles. The workhorses of Detroit would soon be forced to share the streets of Detroit with another kind of horsepower—the automobile. Workhorses toiled in the city as late as the 1960s and were the primary group of animals served by the early Michigan Humane Society. (Courtesy of Burton Historical Collection.)

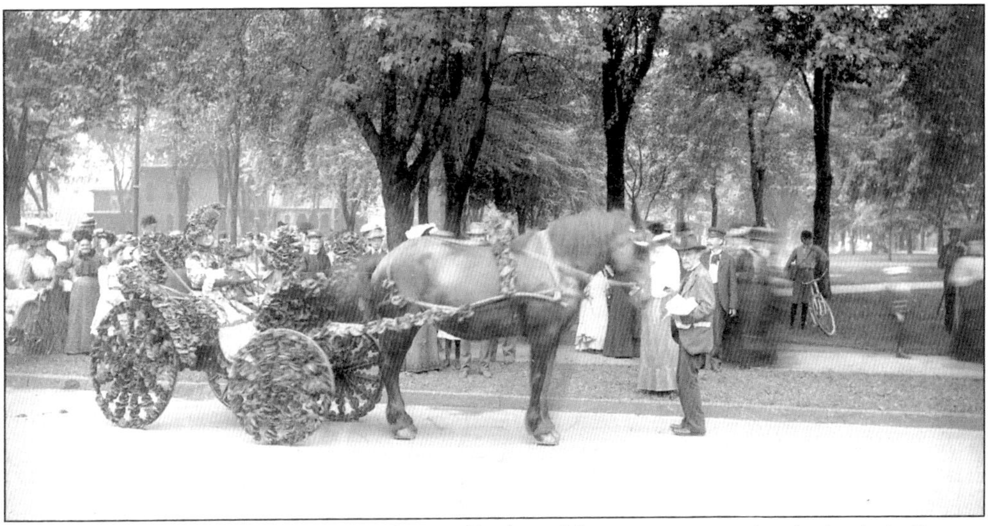

Everybody Loves a Parade. Mrs. George Beck and her son wait patiently in their flower-decorated carriage for the 1901 Bicentennial Parade to begin. The city of Detroit celebrated its 200th birthday with a huge parade to show itself off. Early supporters of anti-slavery and other social movements were the affluent and well-to-do. The early success of the Michigan Humane Society would depend on support from the more affluent Detroiters. (Courtesy of Burton Historical Collection.)

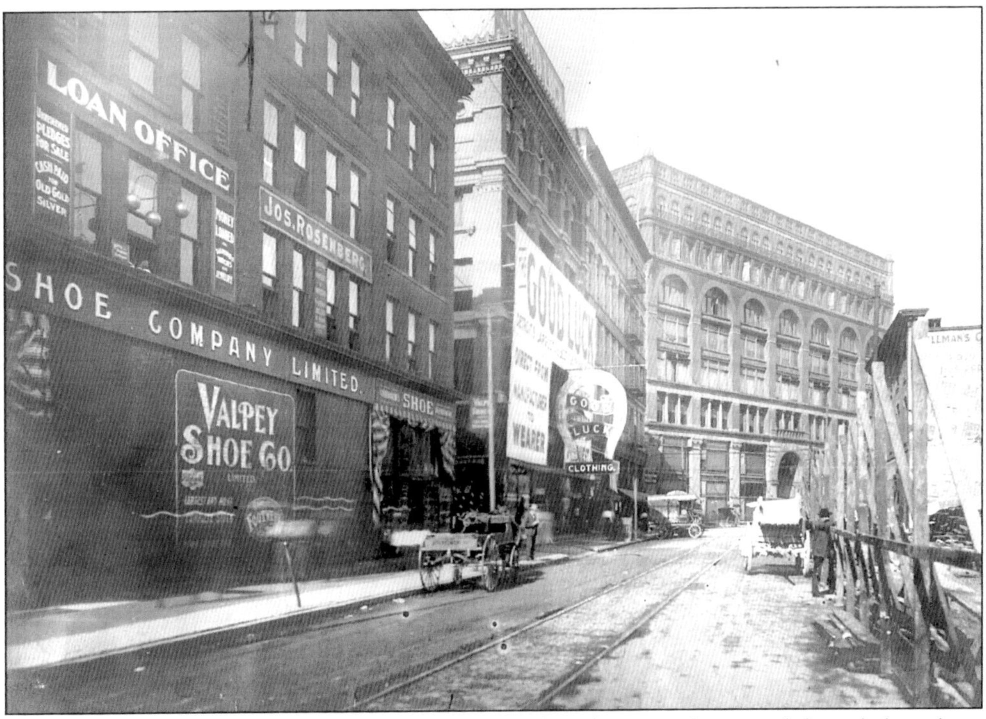

Good Luck Indeed. One of the earliest photos to show horses and automobiles side by side in the city is this one, taken around 1905 at Farmer Street, looking north from Monroe Avenue. Dilapidated conditions in some sections of the city were more hazardous to the well-being of horses than the introduction of the automobile. (Courtesy of Burton Historical Collection.)

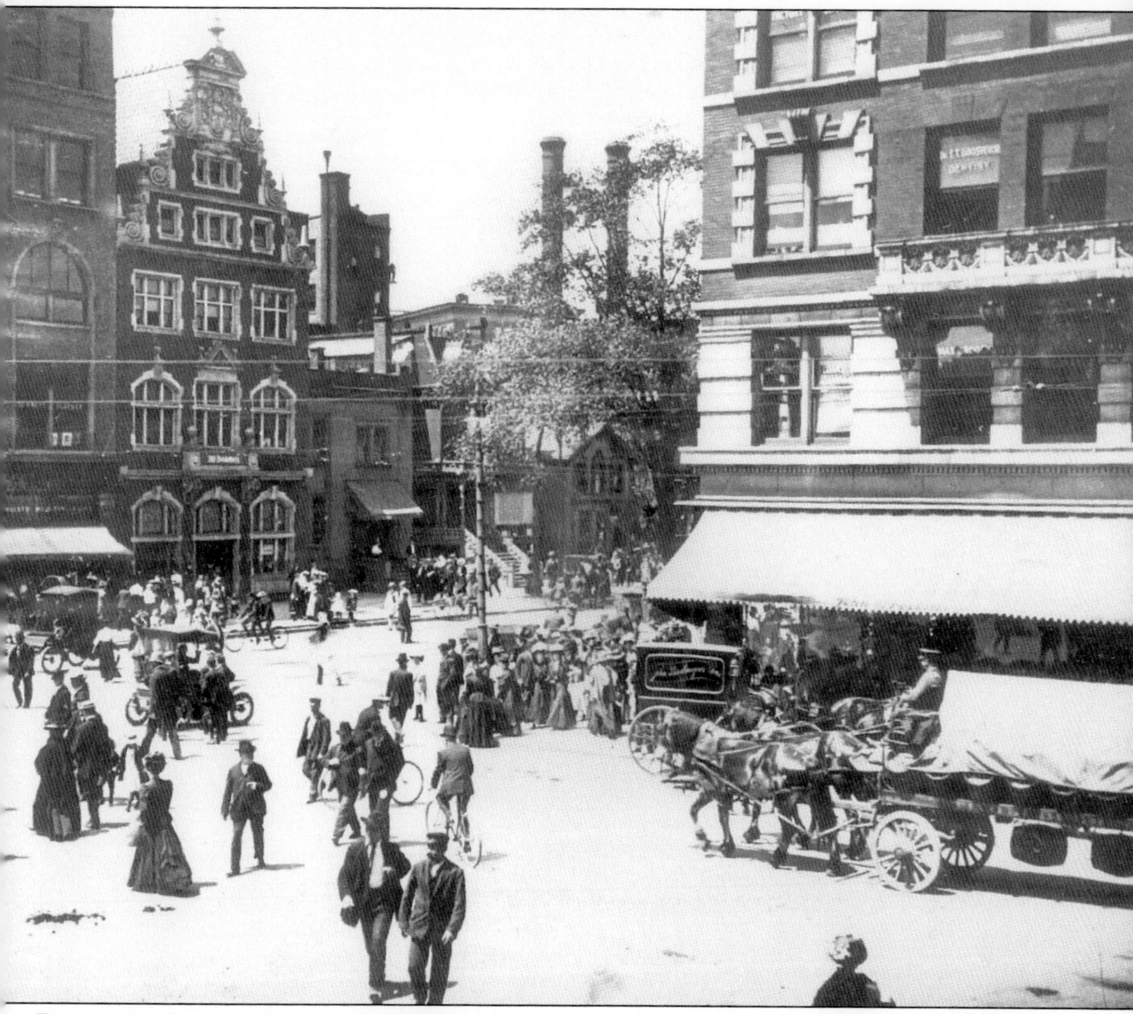

Detroit's Great White Way. The Motor City's own Broadway teems with people as the new Breitmeyer Block opens for business in 1906. Gasoline and electric powered autos are shown sharing the street with bicycles and horse-drawn wagons. In 1917, offices of the predecessor organization of the Michigan Humane Society were housed in Suite 405 of the Breitmeyer Building, at the corner of Broadway and Gratiot Avenue. (Courtesy of Burton Historical Collection.)

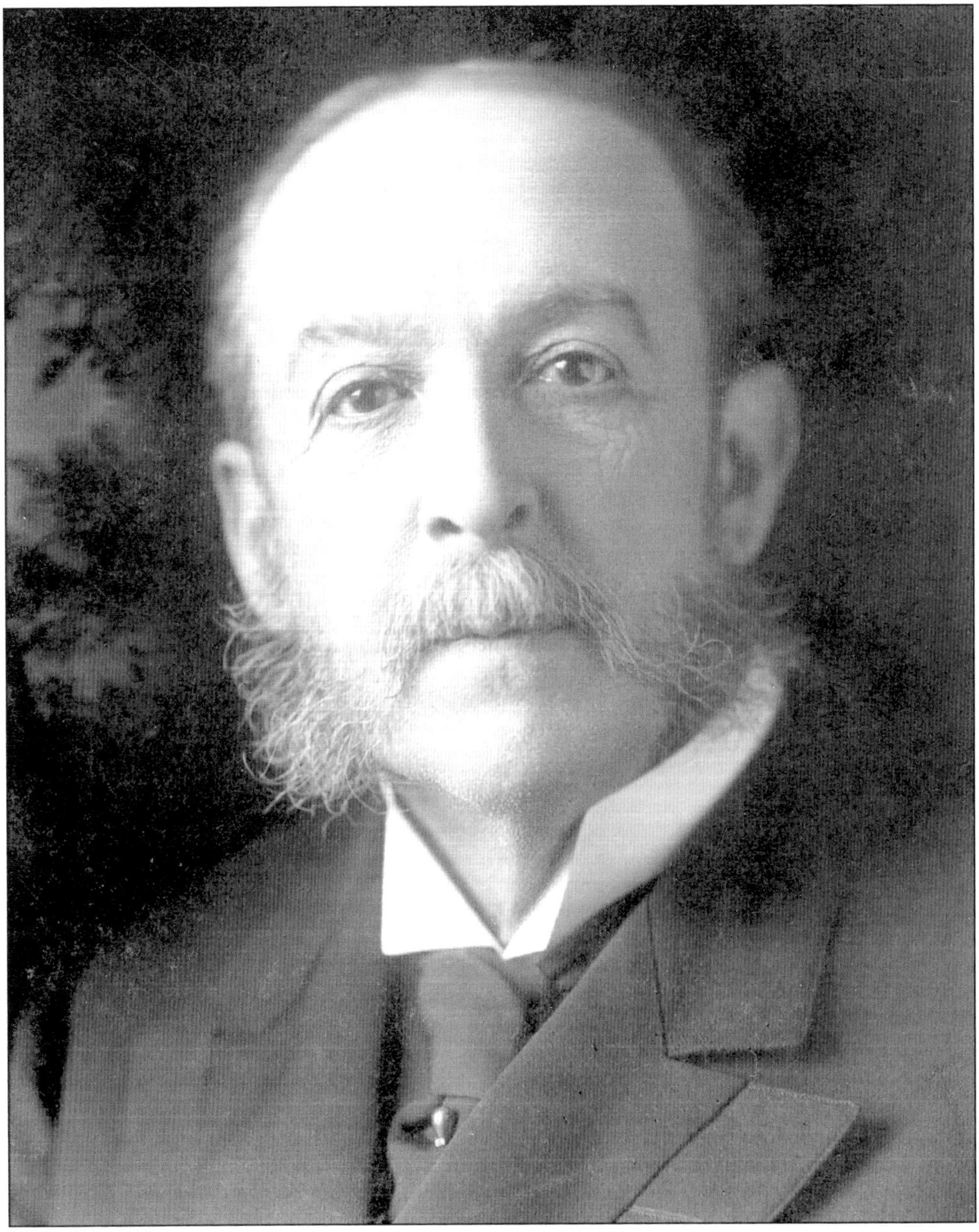

George Harrison Barbour. Born in Connecticut in 1846, Barbour came to Detroit in 1872 to work for the newly organized Michigan Stove Company. In 1886, he became vice president and general manager and developed the company into the largest stove manufacturing institution in the world. In 1913, he built the Michigan Copper and Brass Company and became its first president. Barbour was also socially-minded and served in an official capacity on many boards, including president of the Detroit City Council and president of the chamber of commerce. As is often the case with successful, energetic people, Barbour's devotion to social issues was just as admirable as his commitment to industrial and social growth for the Motor City. The humane movement was in its infancy in Detroit and Barbour served as Vice President of the early Michigan Humane Society for a number of years. (Courtesy of Burton Historical Collection.)

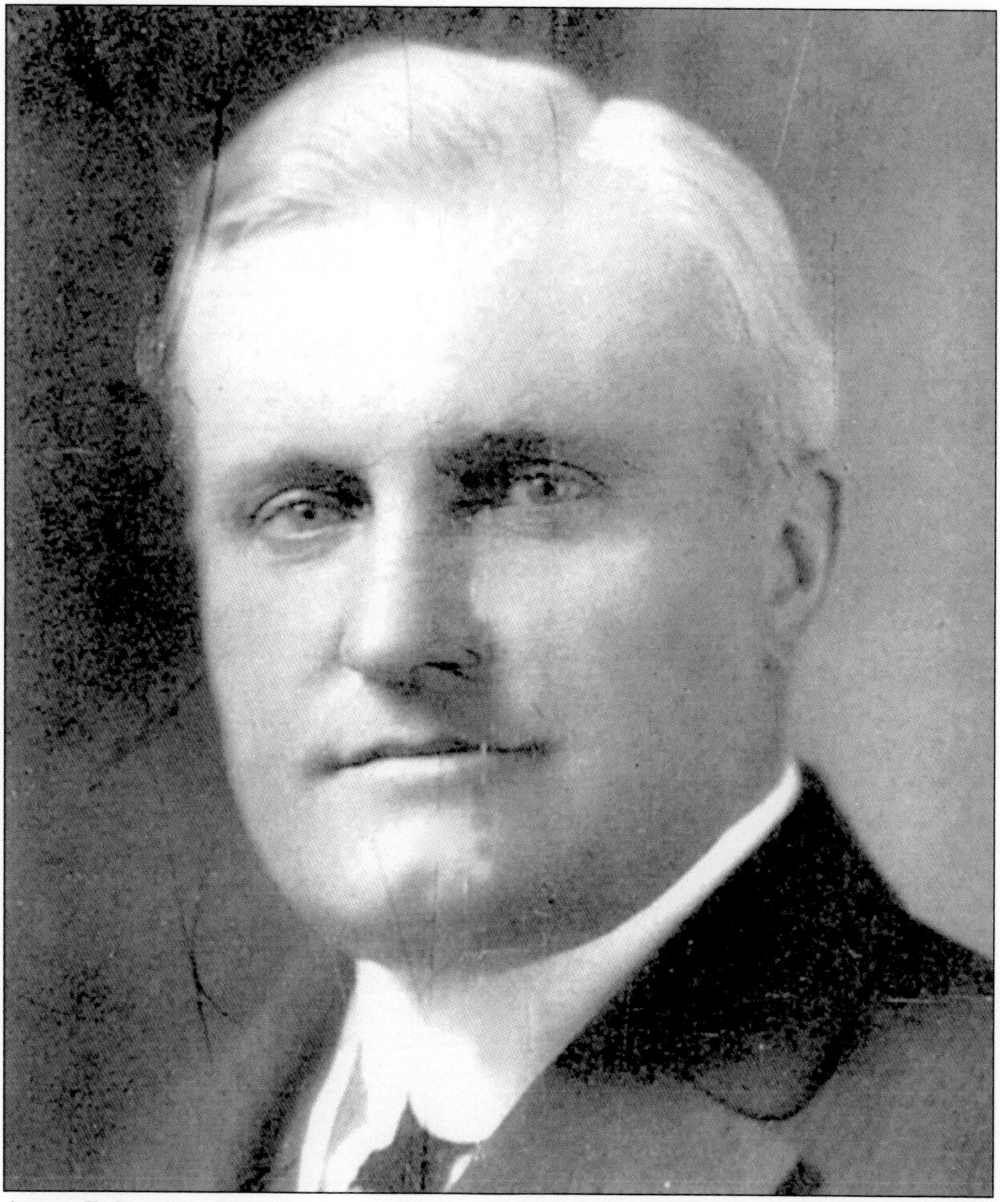

Abner E. Larned. Born in 1871 in Fenton, Michigan, Larned moved to Detroit in the early 1890s and worked for a small retail dry goods company that netted him $6 a week. By 1899, he had saved $1,000 and borrowed another $1,000 to join David Carter in the purchase of a small overall factory. By 1928, Larned, Carter and Co. was one of the largest manufacturers of workers clothing in the country. Both Larned and his wife were well known for their charitable involvement, and they served the Michigan Humane Society for over 20 years. Mr. Larned was a gifted speaker and often spoke at fundraising events for the Michigan Humane Society. In a 1935 newspaper interview about the work of the Michigan Humane Society, he is quoted as saying "All this is a work that no civilized city can afford to be without." Mrs. Larned was President of the early Animal Welfare Association that later incorporated to form Michigan Humane Society. Under her leadership, the Animal Welfare Association far surpassed other humane organizations of the early 1900s. (Courtesy of Burton Historical Collection.)

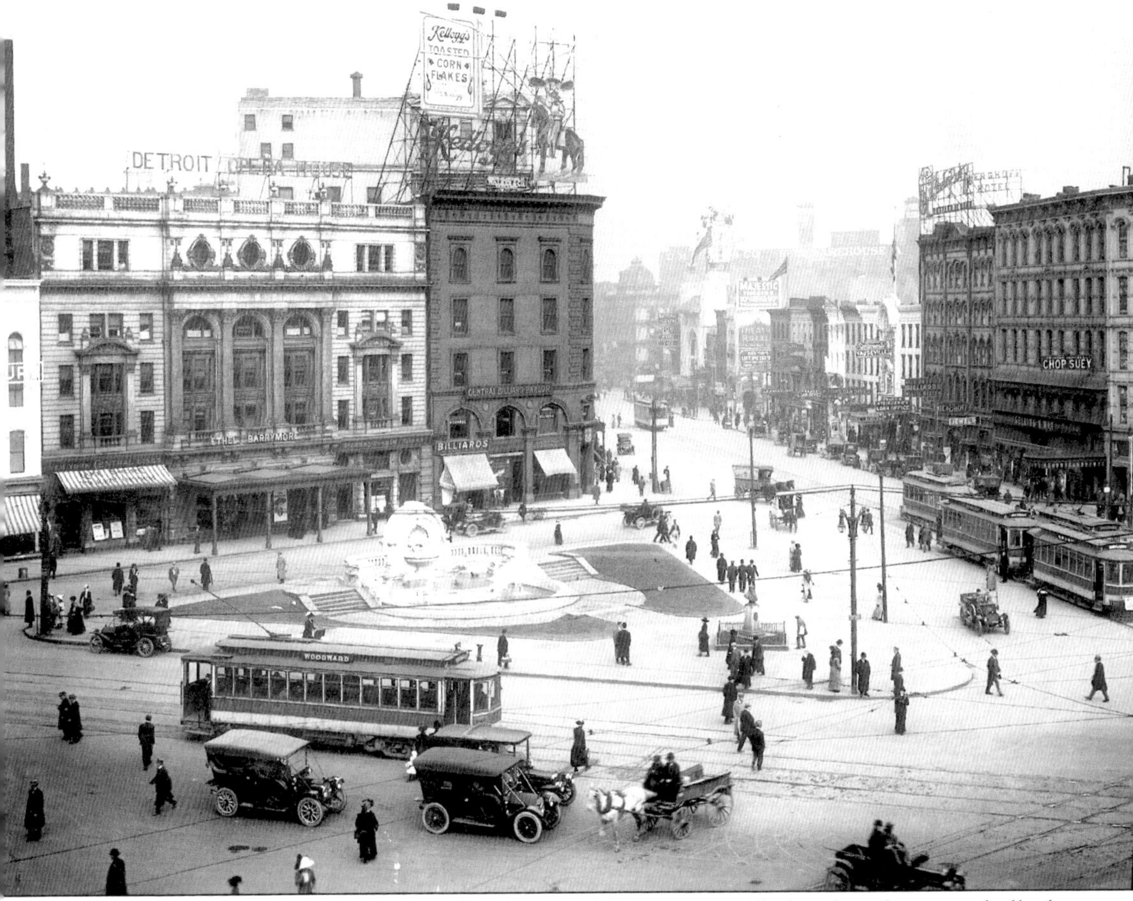

THE CAMPUS MARTIUS, 1910. This Campus Martius view, likely taken from city hall, shows an increasing number of automobiles and electric street cars on the street. Yet, still present are a number of horse-drawn conveyances. Automobile traffic appears to have given the right of way to the couple in the horse-drawn wagon, but soon, automobiles would completely replace horse-drawn equipment and carriages. With automobiles overtaking the workhorses, many horses suffered cruel treatment at the hands of man because of heightened competition for work. Horses were worked when they were too weak, too old, injured, or lame. They were forced to work harder and longer in an effort to keep up with work performed and deliveries made by automobiles. Michigan Humane Society records from 1910 indicate that there were 364 cases of cruelty to horses including beatings, overloading, and being forced to work while lame, crippled, or injured. (Courtesy of Burton Historical Collection.)

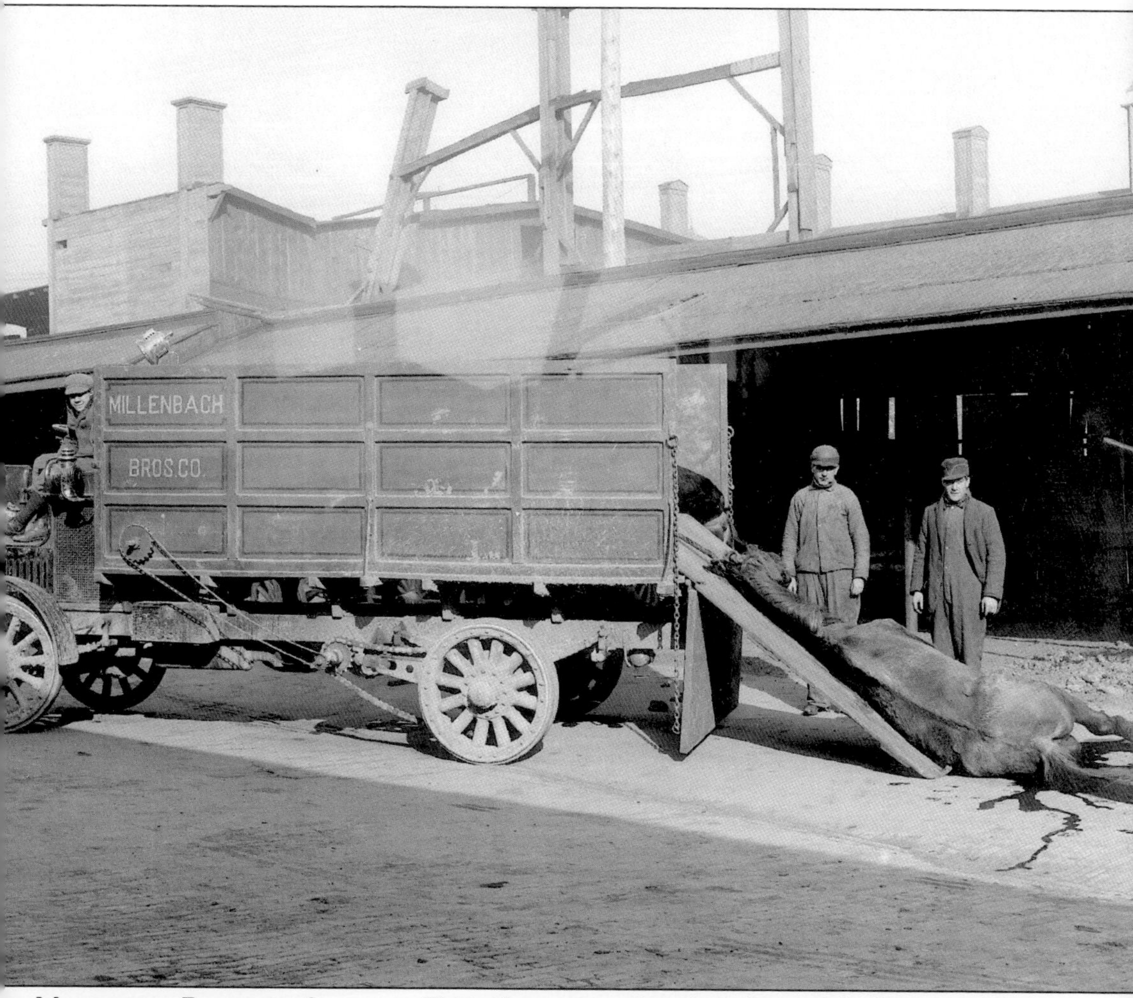

MILLENBACH BROTHERS COMPANY. This otherwise unidentified photograph shows a rather dreadful, yet real scene: the removal of a dead horse from a city street by means of an early gasoline-powered commercial winch with a chain drive. Millenbach Brothers was located on West Jefferson Avenue and dealt in hides, tanning, and grease. This early rendering company provided a needed, albeit not so glamorous, service in the city. The proper removal of dead horses from the streets, liveries, and stables was paramount in disease control and maintaining public sanitation. Early newspaper columns are filled with numerous accounts of sick and injured horses being left in alleys to fend for themselves or abandoned in stables when they could no longer perform the necessary tasks for their driver. The Michigan Humane Society actively pursued those who perpetrated acts of cruelty and neglect and was quite successful in bringing the abusers to justice. (Courtesy of Burton Historical Collection.)

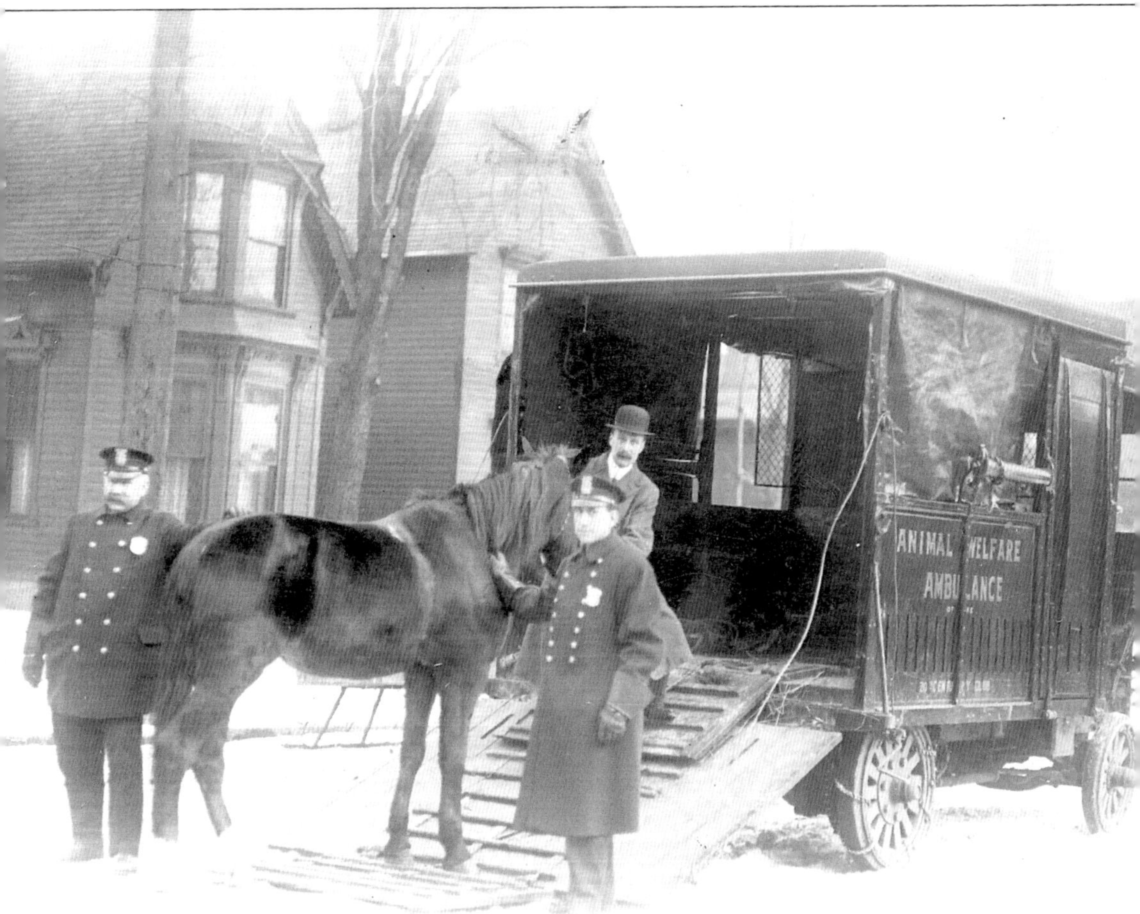

Early Horse Ambulance. Arthur Curtis, Humane Marshall, escorts a work horse into the first horse ambulance of the Animal Welfare Association, a predecessor to the Michigan Humane Society. The Animal Welfare Association was formed in approximately 1912 and was led by Mrs. Abner Larned. This association was formed by the women of the Twentieth Century Club in Detroit and was called "…a jewel in the crown of womanhood in Detroit." This horse suffers from sores on his back left by his harness from pulling overloaded wagons. A generous donor, referred to as Miss Ford, gave a parcel of land to the Animal Welfare Association on the corner of Inkster Road and Michigan Avenue, and the Association developed it into a rest farm for horses. Horses taken by the association that were beaten, maimed, too old for work, abandoned, or lame, were placed at the rest farm for recovery and recuperation. On occasion, Humane Marshall Curtis had the difficult task of euthanizing those horses in the poorest condition.

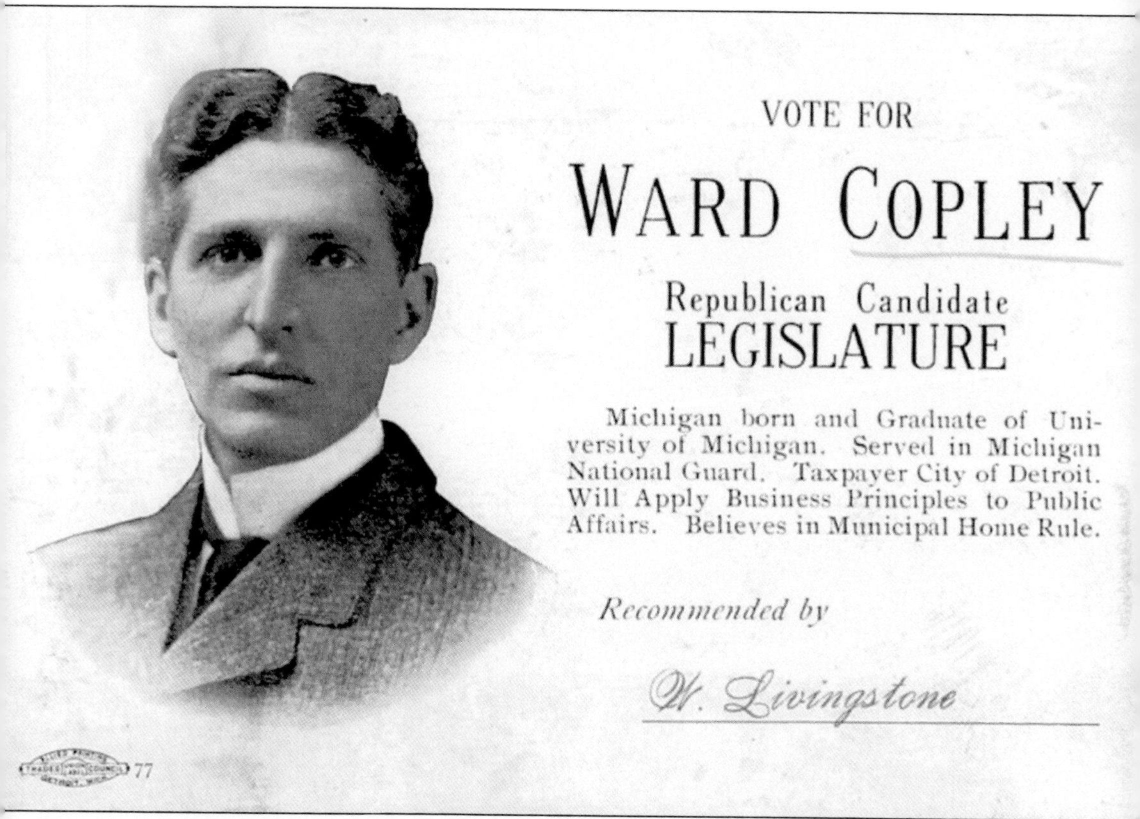

POLITICAL SUPPORT. The Honorable A. Ward Copley, seen here in a 1906 advertisement asking for support in his bid for State Representative, was the driving force behind the passage of a bill prohibiting the trafficking of old, worn-out work horses. Previous attempts to pass this legislation in Michigan had repeatedly failed. This attempt, beginning with the authorship of the Humane Society in 1911, was presented by Ward Copley in Lansing and the bill became law in 1913. Public Act 354 made it unlawful for any person to offer for sale or sell any horse or mule that was deemed permanently unfit for work. Similar laws were already in existence in Pennsylvania, New York, Massachusetts, and Illinois. Copley, who won his seat in Lansing, was a career politician and a four-time husband who continued to support the Society. (Courtesy of Burton Historical Collection.)

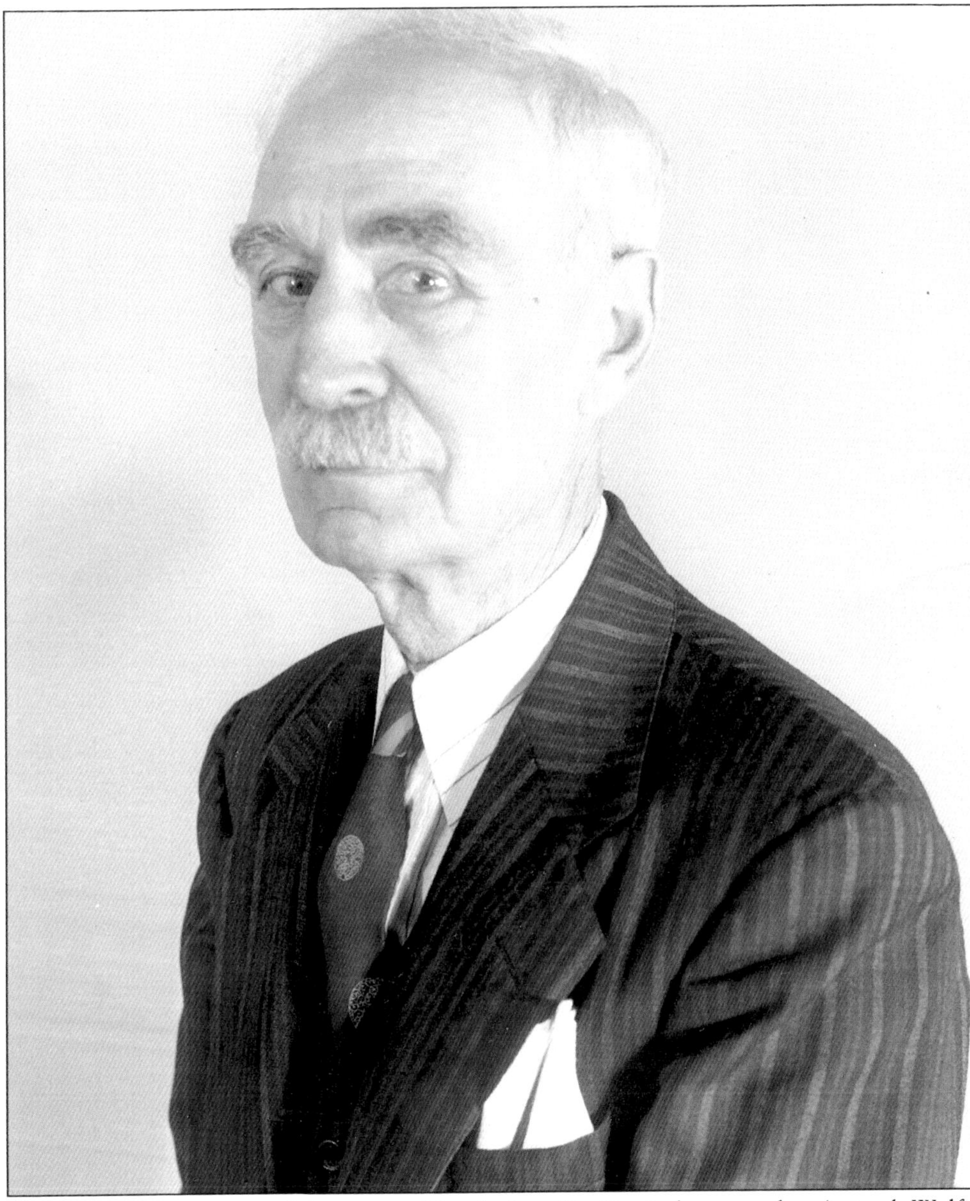

HUMANE MARSHALL FOR MICHIGAN. Mr. Arthur C. Curtis became the Animal Welfare Association's sole employee in 1913 and was later named Humane Marshall by then Governor Woodbridge N. Ferris. He was given statewide authority to investigate charges of animal cruelty. Curtis was born in London, England, in 1880 and came to Detroit with his wife, Emily, in 1911. He was a decorator by trade, but applied for a position with the Animal Welfare Association because of his devotion to animals. Curtis credits his love for animals to his experience in the Boer War in South Africa. As a British cavalryman, both he and his horse were wounded behind enemy lines and his horse carried him back to the safety of British lines despite his own injury. His horse's condition was so grave that he was killed. As State Humane Marshall, Curtis was authorized to carry a gun, both to protect himself from teamsters accused of mistreating their animals and to effect mercy killings as needed. Arthur Curtis worked for the Michigan Humane Society well into his 70s.

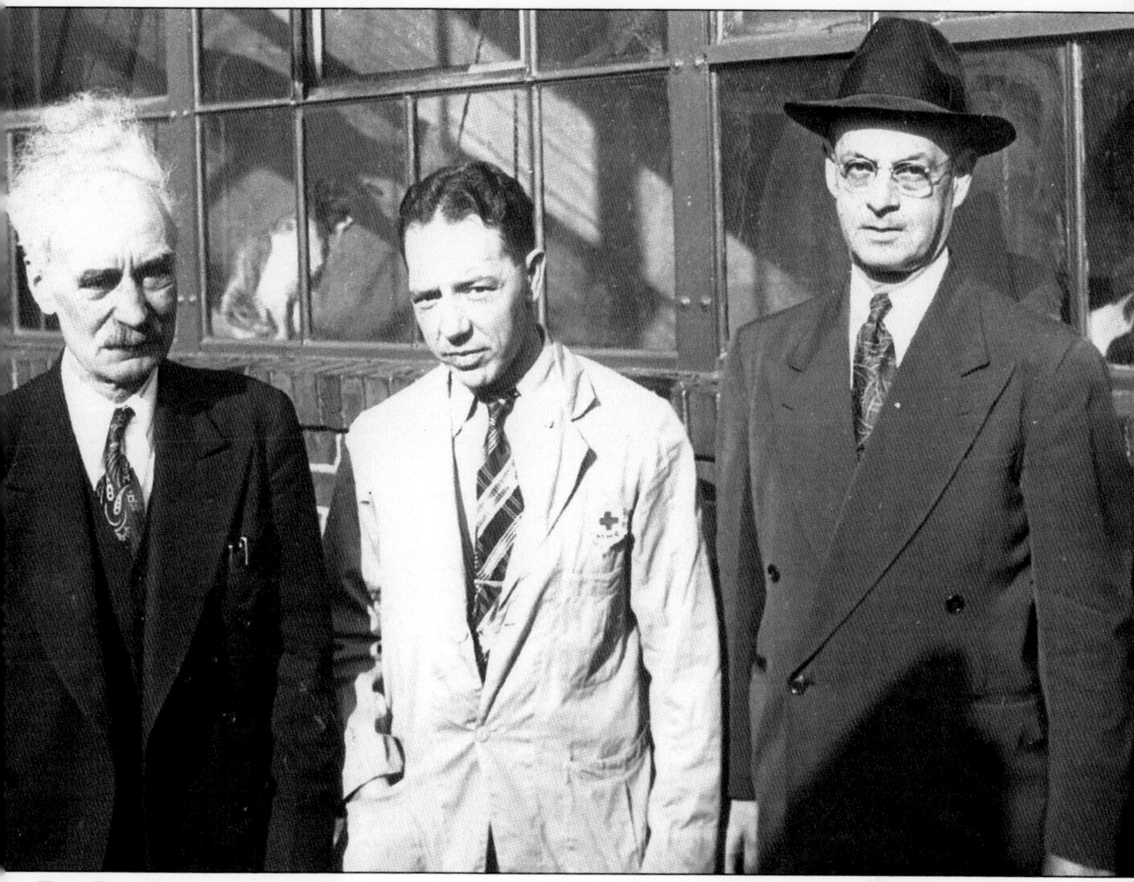

The Big Three. Arthur C. Curtis, Patrick Mack, and Luther King were all driving forces behind animal cruelty investigations for the Michigan Humane Society. Arthur Curtis began his career in 1913 with the Animal Welfare Association. Patrick Mack began his service with the Humane Society in 1933 and became the state's most active and best-known advocate of better treatment for animals. A long-time chief inspector, Mack compiled a handbook on anti-cruelty laws which was widely used by agents in the field. An Arkansas native, Mack retired in 1968, after 35 years of service. Luther King also spent a lifetime in service with the Michigan Humane Society beginning in the late 1930s and enjoyed a fine reputation as an investigator and he retired after a 29-year career. Between the three pictured above, there are well over 100 years of service to the betterment of the animals.

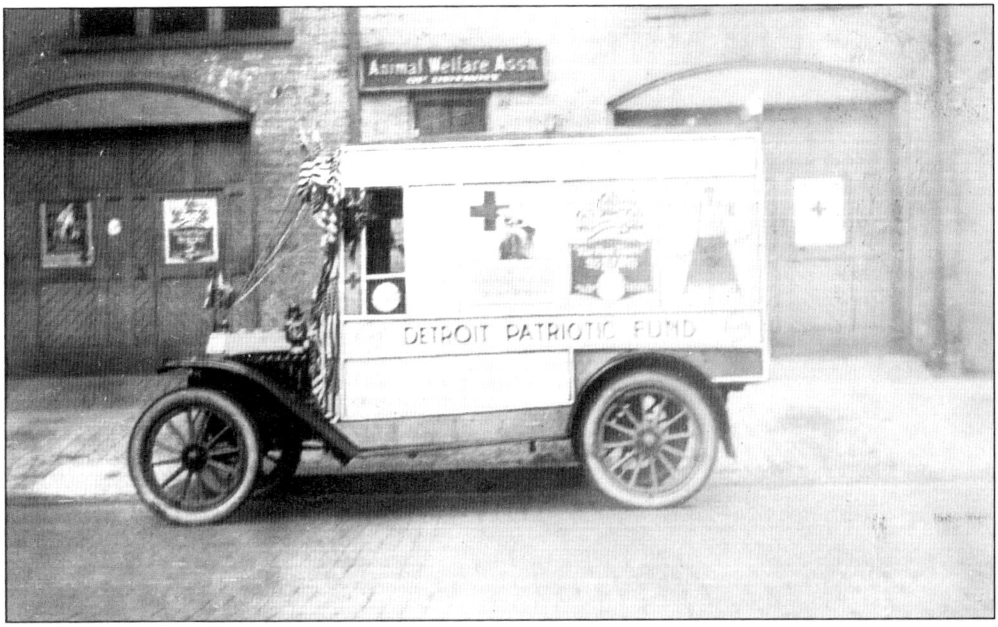

FOUR-WHEELED ADVERTISING. Parked in front of the Animal Welfare Association's Detroit headquarters on East Larned Street sits this animal ambulance painted up to promote the Detroit Patriotic Fund, the forerunner of the Community Fund. The Association received a small amount of funding from this organization until the 1930s.

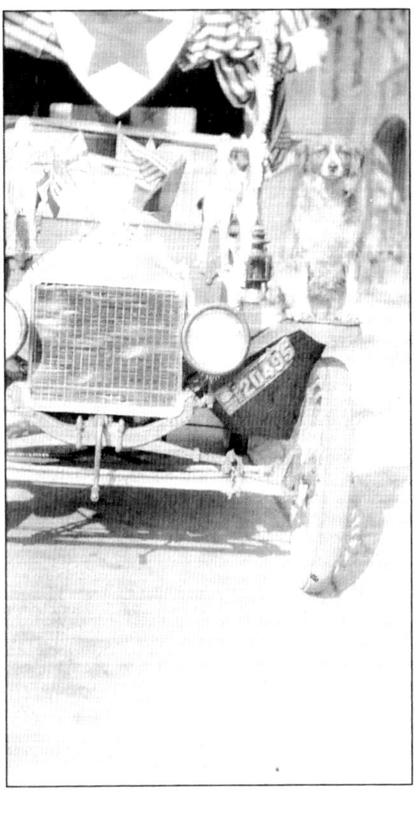

READY TO ROLL. One of the Animal Welfare Association's resident dogs sits perched on the fender of their Ford ambulance as it is prepared for a parade for a fundraising drive.

The Humane Society

FOR PREVENTION OF CRUELTY

Incorporated under the lawc of the State of Michigan.
Affiliated with the National Society.

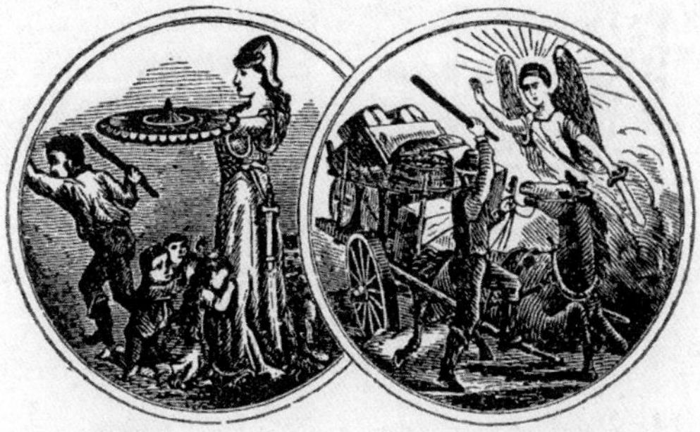

President, - WM. PORATH
Secretary, - P. A. SIDEBOTTOM
Treasurer, . WILLARD BABCOCK
(Manager of Peninsular-State Bank Broadway Branch)

Vice-Presidents,

Jere C. Hutchins, Henry Ford, Geo. H. Barbour
E. L. Ford, F. H. Walker, Dr. C. Bronson Allen
Bishop C. D. Williams, Joseph Boyer

Executive Office

C. E. Bird, William Babcock, Dr. W. M. Bailey
A. C. Paterson, John Henry, P. A. Sidebottom
James F, Hill, John S. Affeld, Daniel Turner

JAMES F. HILL, Supt. and Attorney
HON. T. A, E. WEADOCK, Counsel

Office: SUITE 405 BREITMEYER BUILDING
(Corner Broadway and Gratiot Ave.)
PHONE MAIN 4735

HUMANE SOCIETY FOR PREVENTION OF CRUELTY. A second Humane Society formed in Detroit in 1910 with two special purposes: 1) the protection of human beings from cruelty, abuse, and oppression; and 2) the protection of animals. The list of Society directors reads like a Who's Who of Detroit, with men such as Henry Ford and George Barbour providing direction to the Society. In this 1916 report, the Society reported assisting 103 women in compelling their husbands to support their families, provided for 298 children, and helped 28 men. The Society's agents made 17,130 examinations of horses at stables, sales, and excavations. They found 107 lame horses, 135 horses unfit for work, and 79 horses were humanely killed to end their suffering. Agents made 26 arrests and issued 156 warnings to owners of horses. (Courtesy of Burton Historical Collection.)

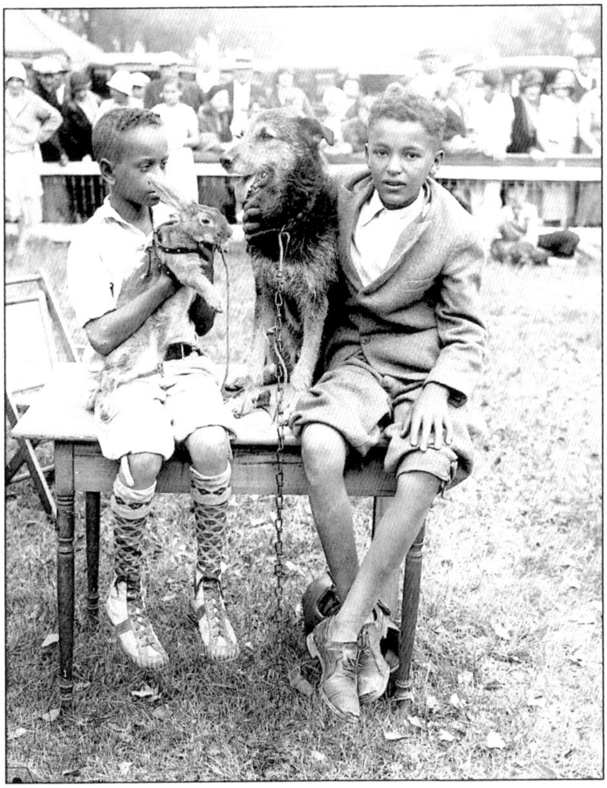

THE FAIR COMES TO TOWN. These two young men brought their pets to the Humane Society booth at the Michigan State Fair in the early 1920s. The Michigan Humane Society was always involved in community outreach and humane education and the Michigan State Fair was a wonderful venue to promote humane values.

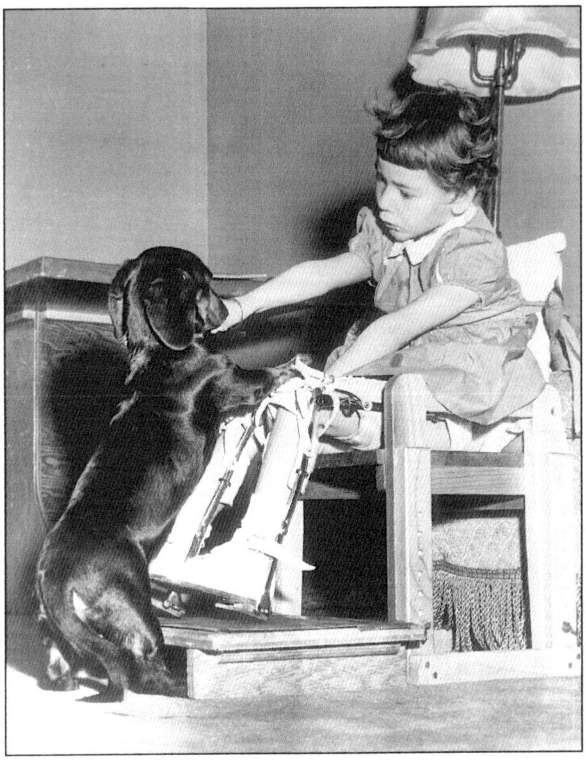

PETS FOR THE INFIRM. In today's society, science agrees that pet ownership helps reduce stress and lower blood pressure. In the early years of the humane movement, those of us in the fight knew the benefits of interacting with pets. This unidentified child is the recipient of some "puppy love" at a Michigan Humane Society open house.

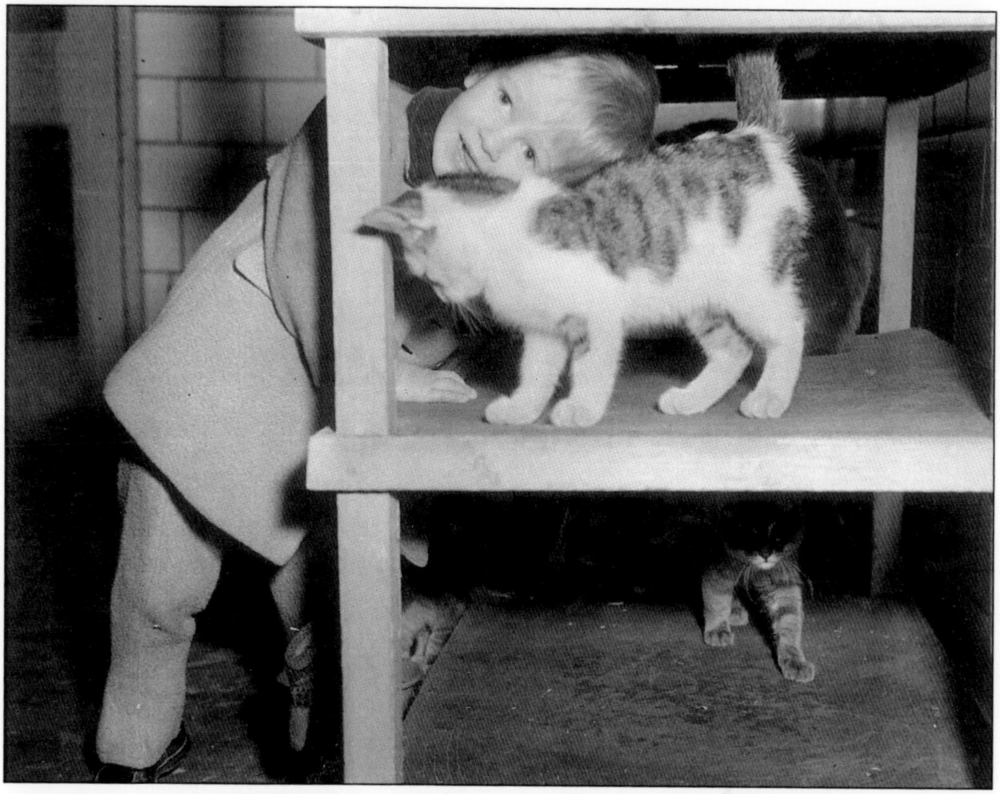

Katzenjammer Kids. Trying to decide which kitten to adopt, this young fellow gets as close and he can to the goods before making his decision. Animal adoption and placement has been a function of the society since 1925 when Board members approved a measure to charge $1 for animals placed in new homes and to keep full records on the animals placed.

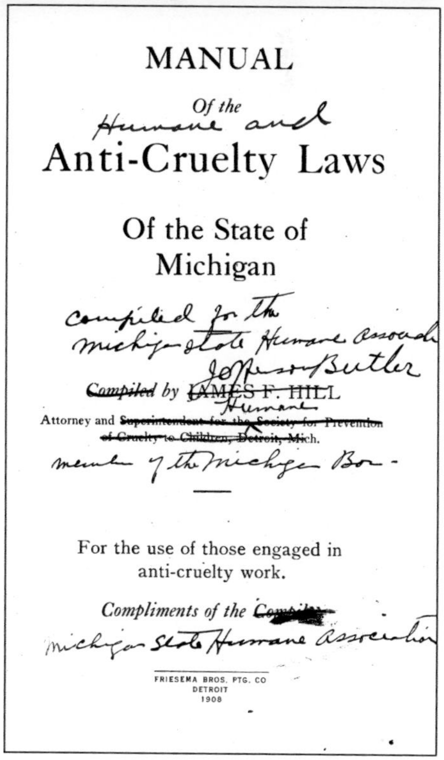

MANUAL

Of the Humane and

Anti-Cruelty Laws

Of the State of Michigan

compiled for the Michigan State Humane Association

Jefferson Butler

~~Compiled~~ by ~~JAMES F. HILL~~

Attorney and ~~Superintendent for the Society for Prevention of Cruelty to Children, Detroit, Mich.~~

For the use of those engaged in anti-cruelty work.

Compliments of the ~~Compiler~~ Michigan State Humane Association

FRIESEMA BROS. PTG. CO DETROIT 1908

Laws We Can Live With. Initially compiled by Humane Society Director James Hill in 1908 and revised and annotated by Society attorney Jefferson Butler, the working document pictured here brings together all of the laws and ordinances relating to anti-cruelty to both humans and animals. It gave field agents a handy reference guide in citing violators. (Courtesy of Burton Historical Collection.)

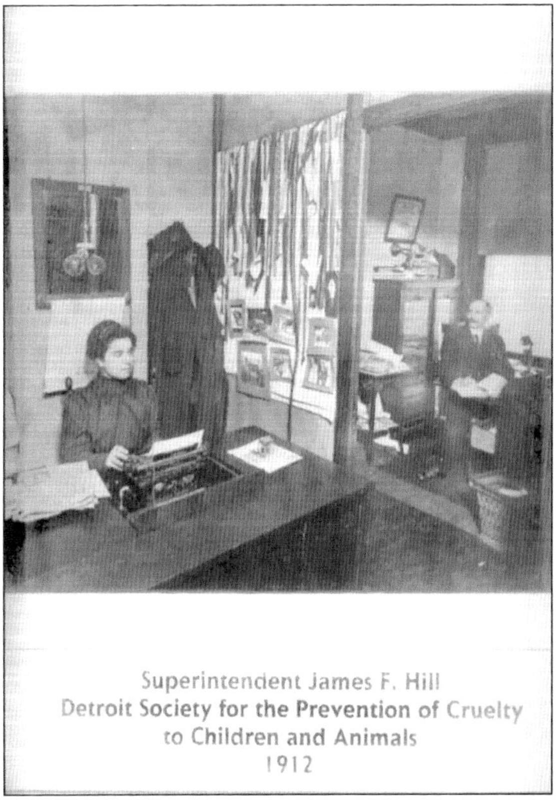

HEADQUARTERS OF THE EARLY SOCIETY. At the time James Hill was the Director of the Society, its office was located in the McGraw Building. In this 1912 photograph of James Hill and his secretary, one can see some of the chains, whips, and other paraphernalia seized in investigating incidents of cruelty toward animals and children. Newspaper clippings as far back as 1914 report charges of cruelty toward children, such as whippings and brandings, and subsequent investigations by the Society. Hill, who would serve as attorney, agent, and President of the Society, compiled the Manual of the Anti-Cruelty Laws used by field agents. Hill's dedication to the protection of animals and children overcame day-to-day conflicts and he took a very active post in securing the passage of laws establishing the juvenile court system. Hill died suddenly in 1917 at the age of 54.

SUPPORT FOR THE CAUSE. Frank Cody, a long-time officer of the Michigan Humane Society, was born in Belleville, Michigan, in 1870. Cody taught in the Belleville school system and then at the old Willow School near Ypsilanti while he attended Michigan State Normal School. In 1891, Cody became superintendent of the Delray Schools and principal of the McMillan School. Gaining national recognition for his pioneering work in social education for crippled and handicapped children, Cody was named superintendent of Detroit Schools in 1914. A refined yet humorous speaker, Cody was master of ceremonies at the 60th Anniversary of the Michigan Humane Society held at the Statler Hotel in 1937. Cody's long association with the Michigan Humane Society furthered his goals for humane education programs and in 1927, humane education was in effect in all Detroit public schools through a program of the Michigan Humane Society. (Courtesy of Burton Historical Collection.)

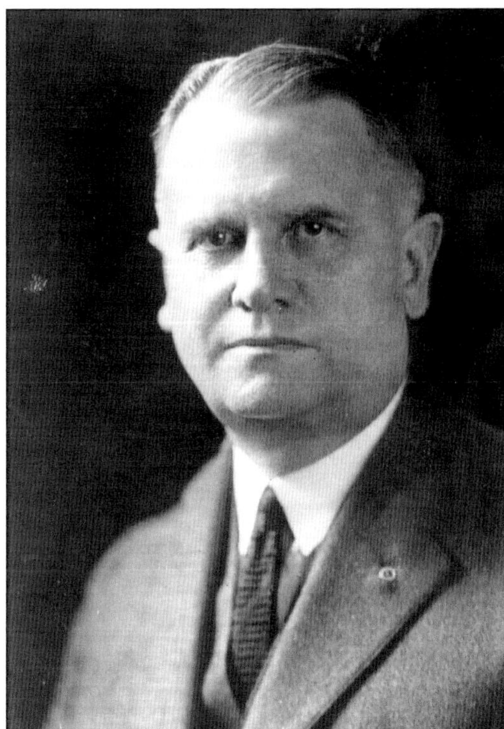

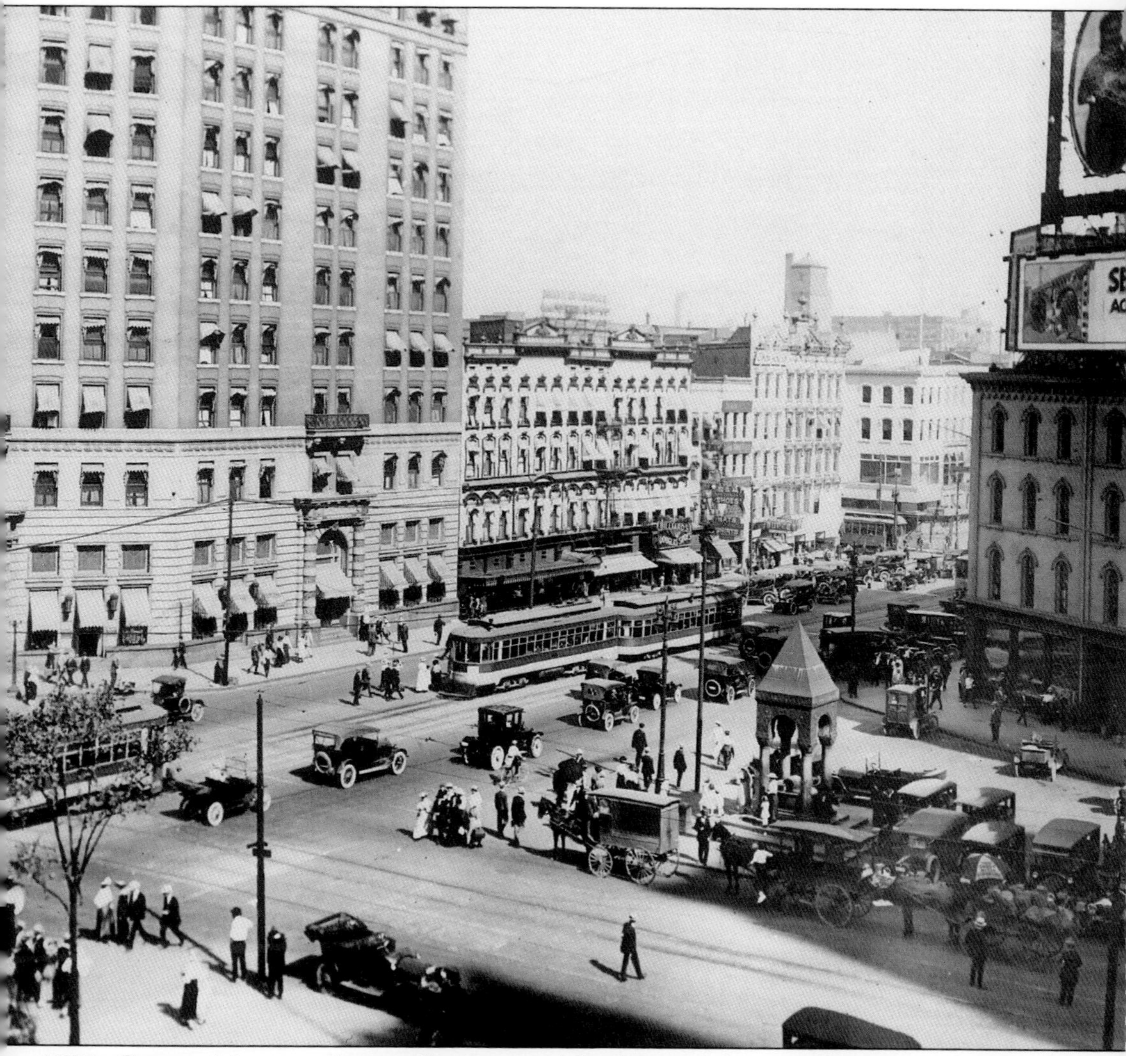

1920s Campus Martius. An excellent view of the heart of the city during the Roaring Twenties illustrates the co-existence of horse and machine. Sight-seeing and delivery wagons line Campus Martius, as motorized vehicles of all kinds move up and down Woodward Avenue. At its height, the number of work horses in the city of Detroit was over 60,000. (Courtesy of Burton Historical Collection.)

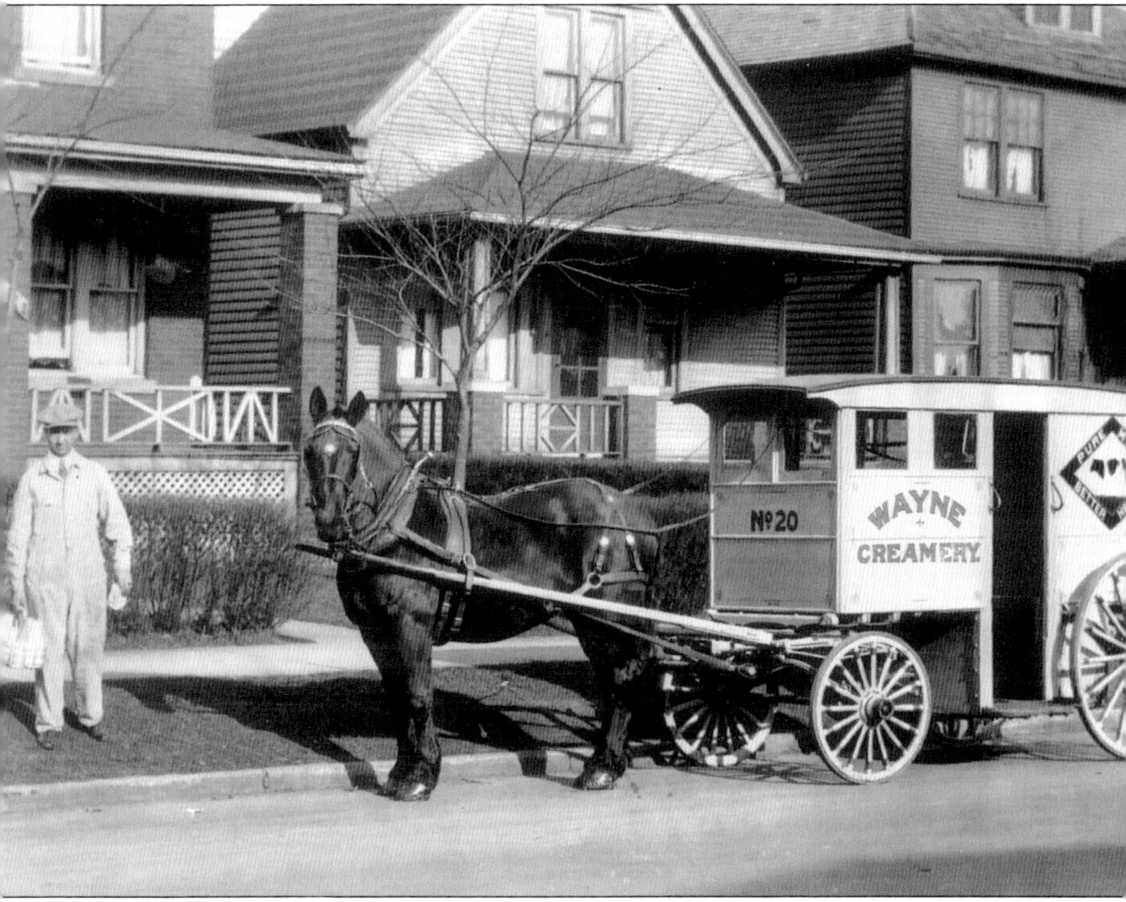

HOME DELIVERY, 1925. "Pure Milk, Better Health" reads the Wayne Creamery delivery wagon. Horse and driver pose proudly on their route through the neighborhood. Scenes like this were common enough through the 1930s and made a comeback with World War II rationing of petroleum products. (Courtesy of Burton Historical Collection.)

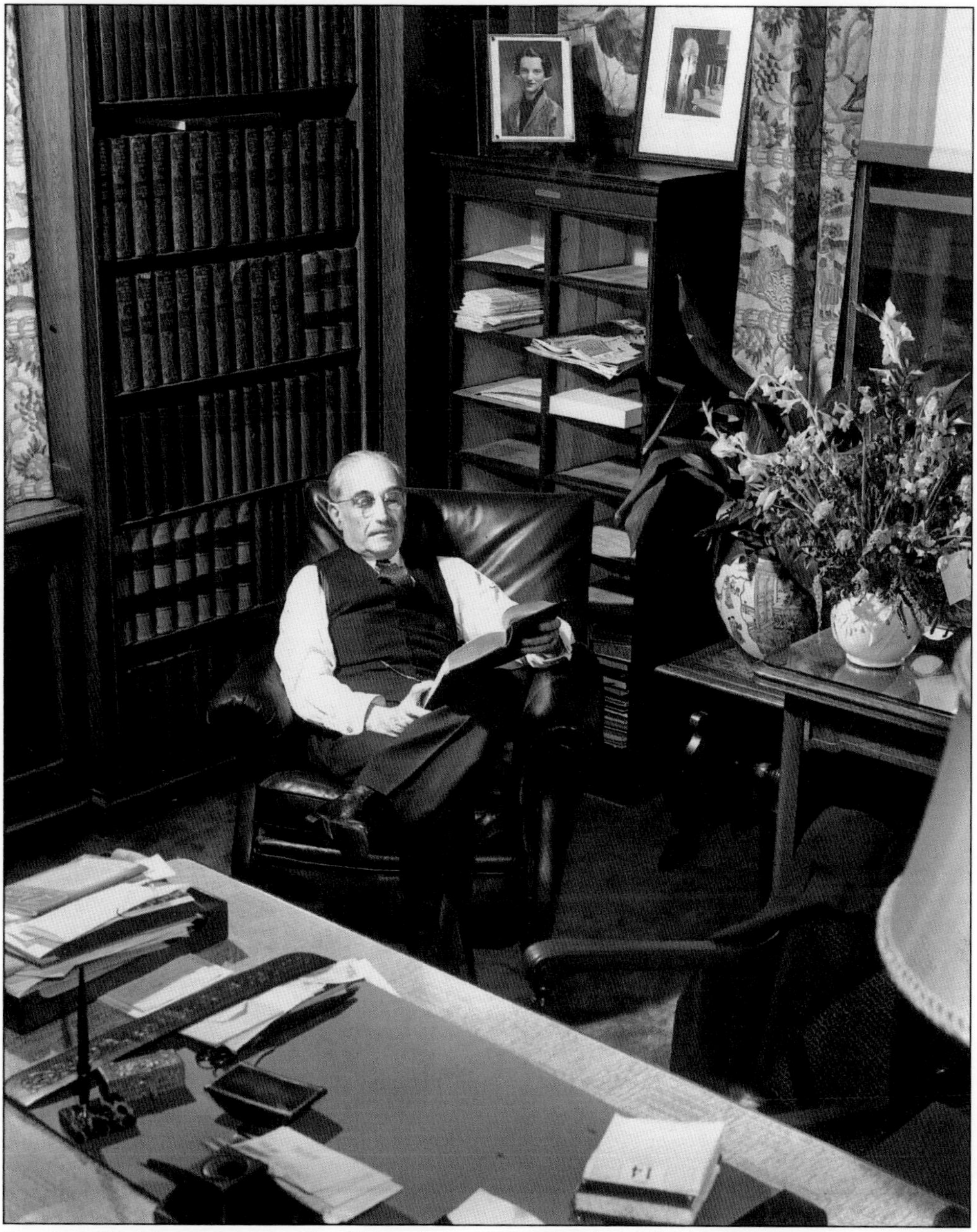

Dr. Leo M. Franklin. Dr. Franklin relaxes with a book in the study of his home in 1941. Rabbi Franklin was at Temple Beth El for 42 years and was Rabbi Emeritus for 7 years after that. Born in Indiana in 1870, Franklin arrived in Detroit in 1899 after a short time as a Rabbi in Nebraska and graduation from the Hebrew Union School in 1892. Already known as one of the most promising of the younger Reform Ministers, Franklin was invited to Detroit to deliver a sermon that was so well received, he was invited to lead the Beth El congregation. Franklin organized the United Jewish Charities and founded the Detroit Round Table of Catholics, Jews, and Protestants. In addition to these accomplishments, Franklin was also an outstanding officer of the Michigan Humane Society and served the Society for many years. (Courtesy of Burton Historical Collection.)

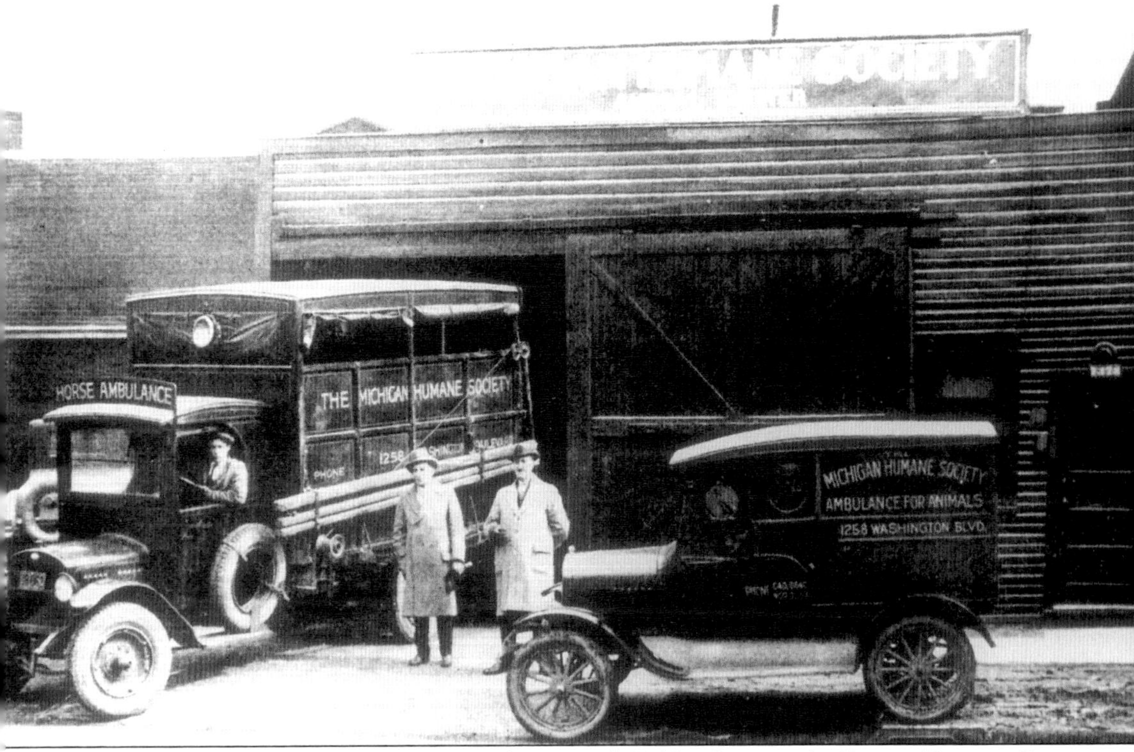

MICHIGAN HUMANE SOCIETY, 1925. The Animal Welfare Society, the Detroit Humane Society, and the Michigan Society for the Prevention of Cruelty to Animals incorporated in 1925 to form the Michigan Humane Society. The horse ambulance and small animal ambulance stand outside the Michigan Humane Society temporary animal shelter at 7378 Richmond. Administrative offices were located at 1258 Washington Boulevard, as indicated on the vehicles. The Animal Rescue Division of the Society had a very busy year in 1925. The Society rescued 6,586 cats, 863 dogs, and 70 horses. Over 200 animals were placed in new homes. Placement of animals in new homes became an official function of the Society in 1925. The horse ambulance responded to 74 calls while the small animal ambulance responded to over 7,500 calls. The Society was only allowed to pick up injured animals, as the responsibility for stray dogs in the city was diverted to the Detroit Police Department.

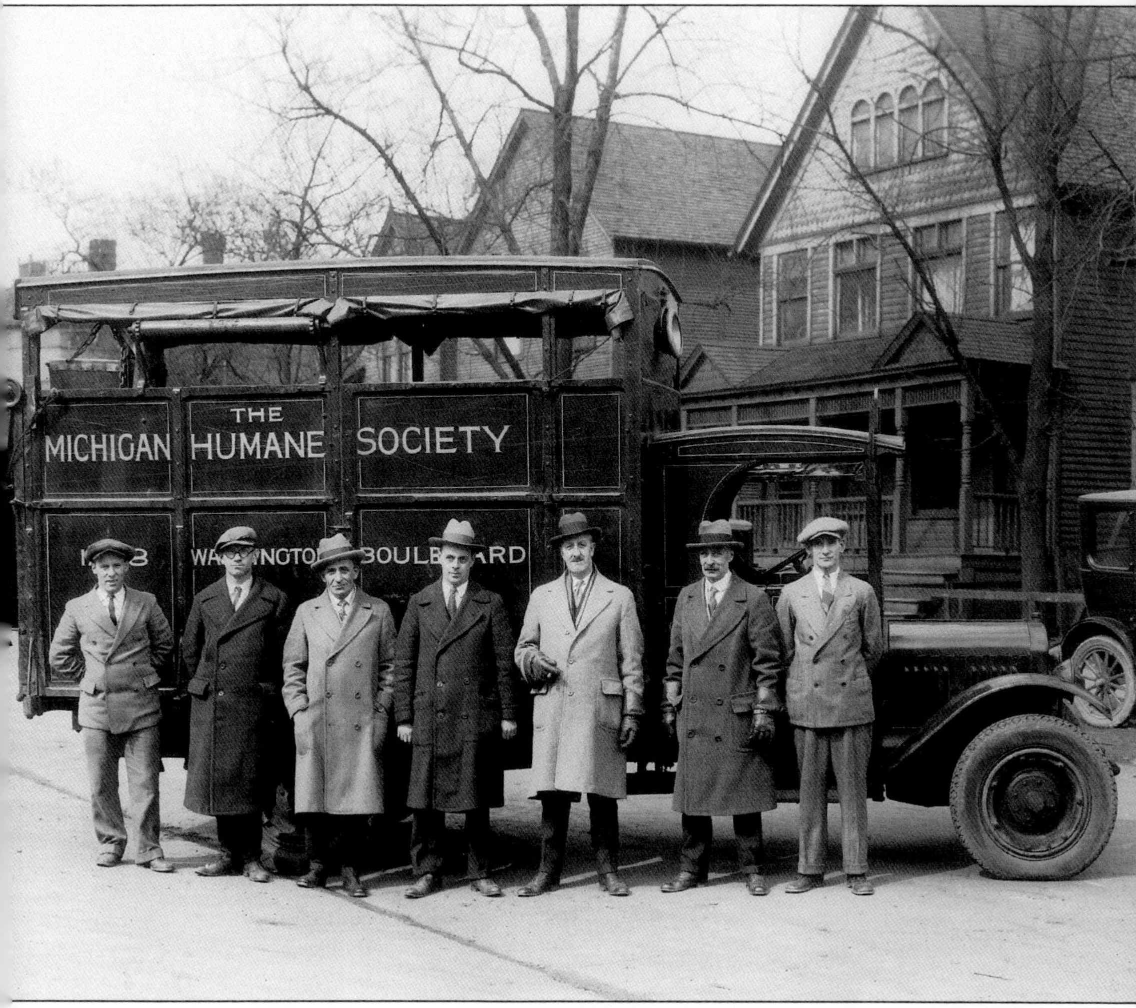

STANDING TALL. Looking like a squad of "Untouchables," the outdoor staff of the Michigan Humane Society poses for this photo with the horse ambulance. Pictured from left to right are as follows: W. Wilds, H. Decker, C. Ford, L. King, F.G. Tetley, Arthur Curtis, and Stan Doner. These were the men responsible for responding to charges of animal cruelty, injured animals in distress, the inspection of stockyards and livestock haulers, and the education of the public on animal welfare. Luther King served the Society for almost 30 years, Arthur Curtis served for over 40, and F.G. Tetley went on to become an officer of the Board. In 1926, there were 62 prosecutions at the municipal and county courts for various offenses resulting in 48 convictions. Nine of the remaining 62 prosecuted fled after posting bond.

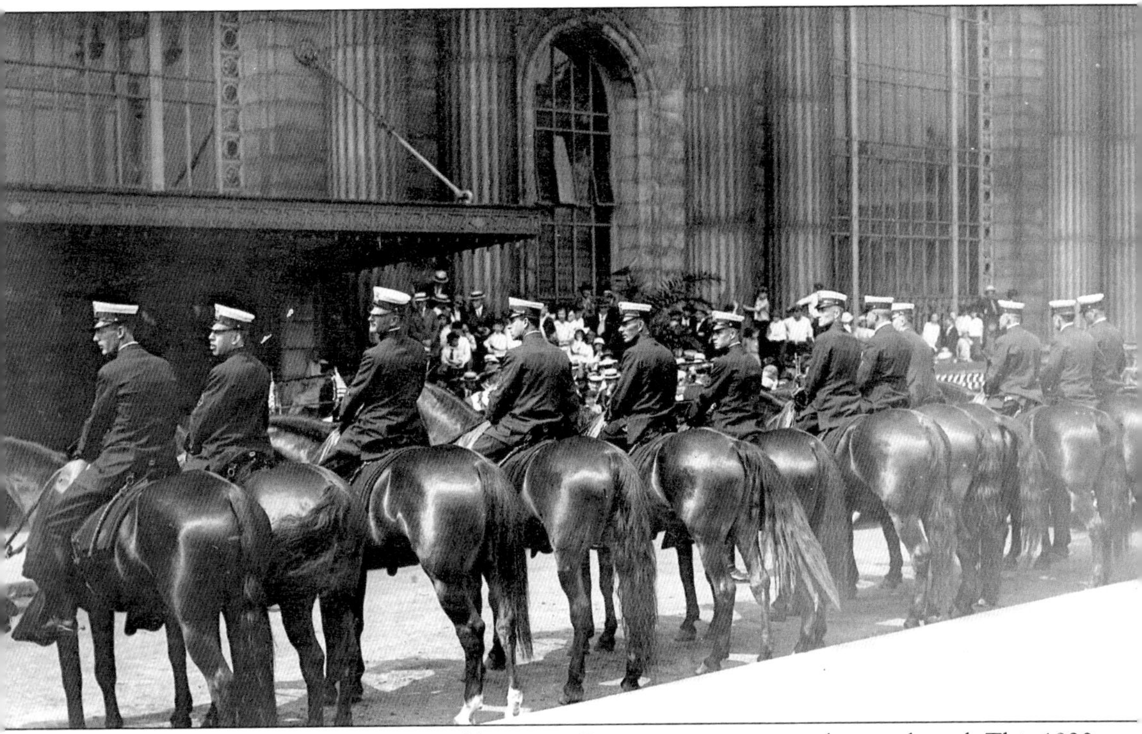

Fine Equines. Not all of the workhorses in Detroit were mistreated or neglected. This 1920s photo of a company of the Detroit Police Department's Mounted Unit shows horses in excellent condition and cared for properly. The field division of the Michigan Humane Society was responsible for inspecting livestock, stables, liveries, and transportation of livestock throughout the Motor City and often worked closely with the police department. In one year, the field staff of the Michigan Humane Society inspected 10,736 horses and mules for fitness, destroyed 128 aged and diseased horses, stopped 77 horses at work and sent them to veterinarians, and relieved 94 overloaded horses from work. (Courtesy of Burton Historical Society.)

Three

LEADING THE MOVEMENT

1920–1950

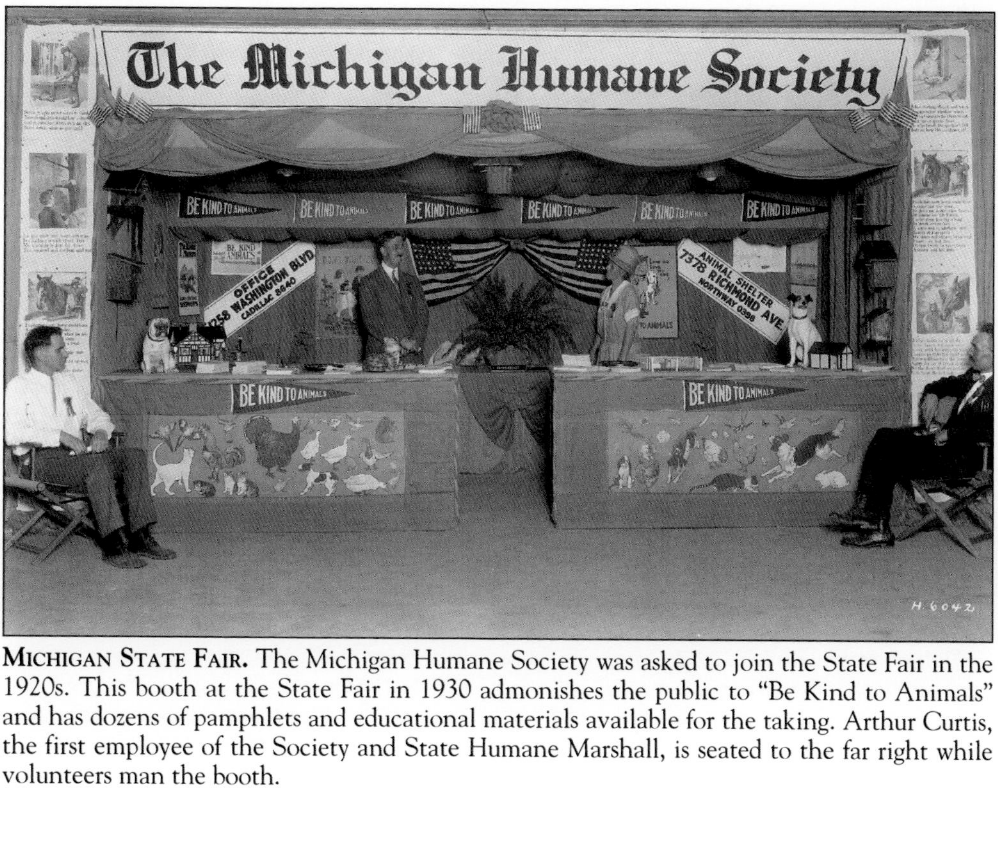

MICHIGAN STATE FAIR. The Michigan Humane Society was asked to join the State Fair in the 1920s. This booth at the State Fair in 1930 admonishes the public to "Be Kind to Animals" and has dozens of pamphlets and educational materials available for the taking. Arthur Curtis, the first employee of the Society and State Humane Marshall, is seated to the far right while volunteers man the booth.

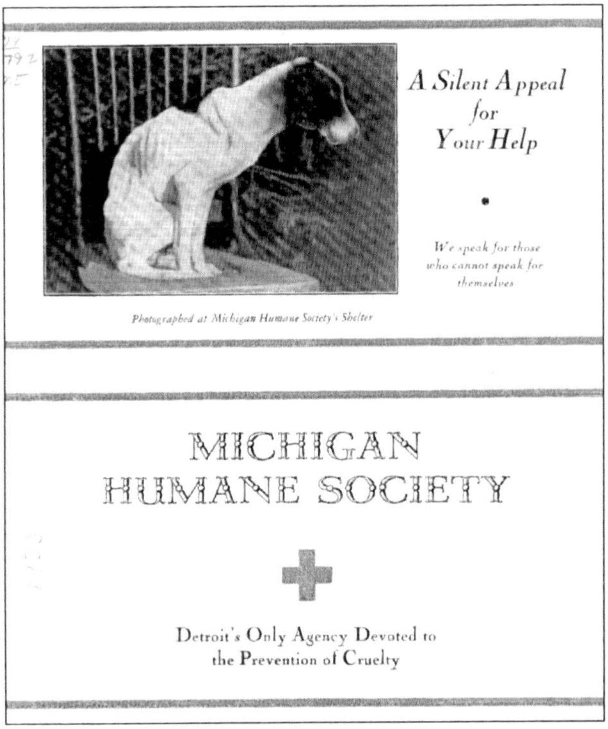

THE BITTER TRUTH. This 1933 pamphlet illustrates the plight of dogs and cats in the city of Detroit. The Society was fully dependent on donations from the public to keep operating, because the Community Fund withdrew the small stipend granted the Society in earlier years. With the development of federally-funded human welfare agencies, the Society turned its focus to entirely serving animals. Appeals such as this one were a successful means to ask for needed funds. (Courtesy of Burton Historical Collection.)

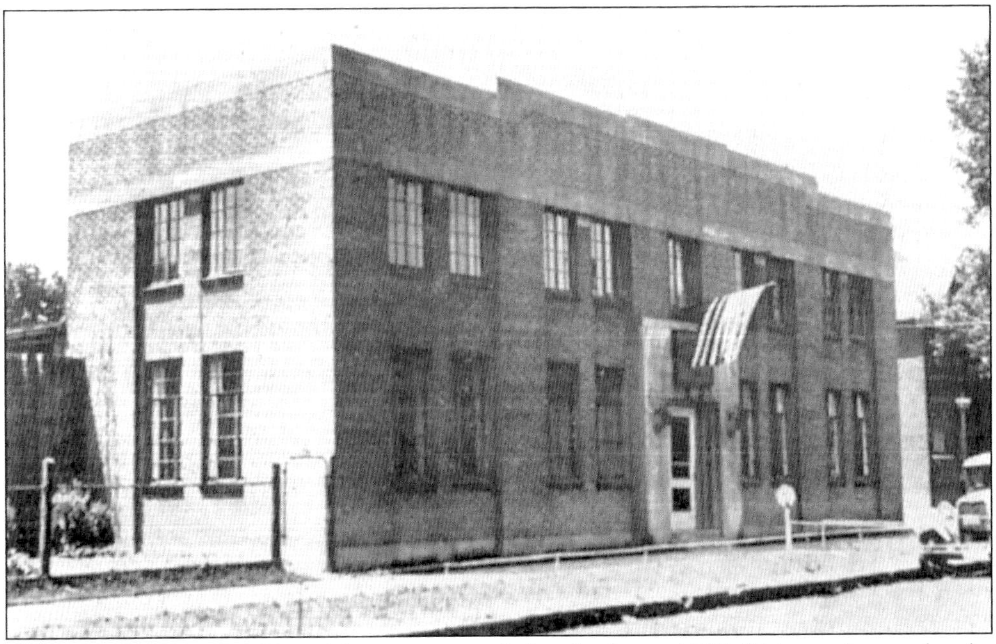

THE DETROIT SHELTER. Use of the temporary shelter facility at 7378 Richmond proved to be inefficient and costly. In 1931, Michigan Humane Society purchased the old Detroit Piston Ring building at 7401 Richmond and still maintains that shelter site in the heart of the city today. The building was in disrepair, and in August of 1931, Dr. Myra Babcock, serving as Director of Operations, oversaw many renovations and improvements to make the facility a sanitary and functional shelter. (Courtesy of Burton Historical Collection.)

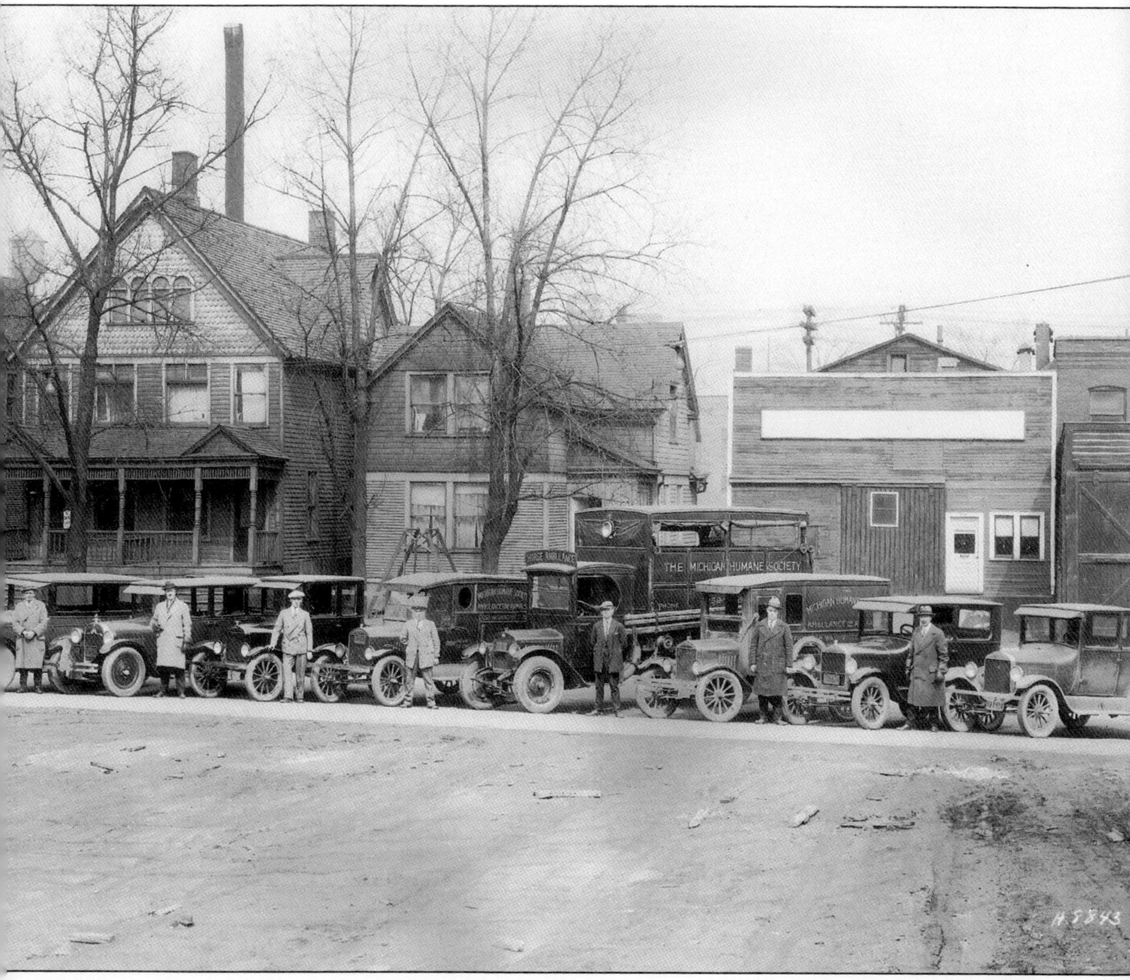

READY TO SAVE LIVES. A fleet of vehicles, some of them donated, and the outdoor staff, stands ready to respond to calls about animals in distress. The horse ambulance, small animal ambulances, and staff cars belonging to the Society responded to well over 10,000 calls per year during the 1930s. In 1934, over 14,000 calls were made involving some 22,000 animals. These vehicles logged 43,441 miles of travel in responding to these calls. The busy season hit right after the summer holiday and Labor Day weekend. Often, summer visitors would pack up to go home and abandon dogs and cats they cared for at their summer cottages. Funds were lacking for the Society to cover the outlying areas of the city, so the Society encouraged people to take their "summer pets" back home or at least make the drive to the shelter to surrender them.

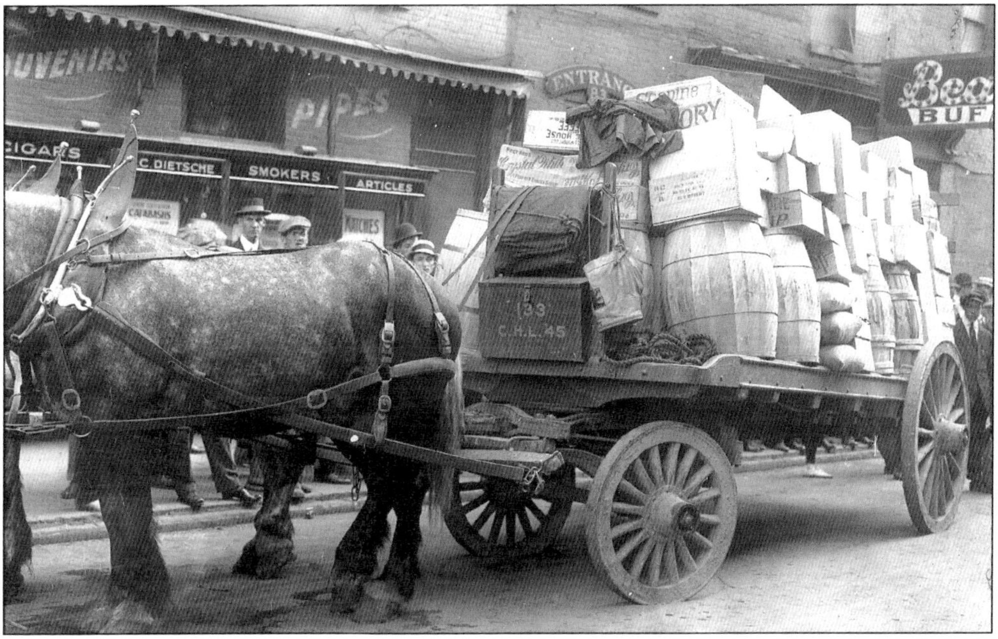

Overloaded! Sights such as this overloaded horse and wagon were not uncommon in the city. In one of the largest fines of the time, Judge William Heston fined a teamster $110 for forcing his horses to wear work harnesses that tore the skin from their necks. Another teamster was prosecuted for malicious injury to personal property, a felony statute, when he tore out the tongue of a horse belonging to a man who refused to give him work.

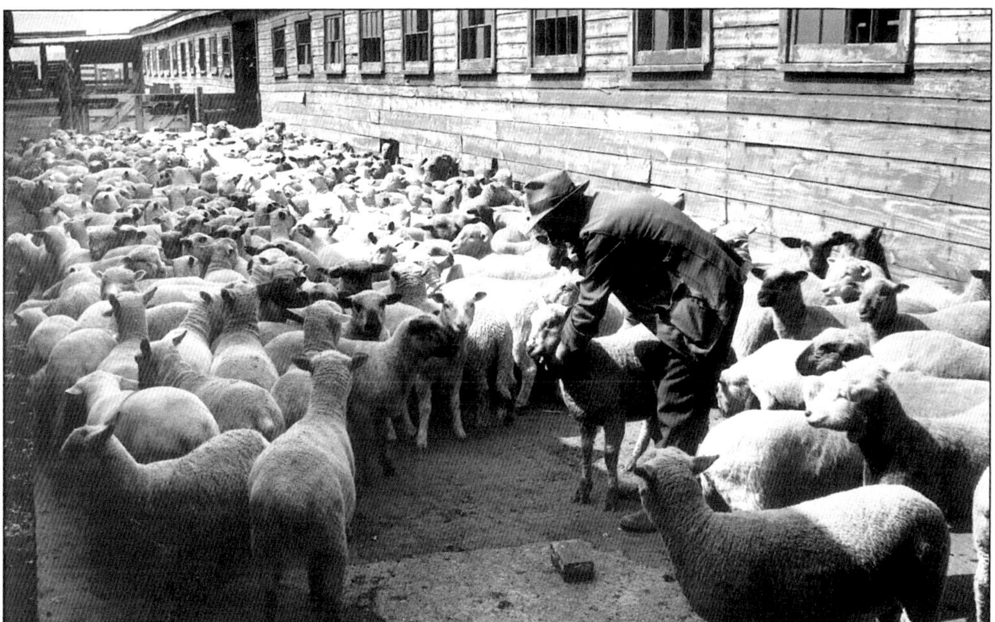

Livestock Inspection. Another duty of the early Michigan Humane Society was the inspection of auctions, markets, slaughterhouses, and stockyards, such as this one where sheep were held prior to shipment. Over 1000 such inspections took place each year.

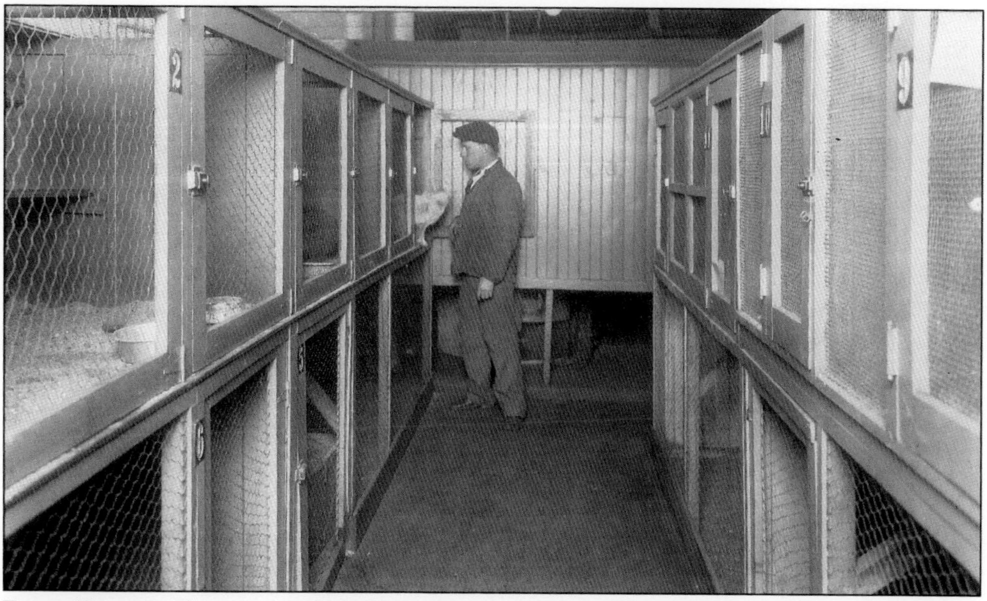

Feline Friends. The renovated Michigan Humane Society Detroit Shelter contained temporary living kennels for the animals. Of the animals brought in, cats far out numbered dogs. Here, a prospective cat owner looks over a tabby as a possible addition to his family. Cats able to regain their health or recover from their injuries were placed up for adoption while those whose conditions were more serious were humanely destroyed.

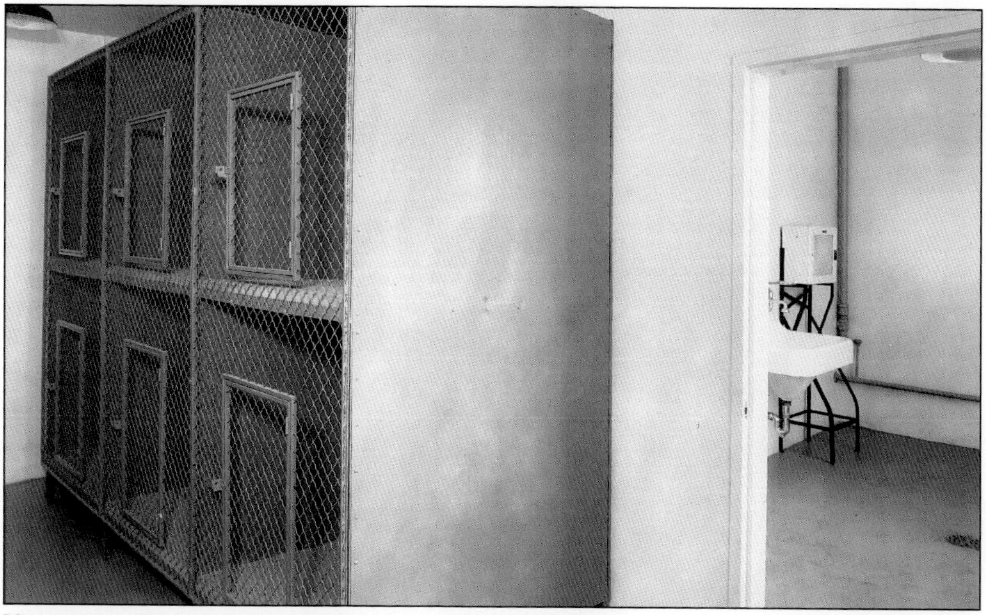

Veterinary Examination. During the 1930s and 1940s, the Michigan Humane Society was not able to provide veterinary services to the pet-owning public, only for the animals in their care. Twenty-two area veterinarians approached the Society in 1933 with this resolution: "We agree to treat any charity case referred to our respective hospitals by your Superintendent, Dr. Cass Kershaw, when, in his opinion, charitable action is required." Thus began an elaborate referral system for indigent veterinary care in Detroit.

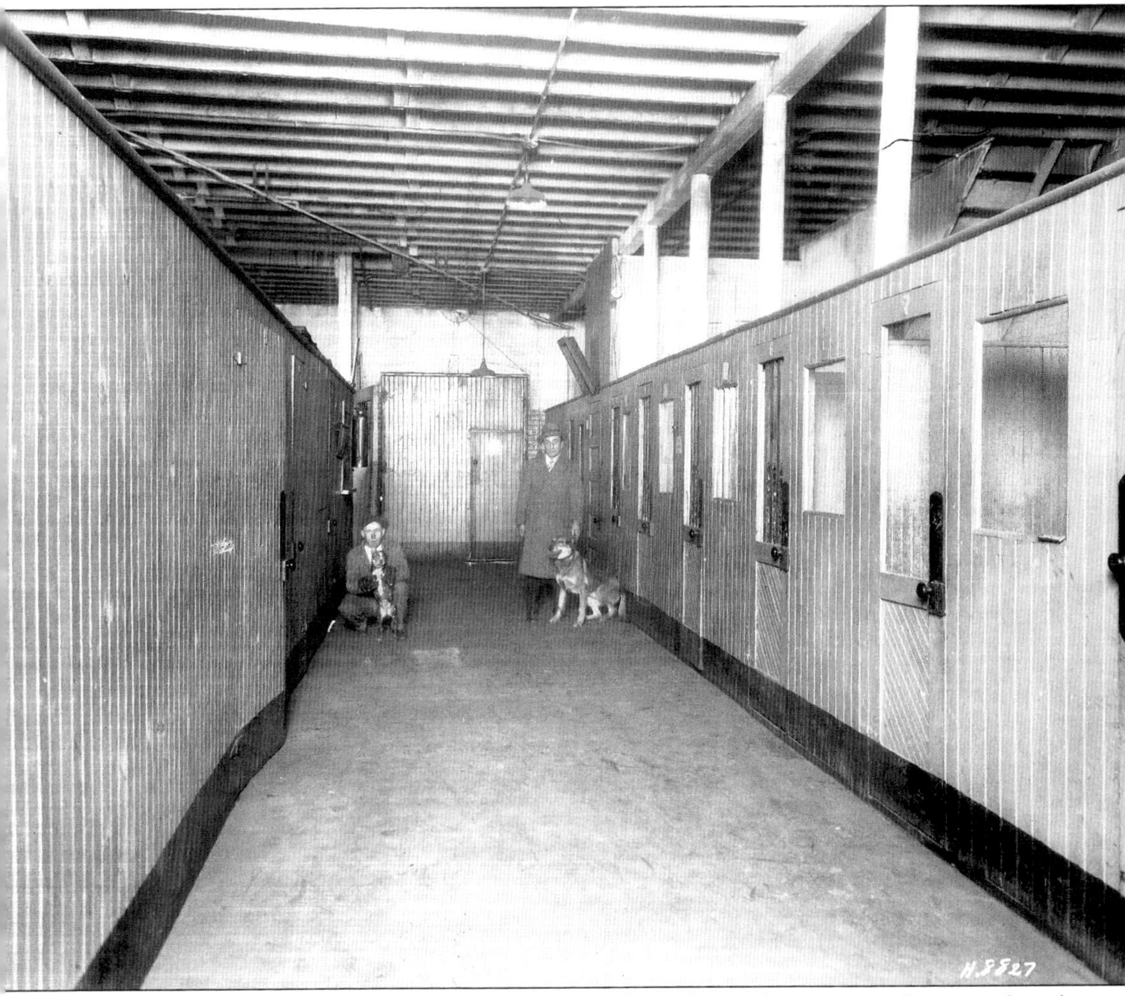

DOG KENNELS. Two Michigan Humane Society kennel attendants pose with canine boarders during the 1930s in the recently improved kennel area. Dogs of all breeds, shapes, and sizes were brought to the shelter or picked up by the field staff. During the 1930s, upwards of 5,000 dogs were housed each year at the Society's Detroit Shelter. Homes were found for many, but not all. Even then, the animal population was outpacing the human population. In order to keep up with the demand for services, the Society appealed to the public to provide materials such as rope for leashes, blankets, old newspaper, dog food and biscuits, and dog dishes. In spite of the harsh economy, the response of the community was overwhelming. Dozens of newspaper articles chronicled the importance of the Society's work and the need for community support.

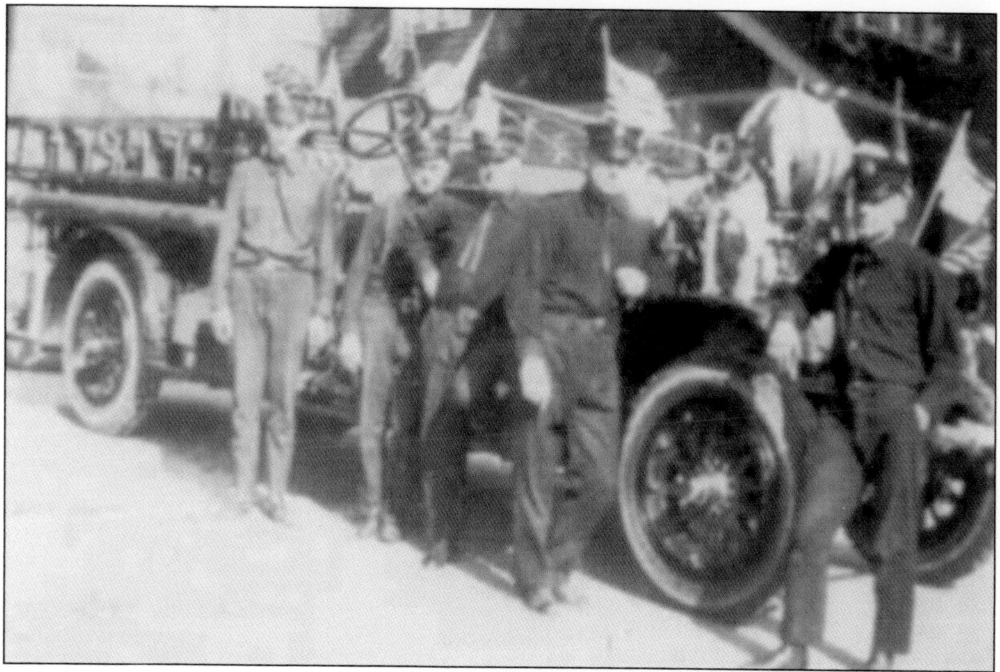

The Pride of Engine Company 45. Engine Company 45 of the Detroit Fire Department, pose alongside their ladder truck and their mascot, Sport, perched on the front fender. The company, located at Mack and St. Jean Avenue, acquired Sport when he climbed up into the seat of the truck and stayed there as the engine pulled out to respond to a fire alarm. (Courtesy of William Cable.)

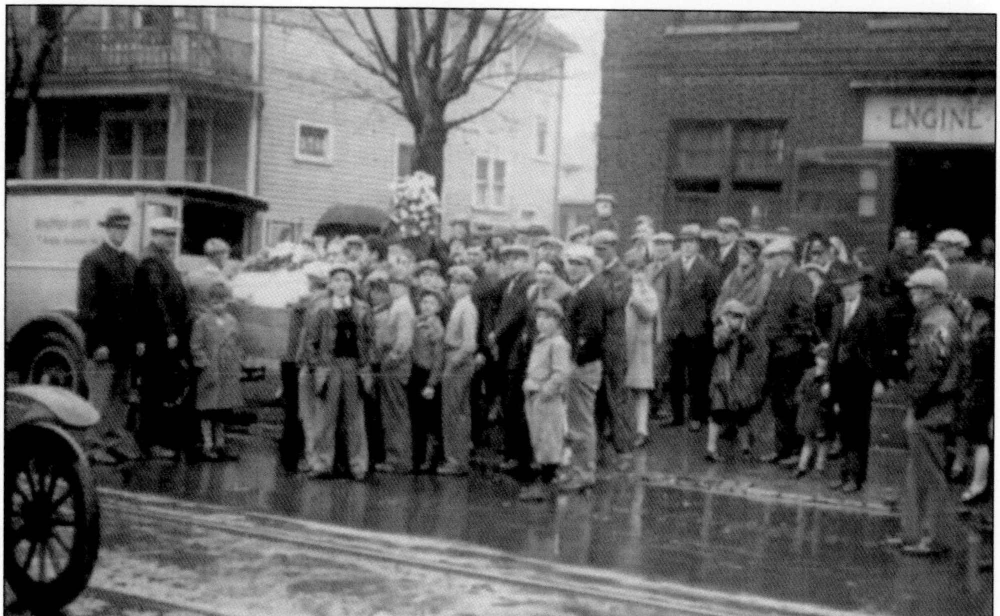

A Hero Mourned. A whole neighborhood turned out to pay their last respects to Sport, who was tragically killed in what he considered to be his line of duty. He was struck and killed by a car while attending a fire on the East Side. Sport had been with Engine Company 45 for more than six years at the time of the accident. (Courtesy of William Cable.)

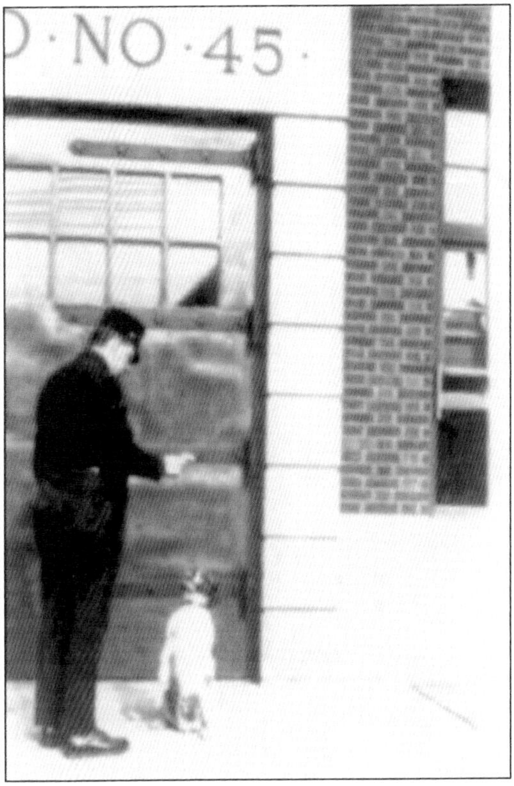

A Warrior's Farewell. Funeral arrangements befitting of a hero were made for Sport, who was much beloved. Sport was a mixed breed terrier who learned to climb ladders and showed no fear in entering a burning building to provide assistance to his comrades. He lost one eye and most of his tail during his firefighting career. (Courtesy of William Cable.)

In honor of Sport, a resident of St. Jean Avenue wrote a poem which reads, in part:

There was a dog, his name was Sport. His color, buff and white.
He loved to ride the fire truck, to fires in the night.
And Sport was ever on the job, to be sure he heard the bell.
A dog of fire was old Sport, how he would bark and yell.
At Engine House number 45, they're mourning night and day.
For all there's left is memories,
for old Sport is laid away.

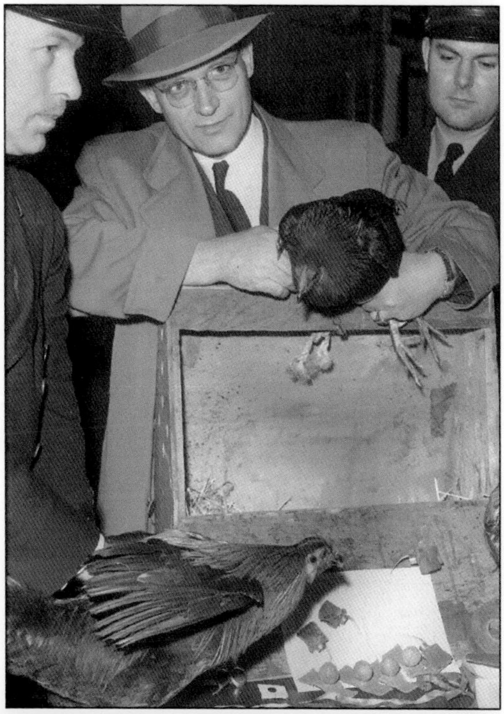

Barbaric and Cruel. Detroit Police Officers and Michigan Humane Society officials seize gamecocks after a raid on a cock fighting ring in Detroit in the 1940s. These roosters fight to the death while onlookers watch and place bets on the outcome. A gruesome and bloody sport, cock fighting is now illegal in 47 states.

Fighters to the End. These roosters, even though held nowhere near the fighting ring, attempt to fight each other anyway, illustrating their combativeness. This raid resulted in the seizure of ten birds and the arrest of nine men and one woman.

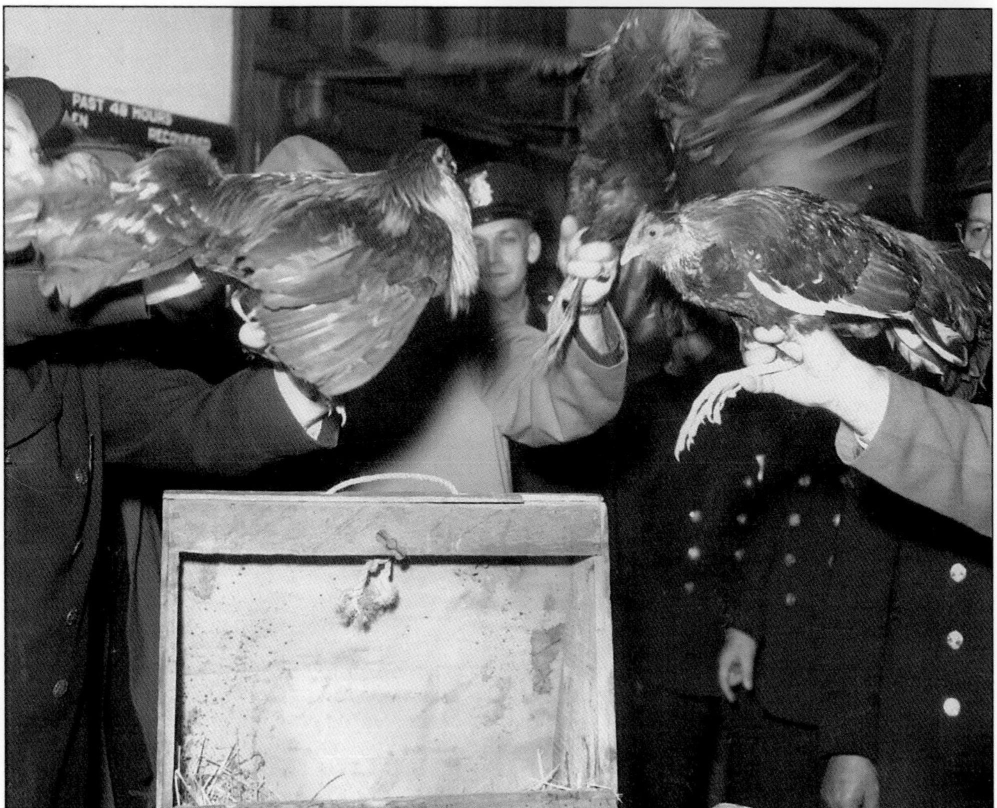

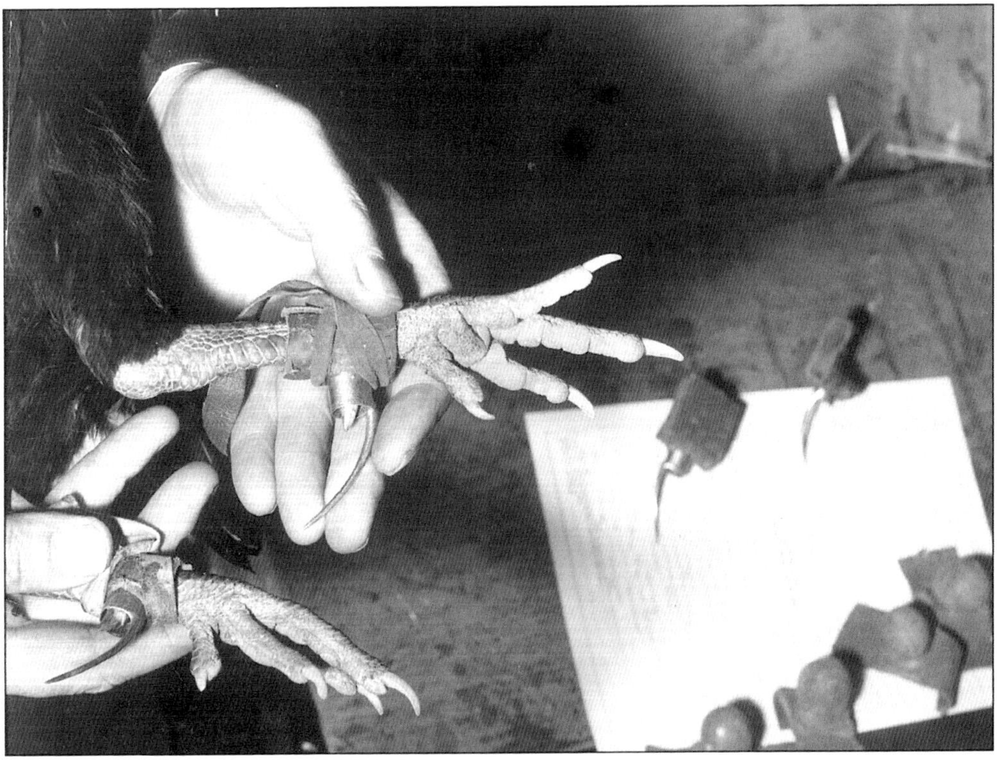

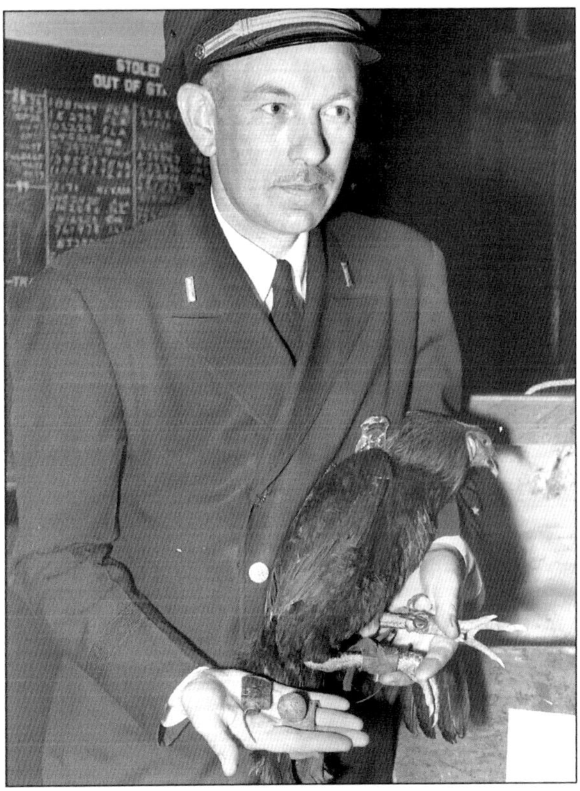

DEADLY TOOLS OF THE TRADE. The spurs and gaffs attached to the legs of the fighting birds can inflict mortal wounds. Fighting birds often suffer fatal puncture wounds. Cockfighting still takes place today, even in states where it is illegal.

A BIRD IN THE HAND. This Detroit Police lieutenant holds a confiscated bird and the weapons of the "sport." A raid in Oakland County in the late 1940s resulted in the arrest of 86 people, the seizure of 75 live birds and 15 dead ones, and fines totaling $4,350.

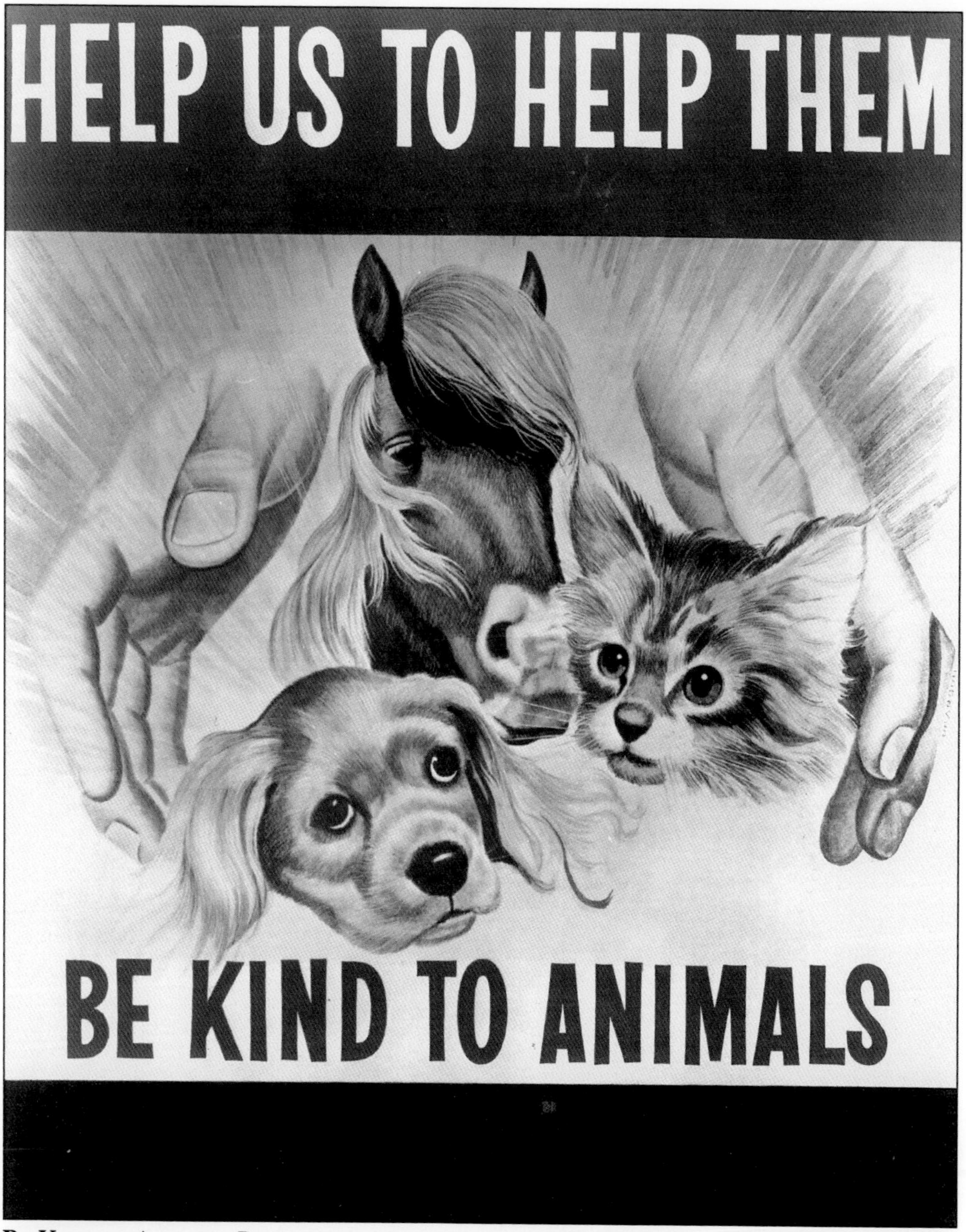

Be Kind to Animals. Beginning some time in the 1920s, "Be Kind to Animals" is the oldest, most recognizable campaign for animals and represents an enduring legacy to animal welfare proponents. In the 15th century, Leonardo daVinci was quoted as saying, "The day will come, when mankind will look upon the killing of animals with the same horror we look upon the killing of our fellow man." Men such as Ghandi, Mark Twain, Bernard Shaw, Louis Carroll, and countless others, both famous and not so famous, have spoken or written similar words concerning the plight of animals in our society. The Michigan Humane Society embarked on a campaign of humane education as early as 1925, to teach and promote humane values for the benefit of all animals. That campaign carries on today with shelter tours and on-site school presentations for children. Though considerable progress has been made, there is much yet to be done.

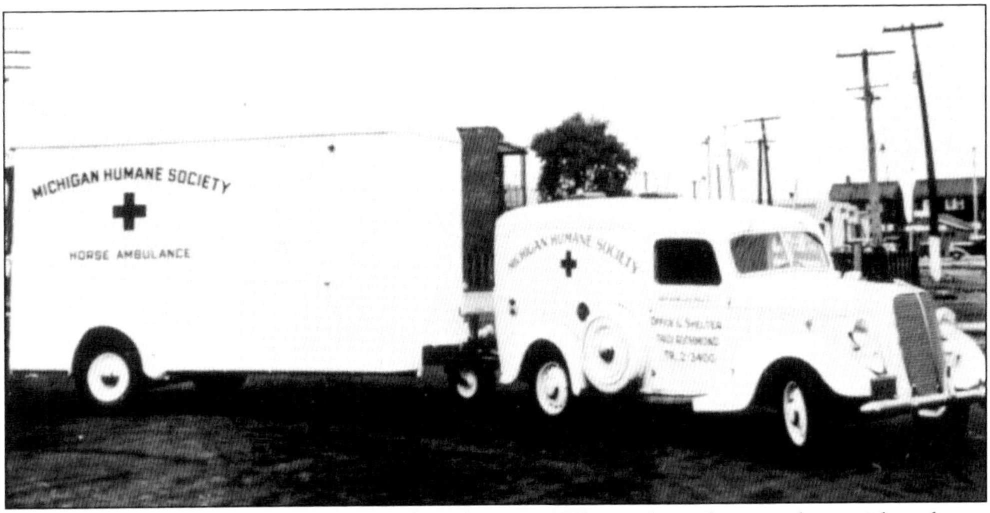

THE AMBULANCES. In this photo, a brand-new 1935 panel truck, complete with a horse ambulance trailer, makes its appearance at the Michigan Humane Society's Richmond Avenue Shelter. Sporting a brand-new white paint job complete with the "Blue Cross" emblem of the Society, the vehicle was the pride of the fleet.

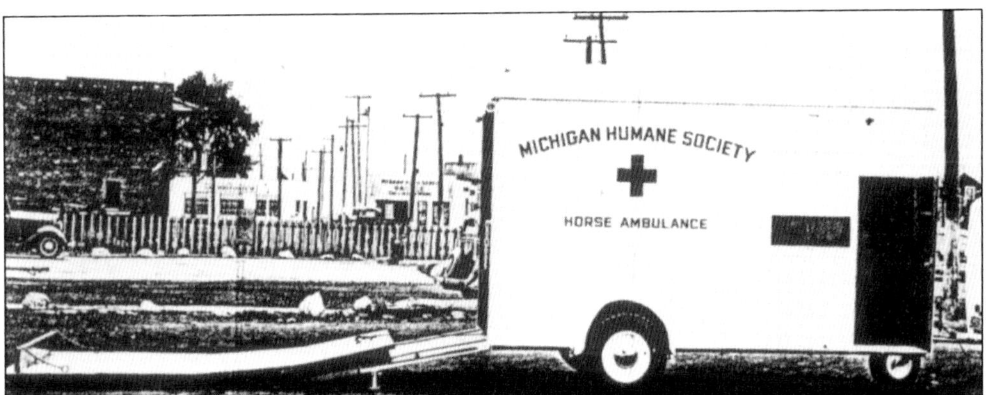

THE HORSE TRAILER. The latest equipment makes this horse trailer ambulance an efficient transport vehicle by which to move lame, injured, or deceased horses from the streets. A stretcher extends from the rear of the trailer and a winch can be used to help move the animal into the trailer for transporting.

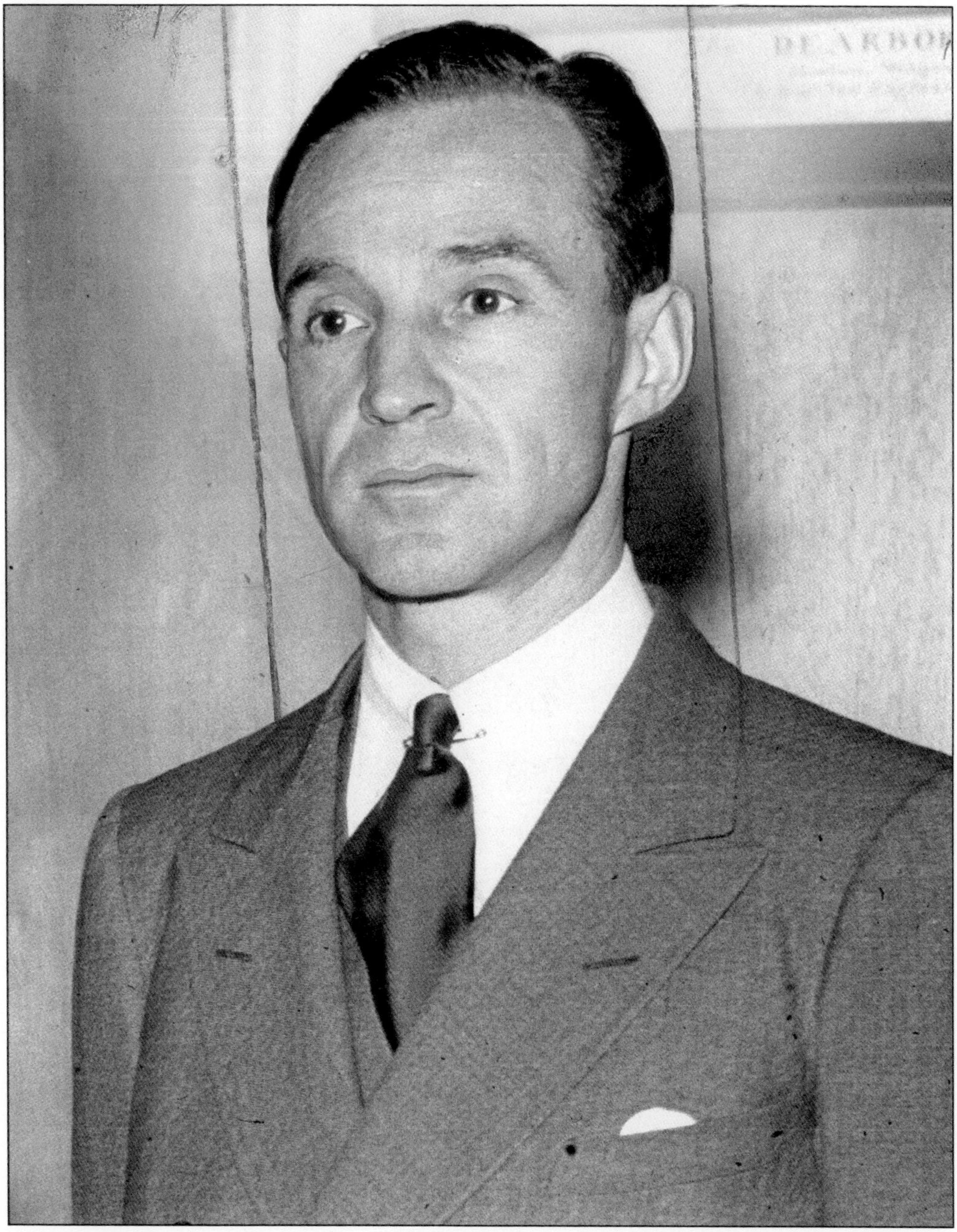

EDSEL B. FORD. The only son of automobile king Henry Ford, Edsel Ford was born in 1893 and followed in his father's footsteps in the automobile manufacturing business. It was Edsel who convinced his father in the 1920s to change the body styles of the Ford vehicles to help with slumping car sales. With his new vision and innovative ideas, Edsel Ford literally saved the company from going out of business. He began to oversee all aspects of the design, color, and construction of the Model A. Henry Ford was a long-time member of the Board of the Michigan Humane Society and Edsel Ford followed his father's charitable endeavors as well. In 1935, he made a monetary donation of $500 to the Michigan Humane Society for the purchase of a new horse ambulance. (Courtesy of Burton Historical Collection.)

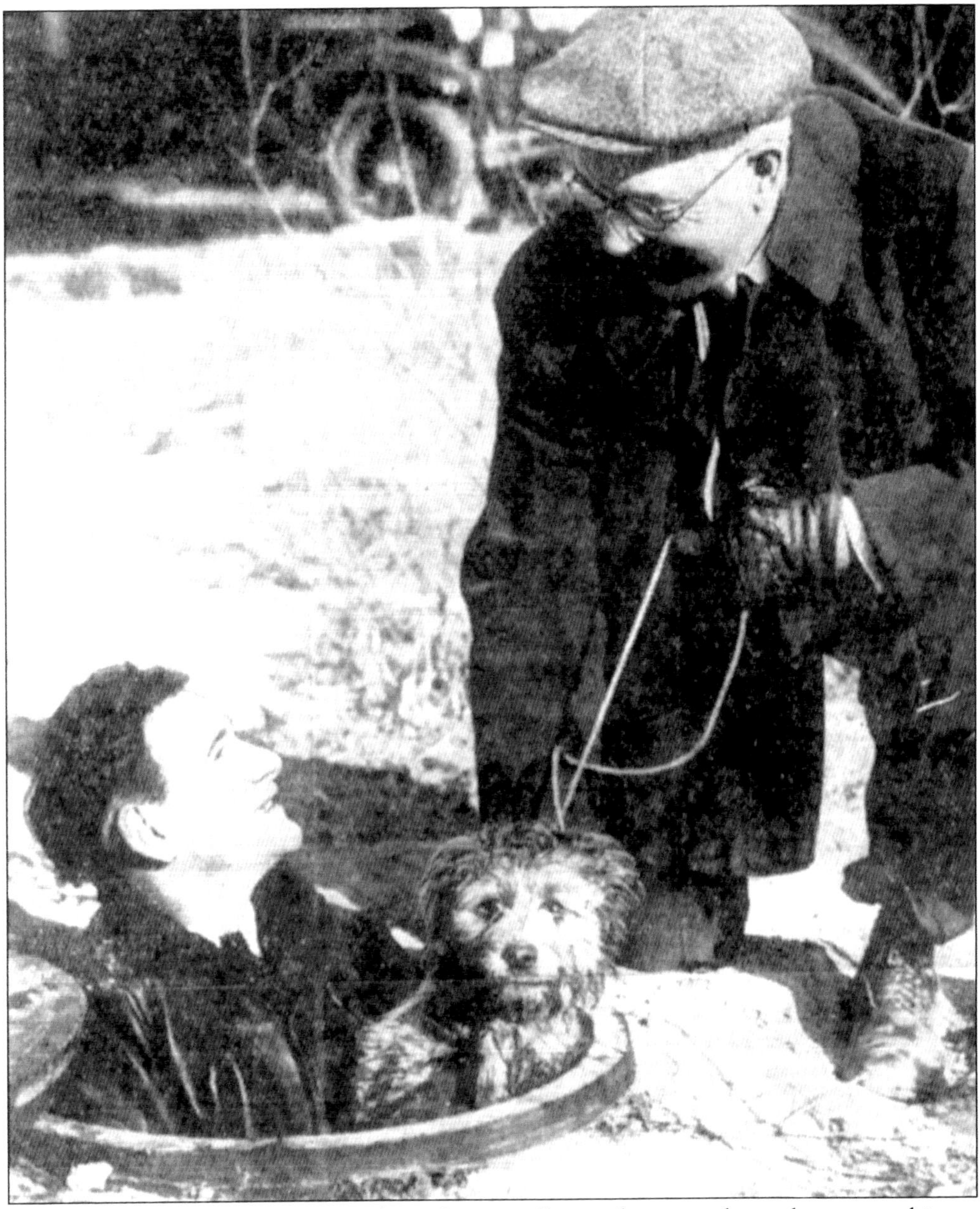

STORM SEWER RESCUE. This story of two Society officers who rescued two dogs trapped in an icy storm sewer is typical of the Michigan Humane Society's efforts to care for those unable to care for themselves. Stanley Doner, left, and Frank Watson, right, spent four days trying to rescue a sizeable German Shepherd and a smaller terrier mix who had fallen down the drainage hole while chasing a rabbit in 1932. With the aid of ropes, ladders, a pistol, and a large board, the rescue attempt was successful on the fourth day. Trying to lasso the dogs from the street-level proved fruitless. Doner then used a ladder to lower himself into the hole. Watson then fired the pistol into the air from street-level and the smaller dog ran straight into Doner's arms, frightened by the sound of the gunfire. The Shepherd was also rescued using this method. Both dogs were taken to the Michigan Humane Society Detroit Shelter for some much deserved love and care. (Courtesy of Burton Historical Collection.)

THE STATELY STATLER HOTEL. In 1937, the Michigan Humane Society celebrated its 60th Anniversary with a gala event at the Hotel Statler in downtown Detroit. Mr. Frank Cody was the master of ceremonies and Abner Larned gave a review of the work of the Society since 1877. A fashion tableaux depicting styles of ladies dresses over the 60-year-period was a highlight, as was the guest appearance of Detroit's first seeing-eye dog, Tello, with his owner Ellsworth G. Smith. (Courtesy of Burton Historical Collection.)

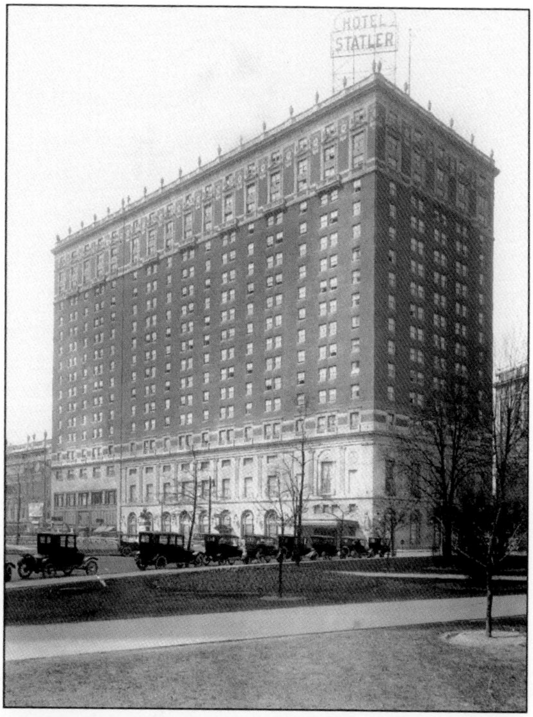

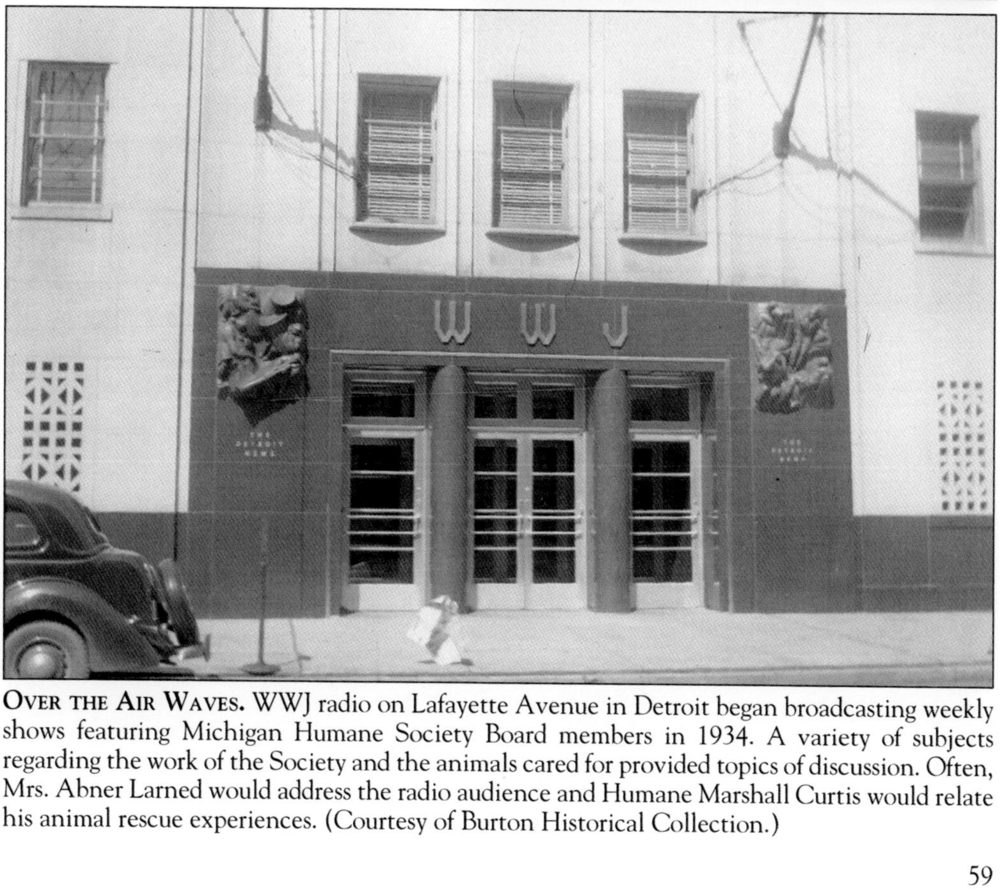

OVER THE AIR WAVES. WWJ radio on Lafayette Avenue in Detroit began broadcasting weekly shows featuring Michigan Humane Society Board members in 1934. A variety of subjects regarding the work of the Society and the animals cared for provided topics of discussion. Often, Mrs. Abner Larned would address the radio audience and Humane Marshall Curtis would relate his animal rescue experiences. (Courtesy of Burton Historical Collection.)

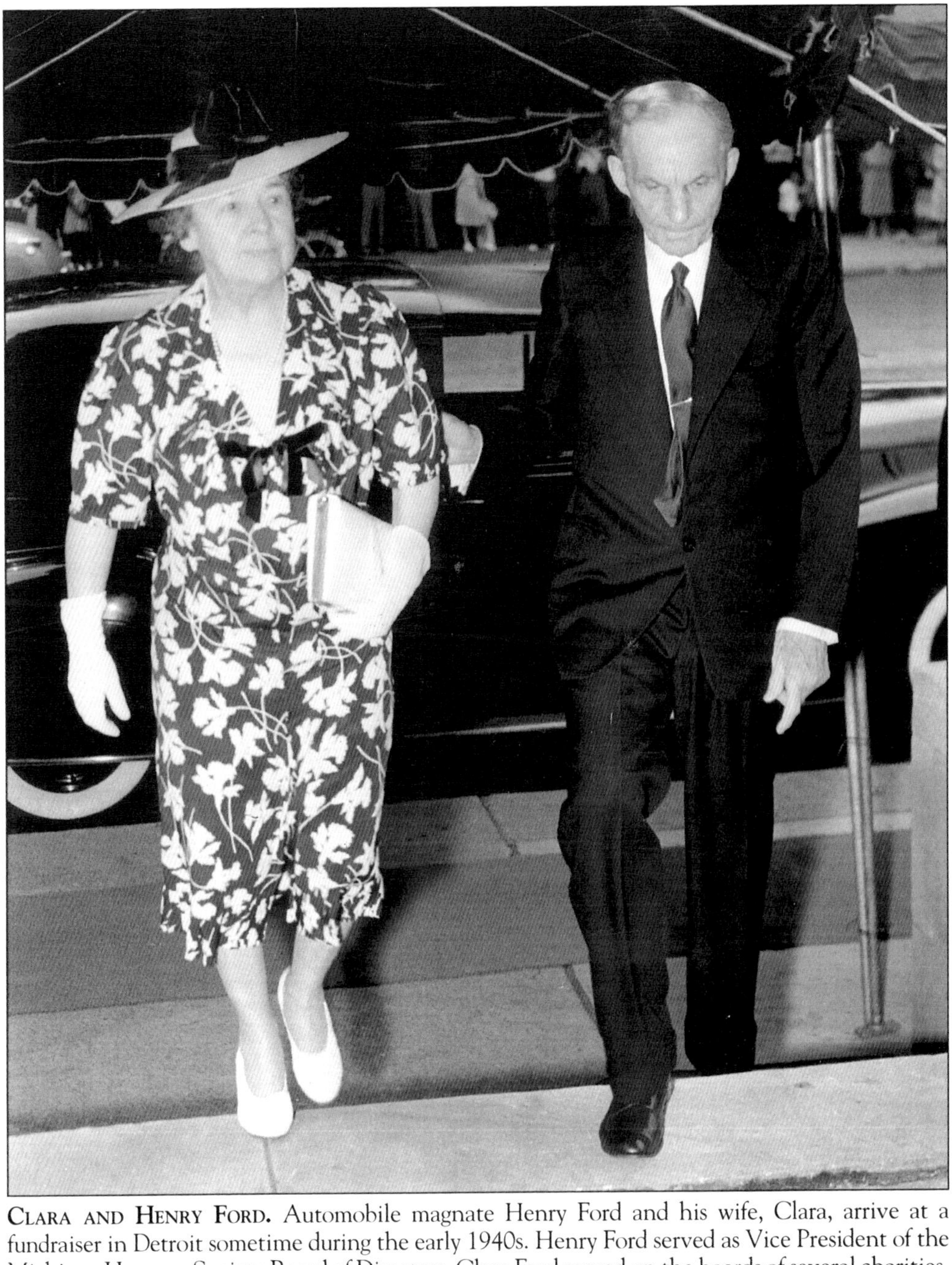

Clara and Henry Ford. Automobile magnate Henry Ford and his wife, Clara, arrive at a fundraiser in Detroit sometime during the early 1940s. Henry Ford served as Vice President of the Michigan Humane Society Board of Directors. Clara Ford served on the boards of several charities, and the entire Ford family was quite supportive of the good work of the Michigan Humane Society. Early in the Society's development, the Ford family donated a parcel of land used as a rest farm for horses. Edsel Ford made monetary donations as well. The generous support of people from all walks of life has greatly aided the Michigan Humane Society in providing much-needed services and programs throughout its 125-year history. Despite the economic distress during the Great Depression, the Society was able to maintain its level of service due to the continued support of those with means. (Courtesy of Burton Historical Society.)

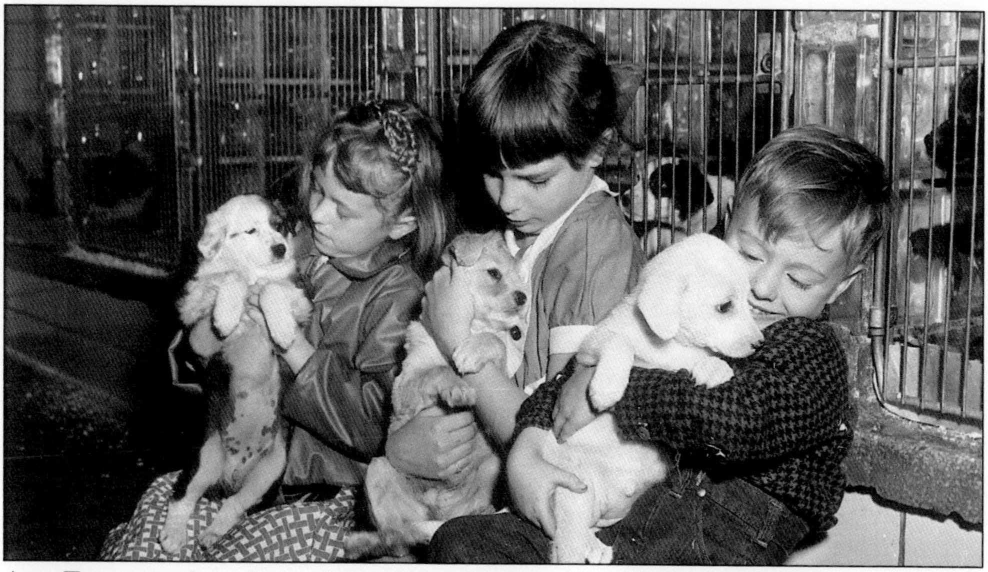

AND THEY CALL IT... PUPPY LOVE! Puppy breath and children's giggles make for smiles all around. These three pups are looking for a new home and these three children are prime candidates. Teaching humane values is paramount to the mission of the Michigan Humane Society, and children have been heavily involved from the very early years. Junior Humane Societies were formed in the 1930s, and these groups brought in much needed funds through concerts, plays, and candy sales.

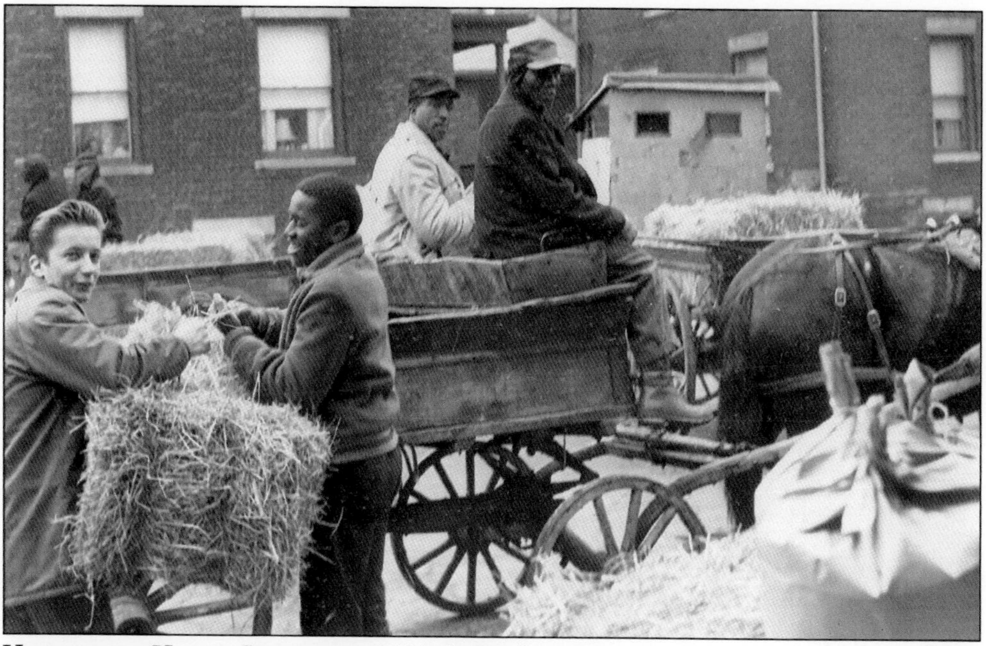

HOLIDAYS FOR HORSES. Beginning in 1931, the Michigan Humane Society hosted Holiday parties for workhorses and their drivers. At these parties, the drivers would line-up their horses on the streets near the Michigan Humane Society shelter at 7401 Richmond. Society officers and city officials would judge the horses and award three cash prizes for the "Best Cared-For Horse." All of the horses received a generous helping of hay, oats, and apples as well as a new blanket.

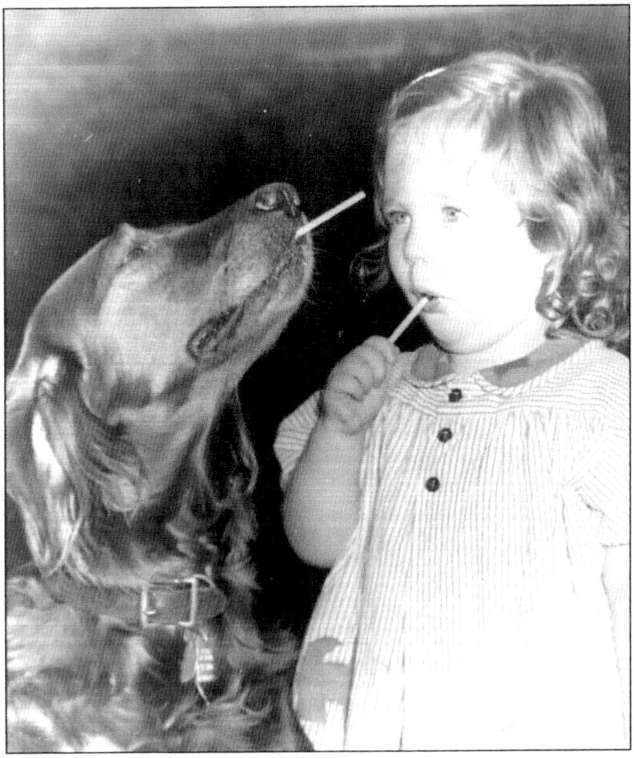

LOLLIPOPS. Everybody's a sucker for a cute kid and a dog. Geraldine Stocker and her Irish Setter, Patty, enjoy a sweet treat on a stick in this 1948 photograph. It's hard to tell who is enjoying their sucker more, Geraldine or Patty.

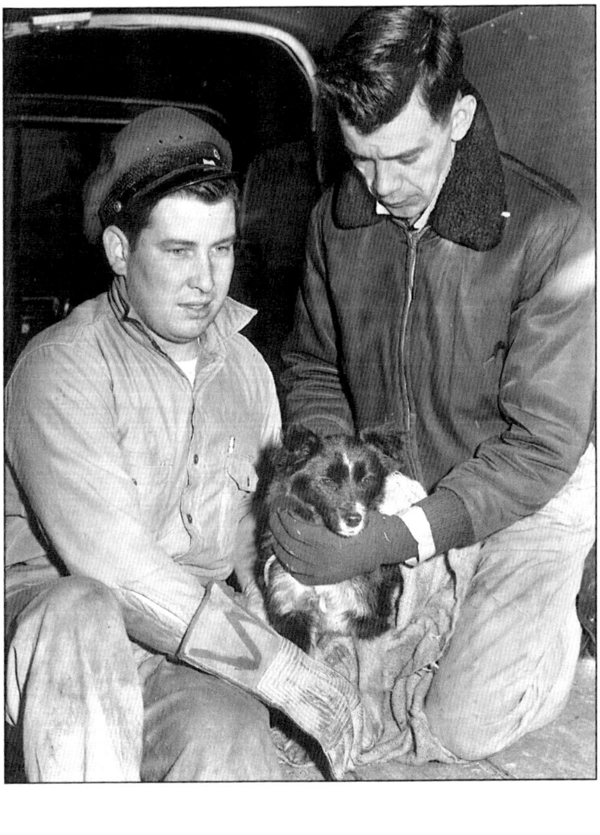

CLOSE CALL FOR A PUP. Michigan Humane Society ambulance driver Woodrow Hastings, at left, takes a breather after rescuing a very lucky dog from a coal silo. Using ropes and ladders, Hastings was able to rescue the poor pup, and Detroit Shelter Superintendent Wallace Cross gave her a quick check for injuries prior to transporting her to the shelter for care.

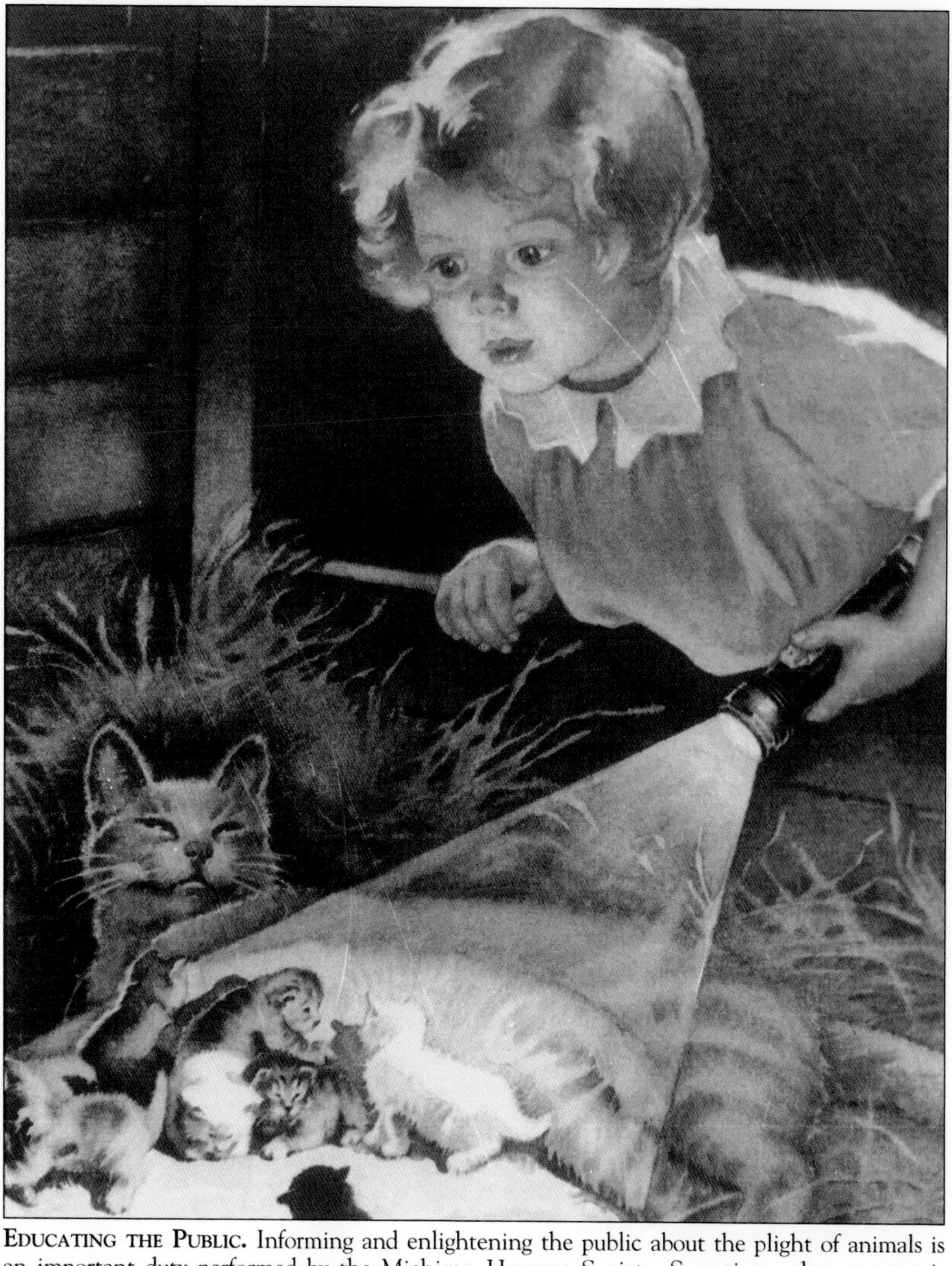

EDUCATING THE PUBLIC. Informing and enlightening the public about the plight of animals is an important duty performed by the Michigan Humane Society. Sometimes, that message is conveyed with subtlety, other times, the use of hard-hitting graphics is warranted. In this Norman Rockwell-like poster, the message is subtle yet timely. The animal population has been outpacing the human population for decades. There will never be enough homes for them all, yet here is what appears to be another stray cat with a litter of kittens in a barn. The Michigan Humane Society enacted mandatory sterilization for all pets adopted from their shelters back in 1983. In the State of Michigan, the law now requires all animals adopted from public or private shelters to be sterilized, thanks to the efforts of the Michigan Humane Society on the legislative front.

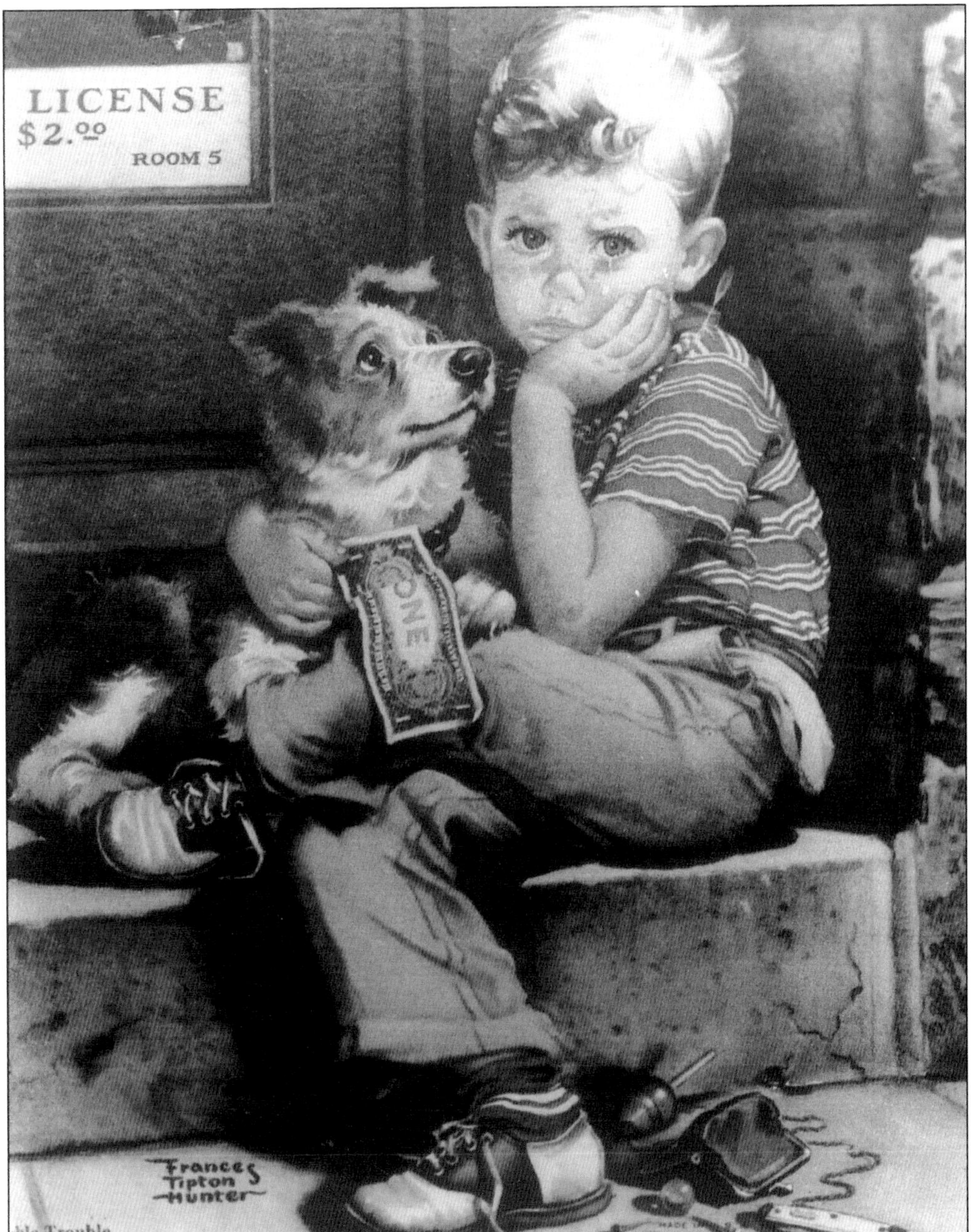

POIGNANT PLEA. The troubled look of this boy who has only half of the $2 dog license fee strikes the heart of many. Not just a heart-wrenching portrayal of a boy and his dog, this illustration by Frances Tipton Hunter sends a number of silent, subtle messages. It serves as a reminder to license your house pet. The city license helps a city determine the number of animals living there, as well as provides identification and can help in the return of your pet, should he become lost. It also illustrates how, in some instances, children are the ones left responsible for taking care of the family pet, sometimes without appropriate means. Over four million pets are lost each year. Under 20 percent of those lost pets are ever reunited with their families. The Michigan Humane Society urges pet owners to identify their pets with a tag and a microchip.

Four

OUTREACH UNRIVALED

1950–1960

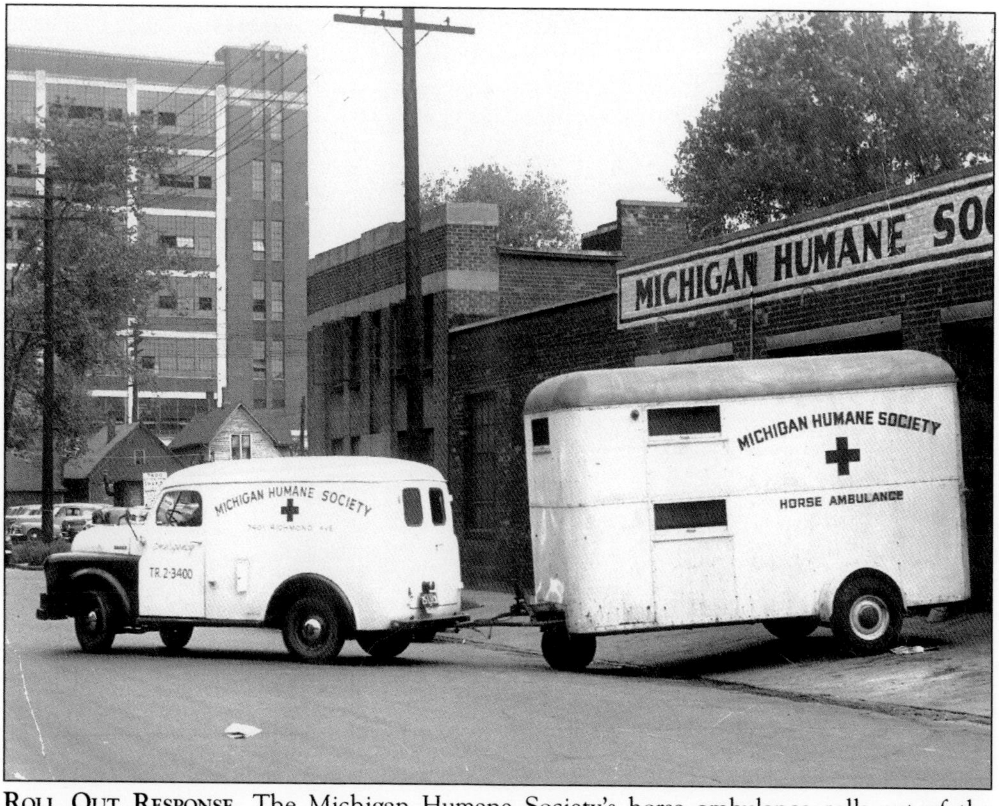

ROLL OUT RESPONSE. The Michigan Humane Society's horse ambulance rolls out of the Richmond Street garage in response to an emergency in the spring of 1953. This is the same ambulance trailer that the society acquired in 1935, but it's now hitched to a 1940s model panel truck with the traditional Michigan Humane Society blue cross emblem. There were still quite a few workhorses in the city of Detroit, and the Society continued to respond to the needs of the work horse well into the 1960s.

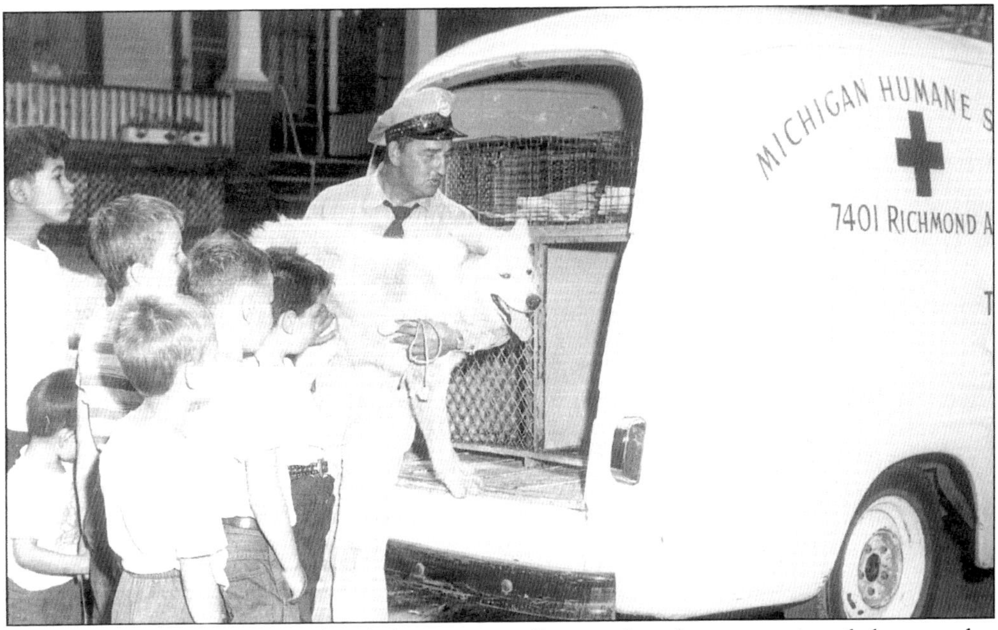

EMERGENCY RESCUE. A typical ambulance run is illustrated in the next series of photographs. After being injured in the street, this white dog is gently lifted into the Michigan Humane Society ambulance by driver Lloyd Schwartz, while neighborhood children watch and worry for the pooch.

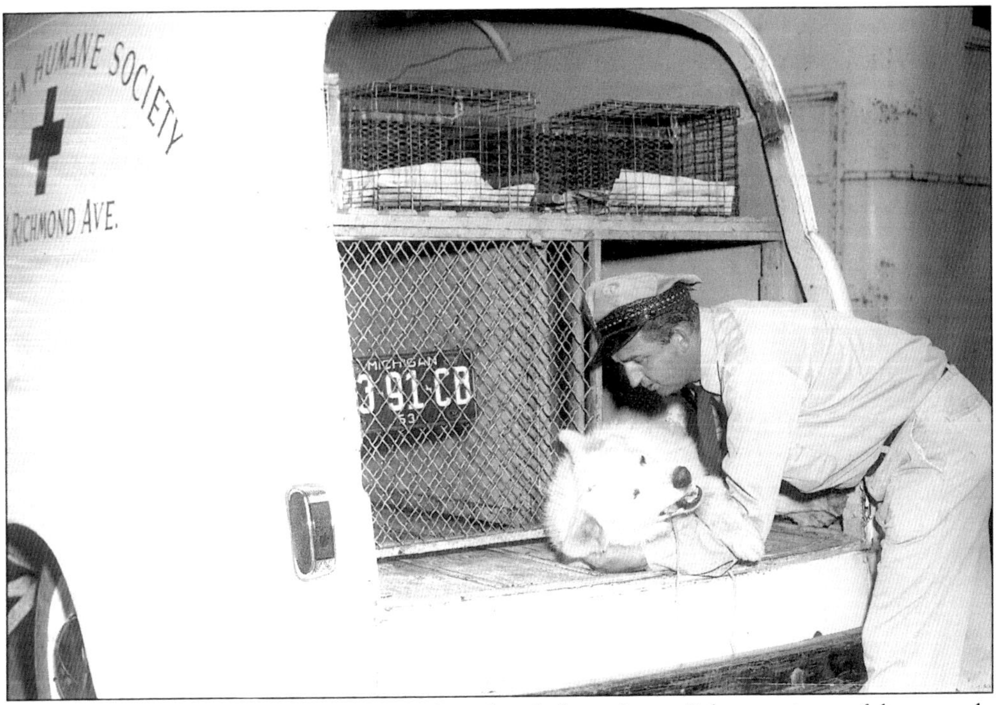

ARRIVAL AT THE SHELTER. Upon arrival at the shelter, driver Schwartz is careful to gently remove the large dog from the back of the ambulance. With the dog's injuries unknown at the time, Schwartz prevents further injury by handling the dog with care and attention.

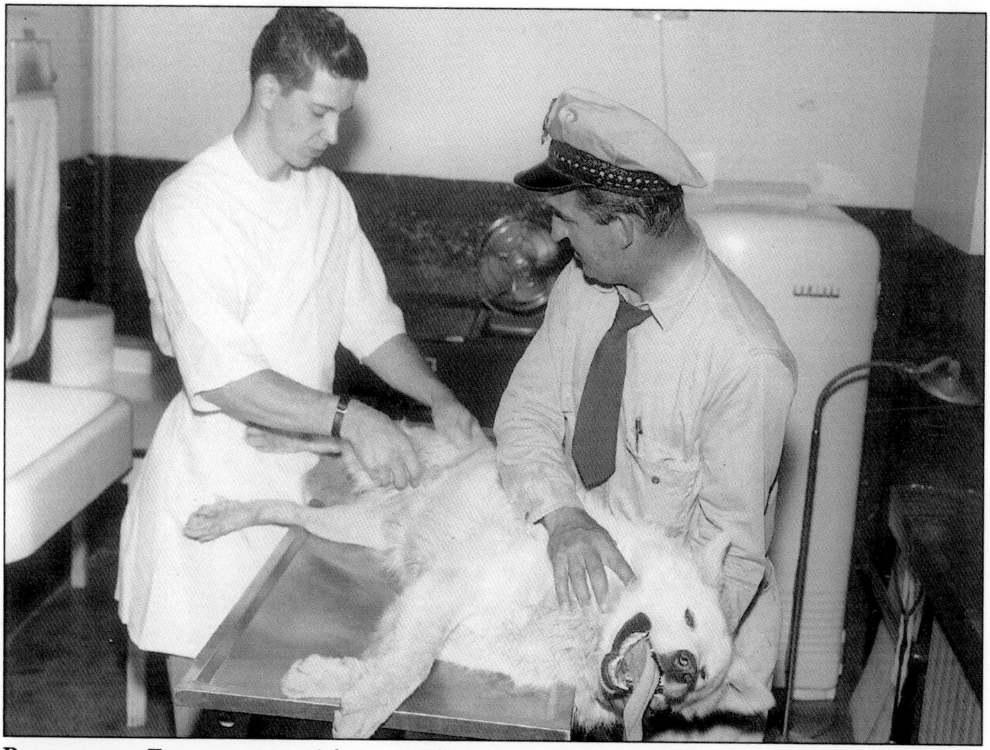

Preliminary Examination. After arrival at the shelter, the dog is examined by Michigan Humane Society veterinarian, Dr. Raymond Dow. He checks for broken bones and open wounds while driver Schwartz keeps the dog comfortable and calm.

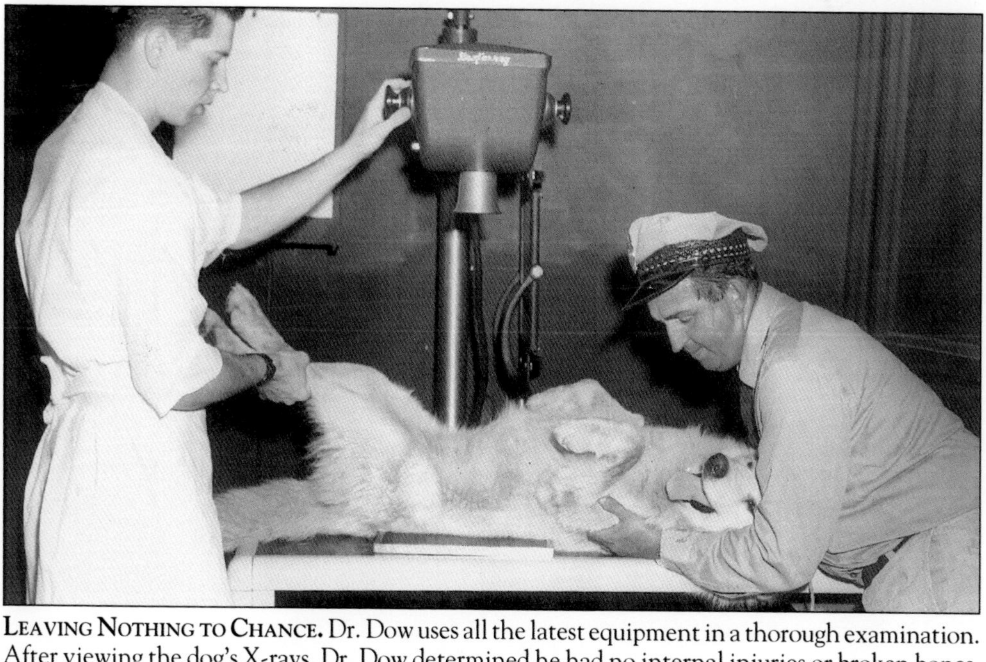

Leaving Nothing to Chance. Dr. Dow uses all the latest equipment in a thorough examination. After viewing the dog's X-rays, Dr. Dow determined he had no internal injuries or broken bones. He gave him a clean bill of health.

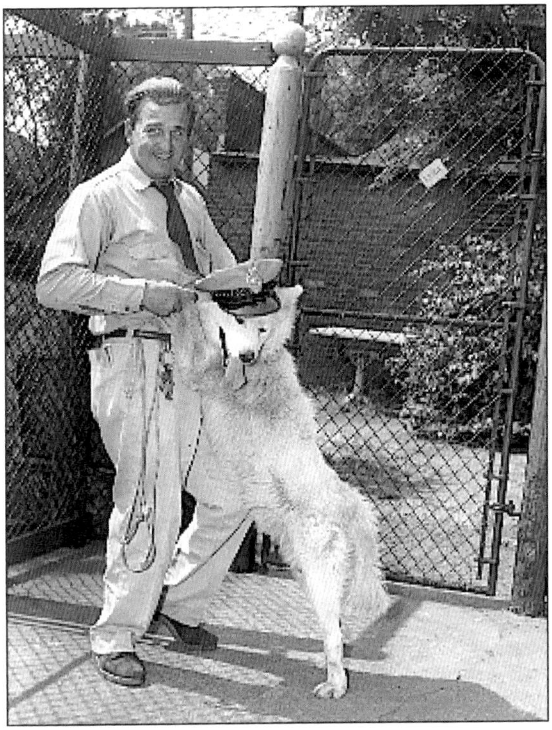

All Is Well That Ends Well. Here, the rescued dog looks fully recovered and ready to assist rescue driver Schwartz in his next call. The dog was kept at the shelter during his veterinary exam and held for observation for a few days. It is not uncommon for ambulance and rescue drivers to become attached to each animal they pick up.

Graduation Treat. Miss Mary K. Kohn, 12, and her mixed breed dog graduated from the Southern Michigan Obedience Training Club, their first obedience class, in 1953. The classes were held in the Grosse Pointe High School Gym. He was the only mixed breed dog to graduate in a class of pure bred dogs. The Southern Michigan Obedience Training Club was taught by Michigan Humane Society Director Marion K. Kellogg in 1953.

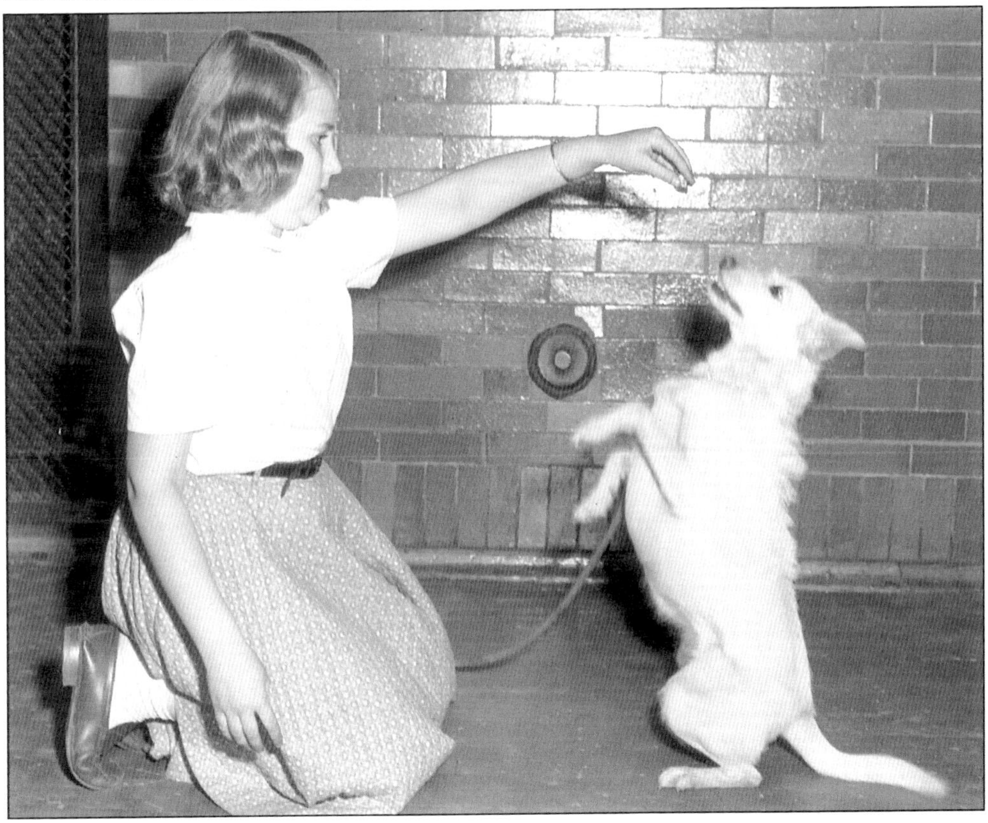

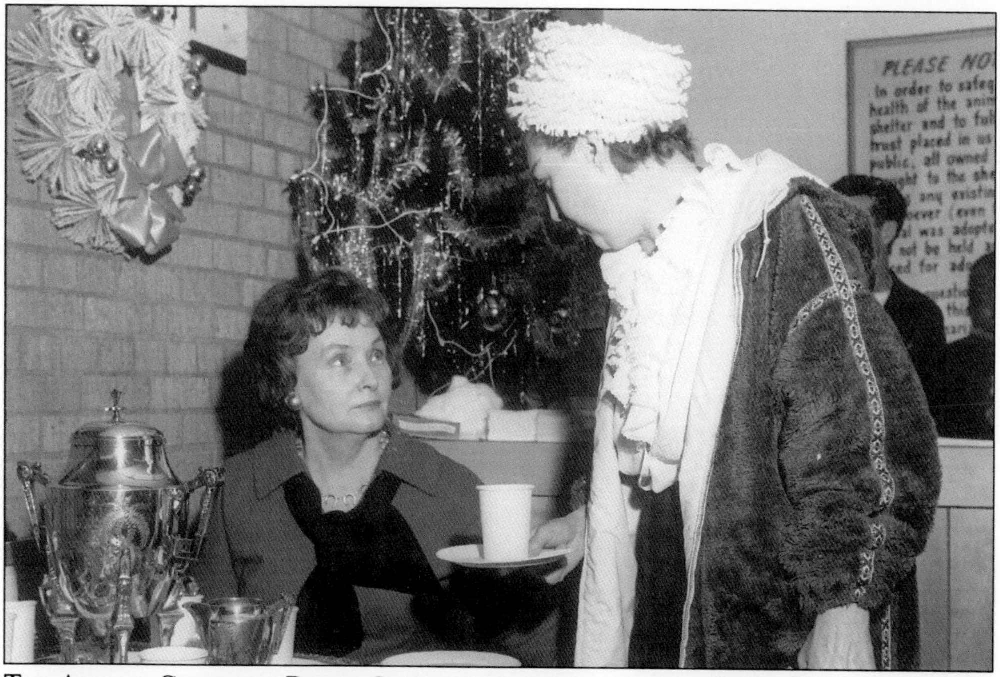

THE ANNUAL CHRISTMAS PARTY. Society matrons take time out during the Holiday Season to help out at the Michigan Humane Society Holiday Party for Horses. The parties were well attended by horses and drivers, as well as people from the community. The neighborhood Christmas Tree, organized by the Michigan Humane Society, often towered over dozens of gifts donated for those less fortunate.

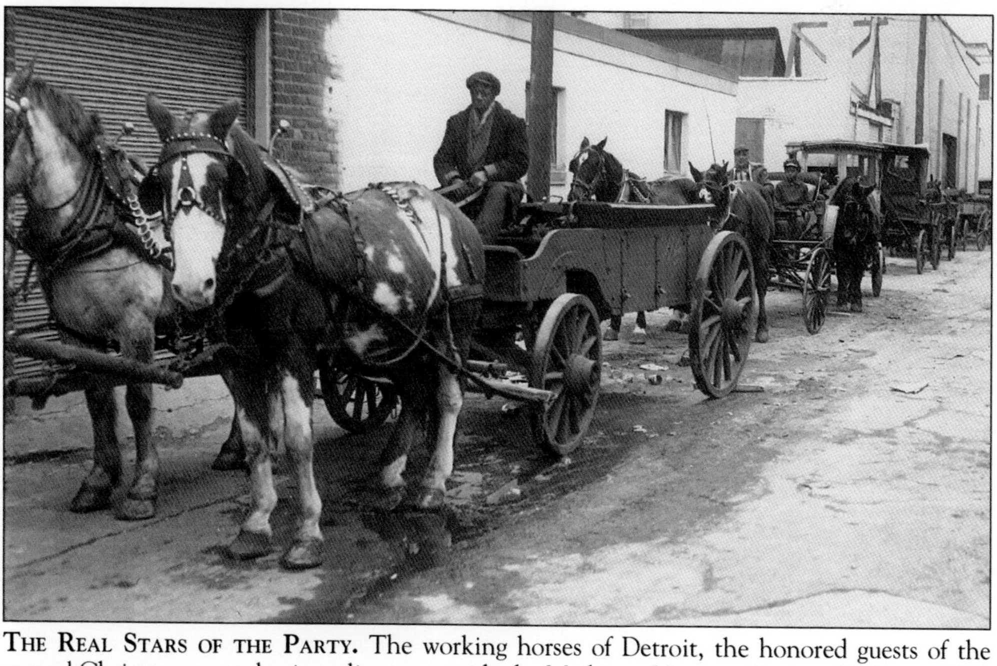

THE REAL STARS OF THE PARTY. The working horses of Detroit, the honored guests of the annual Christmas party, begin to line up outside the Michigan Humane Society Shelter at 7401 Richmond to get their gifts of hay, oats, and apples.

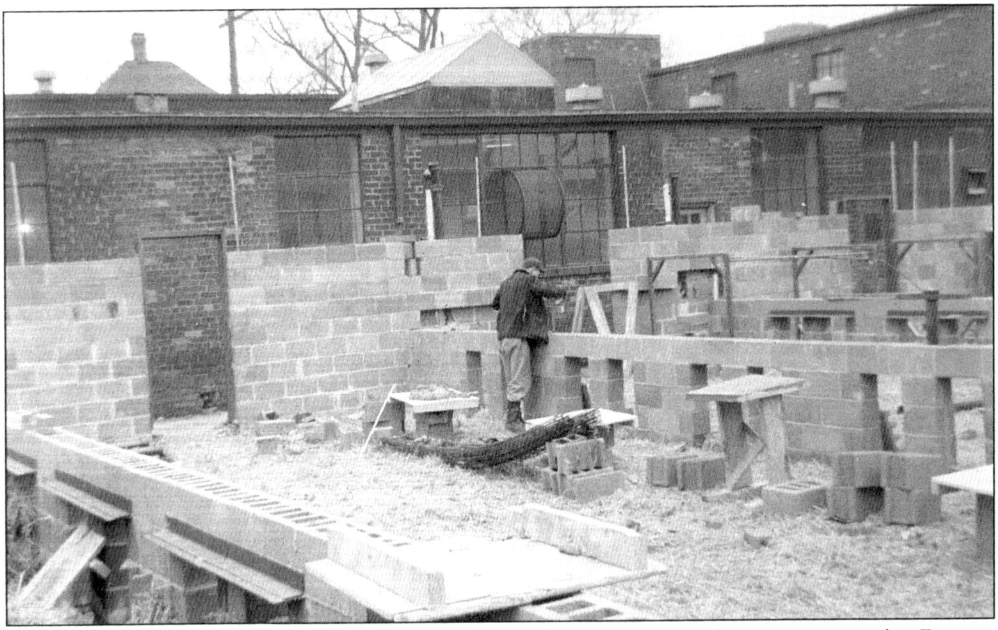

MUCH-NEEDED EXPANSION. There was a climate of renovation and expansion at the Detroit Shelter in the 1950s. New kennels were added to accommodate the ever-increasing number of animals in need of the Society's services, and renovations were made to the existing building to offer veterinary services to the pet-owning public.

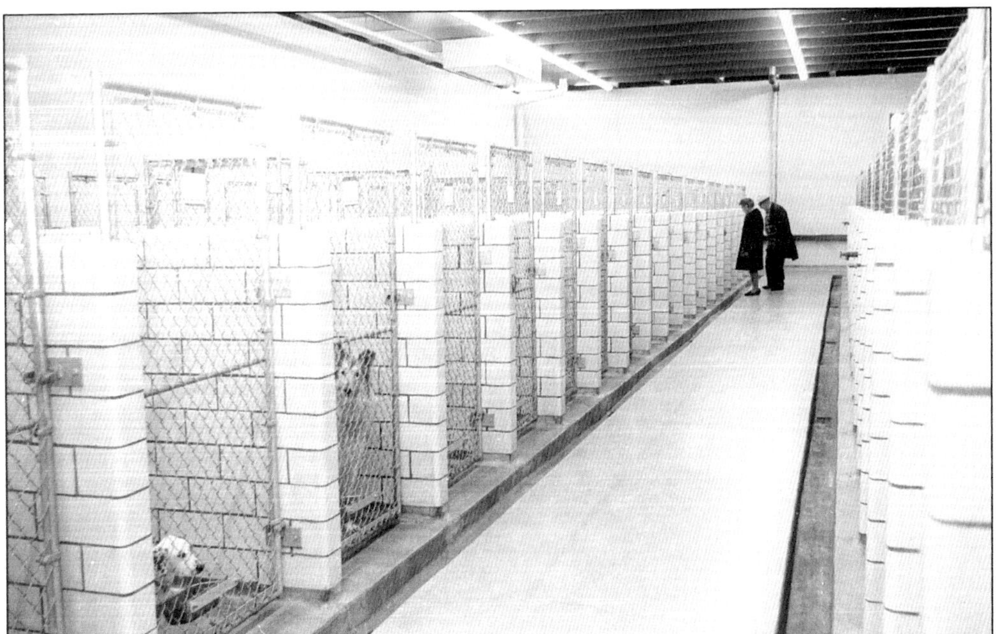

THE NEW KENNELS. These well-maintained kennels provide a clean and safe environment for dogs until animal lovers such as these come to adopt. Thousands of animals pass through the doors of the Michigan Humane Society's three Detroit-area shelters each year. In 2001, over 48,000 animals, both wild and domestic, came through Michigan Humane Society shelter facilities.

CATS: THREE, JOHNSON: ZERO. Michigan Humane Society Director Clifton Johnson tries to keep a handle on these two kittens as they do their best to upset his desk in 1957. Johnson, an Indiana native, was named manager of the Society in 1940.

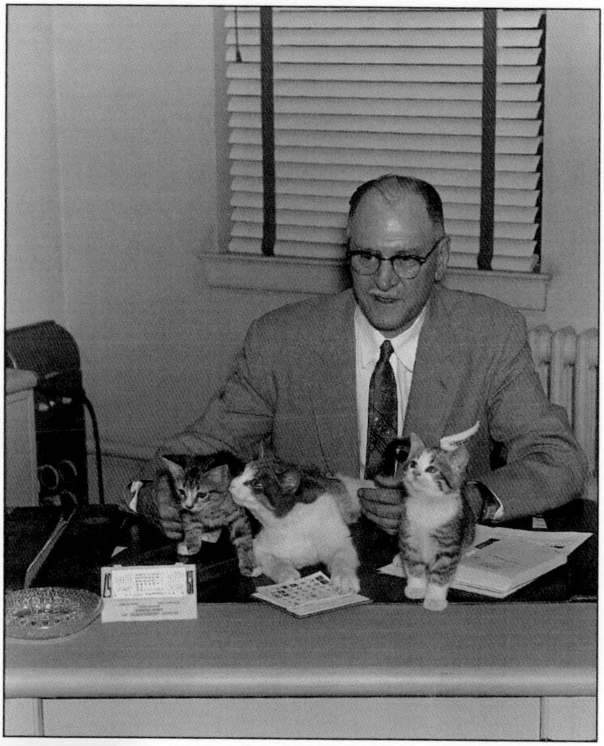

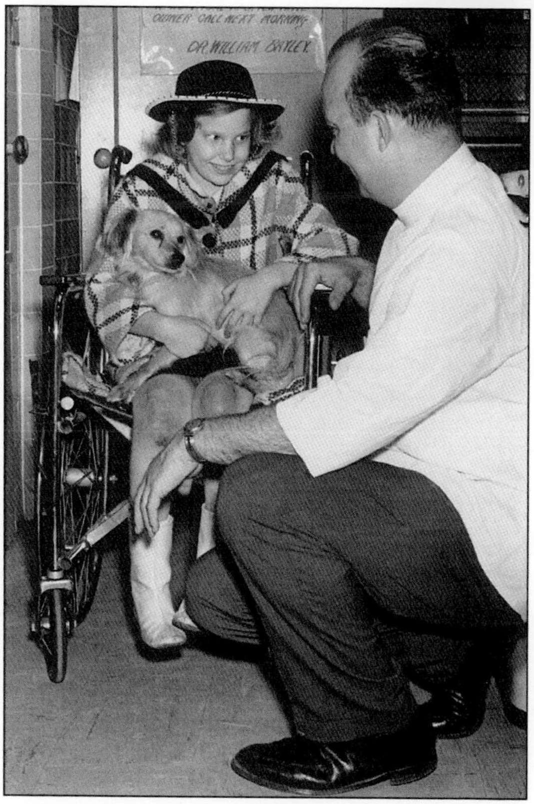

THAT PRECIOUS SMILE. Michigan Humane Society Head Veterinarian William Bayley gets a heartwarming smile from this little handicapped girl as she cradles a newfound friend. There is nothing quite like a new pet to warm the most unfortunate heart and have that warmth reflected in a smile.

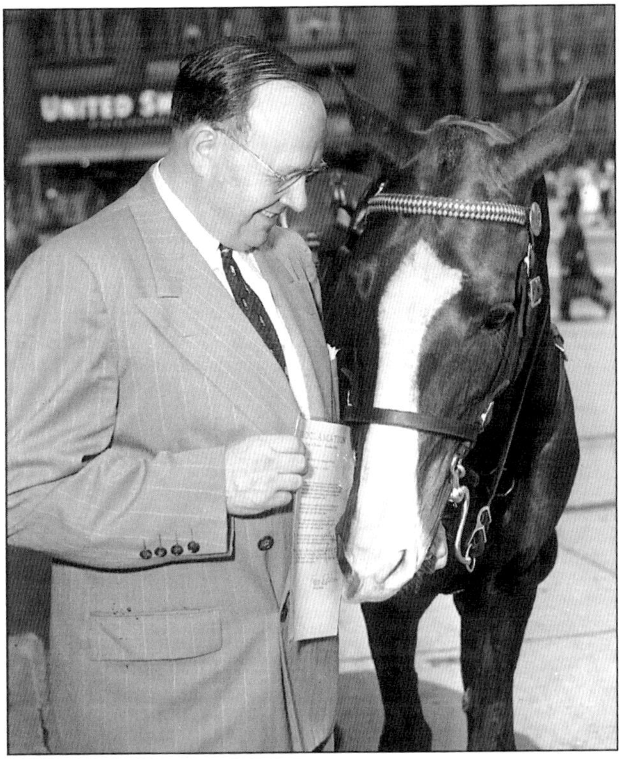

The Mayor's Proclamation. In a proclamation of utmost importance, acting Detroit Mayor Louis Miriani gets it straight from the horse's mouth in officially declaring "Be Kind to Animals Week" in 1953.

Helping Animals In Distress. The Michigan Humane Society has provided ambulance service to injured animals in the city of Detroit since before the rise of the automobile. The winter months prove to be the hardest on the animals, and these ambulance drivers stand ready to provide service. The Society is the only organization in the city that provides rescue service 365 days a year.

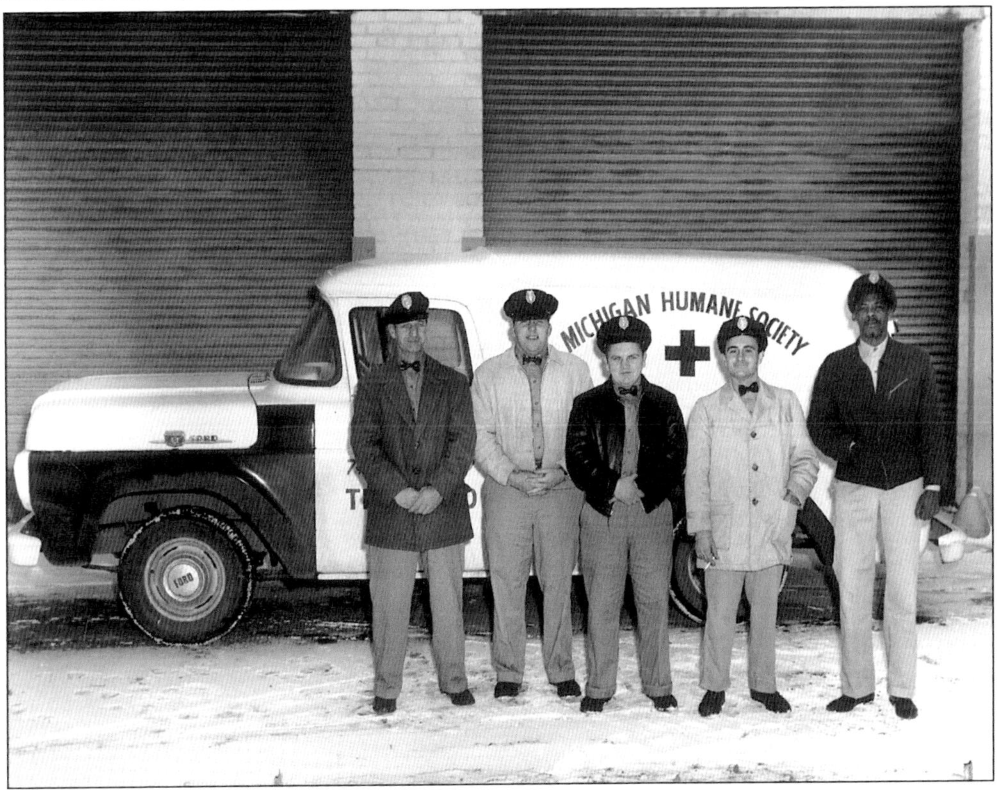

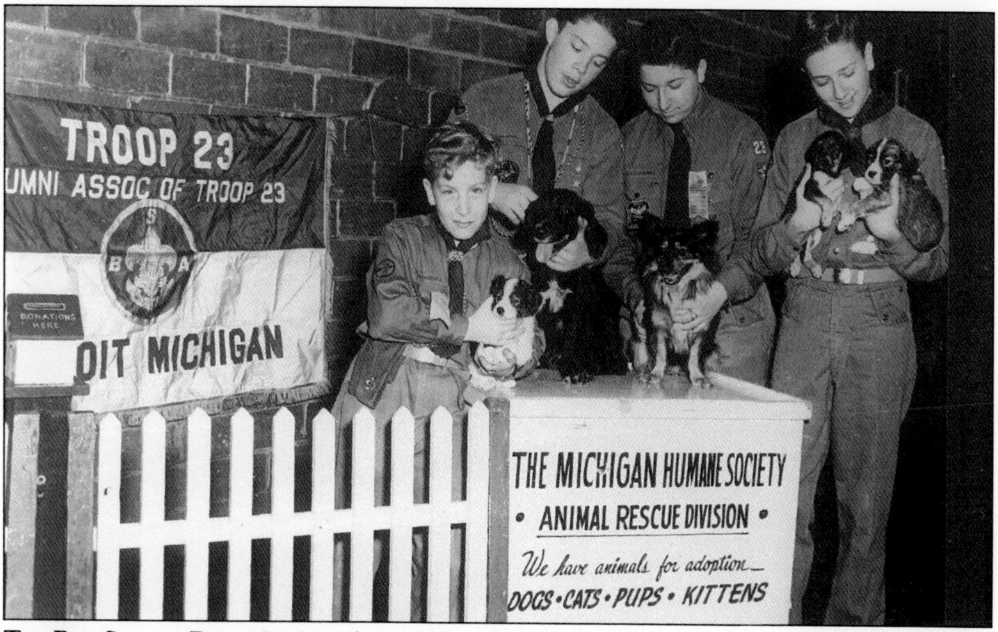

The Boy Scouts Pitch In. Members of Boy Scout Troop 23 of Detroit volunteer their services at a Michigan Humane Society information and adoption booth in the late 1950s. Today, Scouting groups still lend their time and talents to the Michigan Humane Society in the form of building and landscaping projects, pet supply drives, and fundraising events.

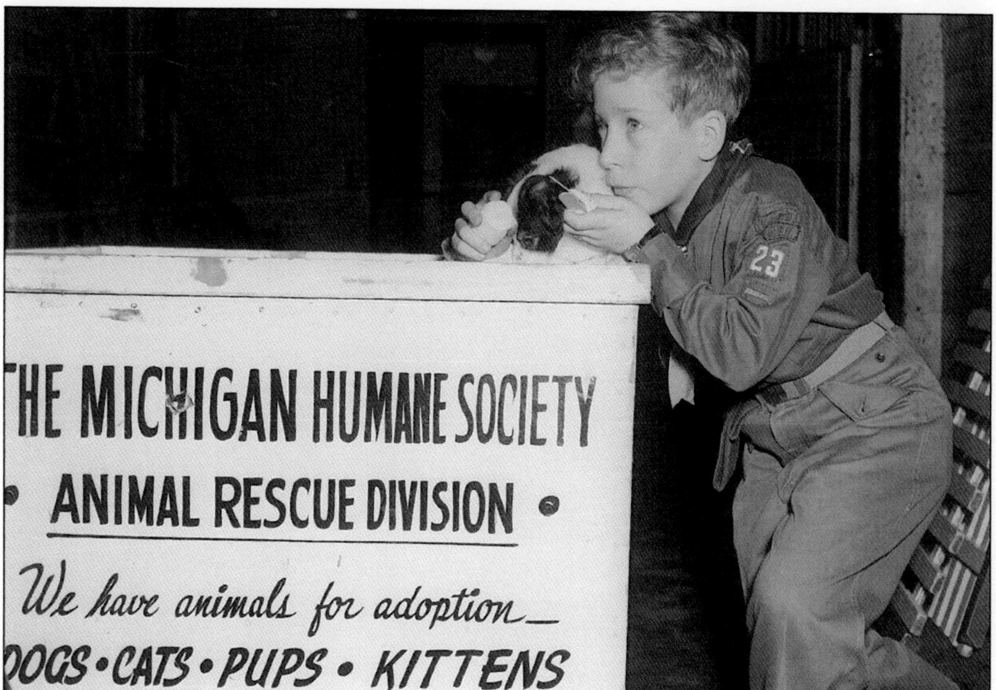

A Boy and a Dog. This Boy Scout comforts an accommodating pup prior to its finding a good home. Volunteers play a key role in helping the Michigan Humane Society place thousands of animals each year through off-site adoption events.

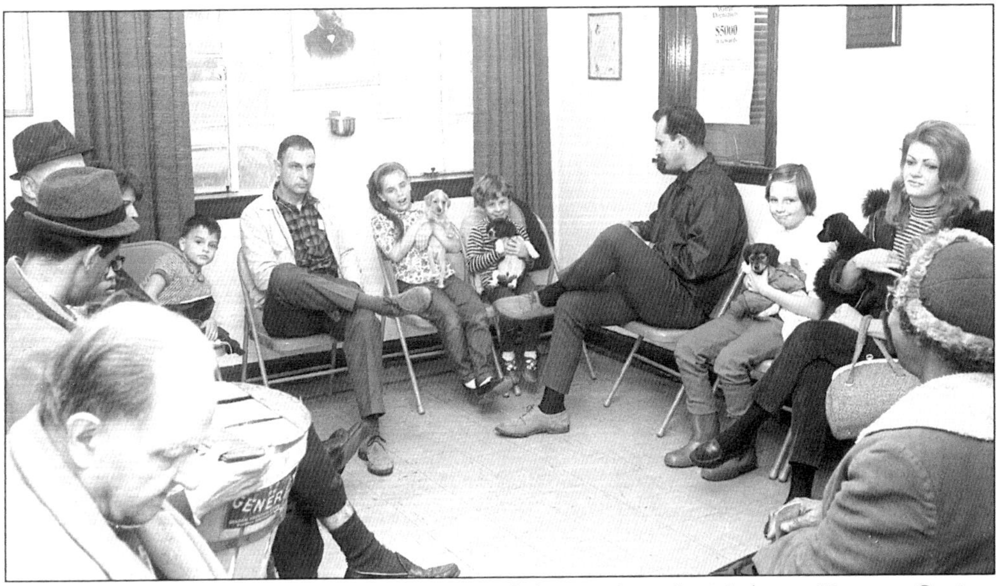

Check Ups for Pets. There was no shortage of clients when the Michigan Humane Society Detroit Shelter opened its veterinary hospital to the pet owning public in the late 1950s. Owners patiently await their turn with the veterinarian.

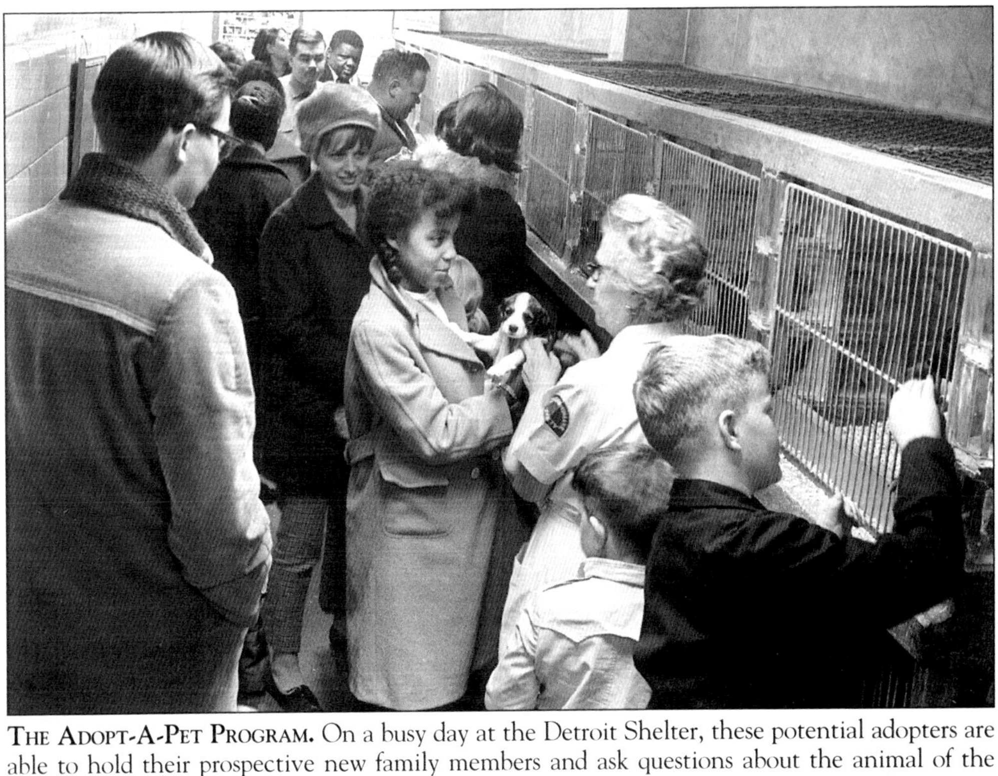

The Adopt-A-Pet Program. On a busy day at the Detroit Shelter, these potential adopters are able to hold their prospective new family members and ask questions about the animal of the Michigan Humane Society staff. Potential pet owners are carefully screened to ensure a long-term, permanent home for the animal, and the Michigan Humane Society adoption package includes first series of shots, sterilization, fecal check, and health and temperament tests.

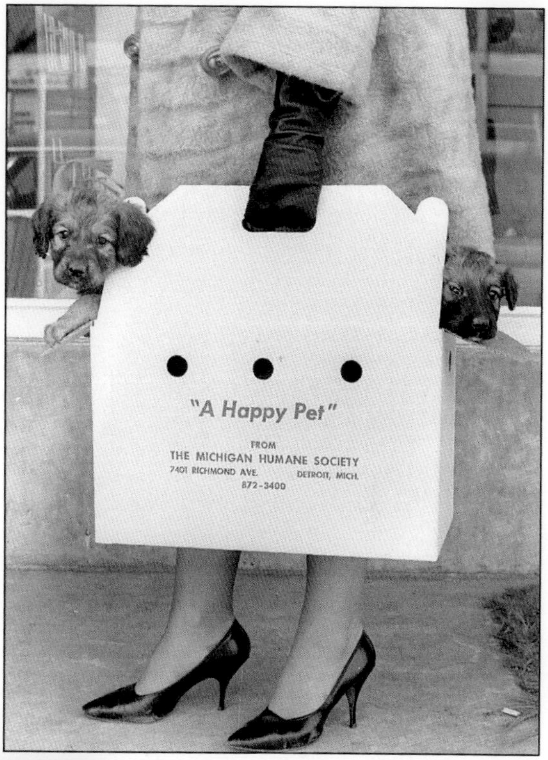

OFF TO A HAPPY HOME. This happy pair of pups is off to a new home after a successful adoption. Adopters are given a complete package of information and materials on the proper care of their new pet, as well as obedience tips and a discount on obedience classes.

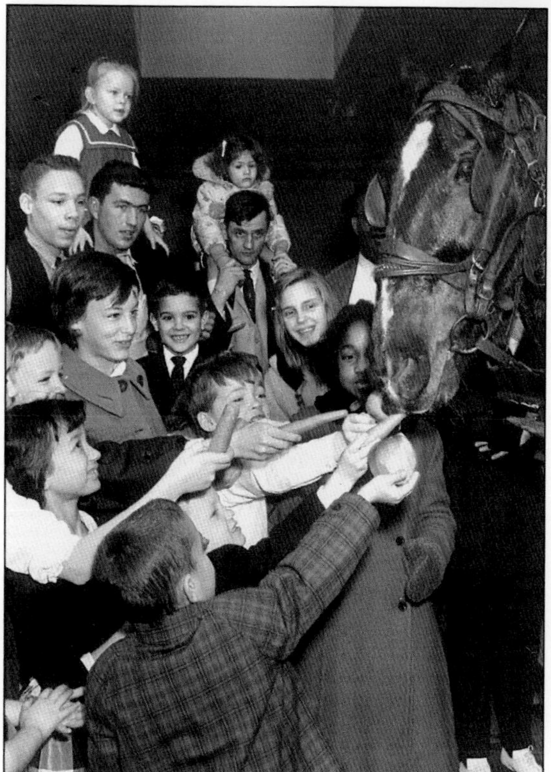

JUST HORSIN' AROUND. These children enjoy the 33rd Annual Christmas Party hosted by the Michigan Humane Society in 1966. The celebration started as a party to encourage proper care of work horses, but soon expanded to include neighborhood children. This was but one more opportunity for the Michigan Humane Society to teach humane values and kindness to animals. For some children, the Holiday party was their only contact with animals.

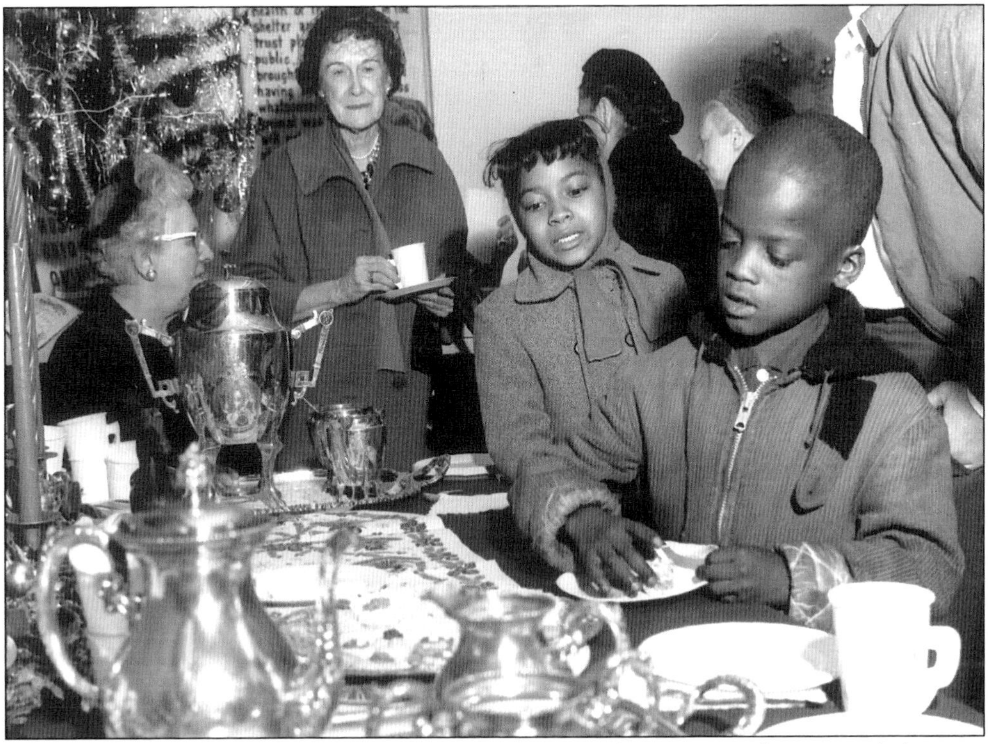

AFTER THE HORSES ARE FED. Once the horses and their drivers were taken care of, the time for the children to "dig in" to a variety of delicious treats came. The annual Holiday Party was always a good time for all who attended. The 1947 Holiday party was attended by 900 people and 63 horses.

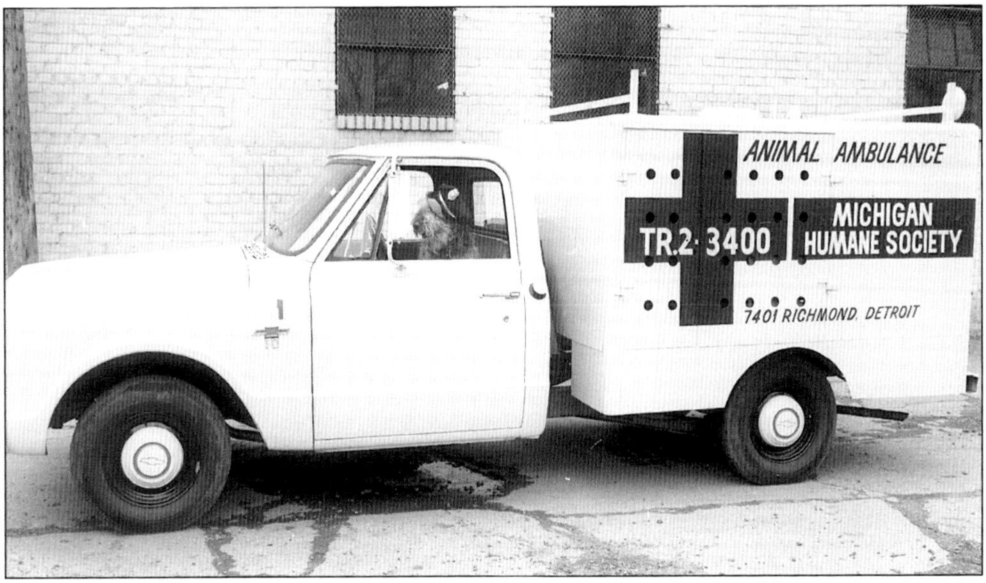

CAN I SEE YOUR LICENSE PLEASE? This small animal ambulance, one of five operated by the Michigan Humane Society in the 1960s, is ready to roll with Rover at the wheel. While all dogs should be licensed, we certainly hope that we don't see them behind the wheel.

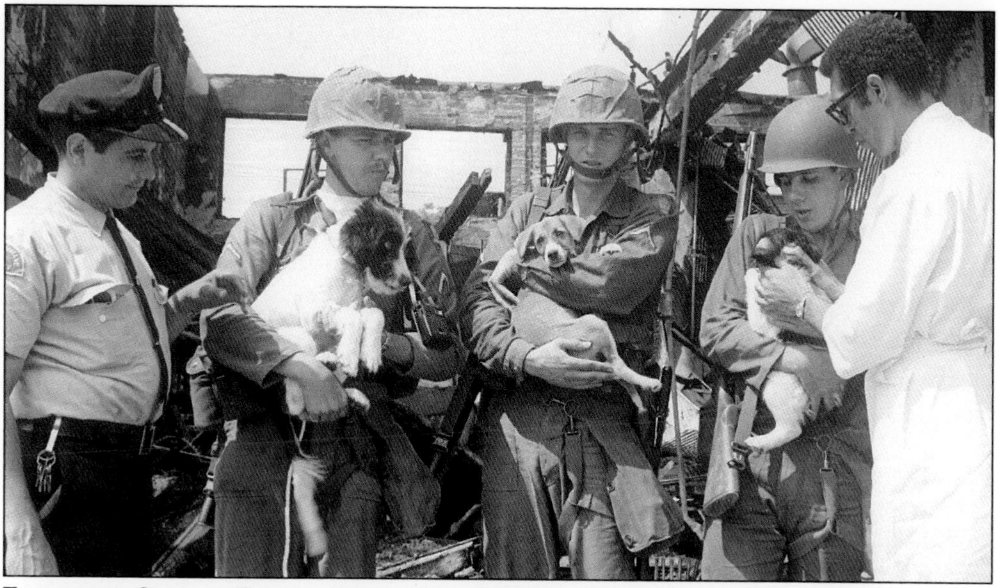

Emergency Care in Time of Strife. The Michigan Humane Society set up an Emergency Animal Relief Station during the 1967 civil disturbance in Detroit. National Guardsmen brought injured and homeless animals to the station for treatment. Michigan Humane Society Veterinarian Dr. Dewdney and ambulance driver Ron Thomas provided emergency care in the streets of the Motor City. Michigan Humane Society staff stayed at the shelter to care for the animals during the height of the burning, looting, and sniping.

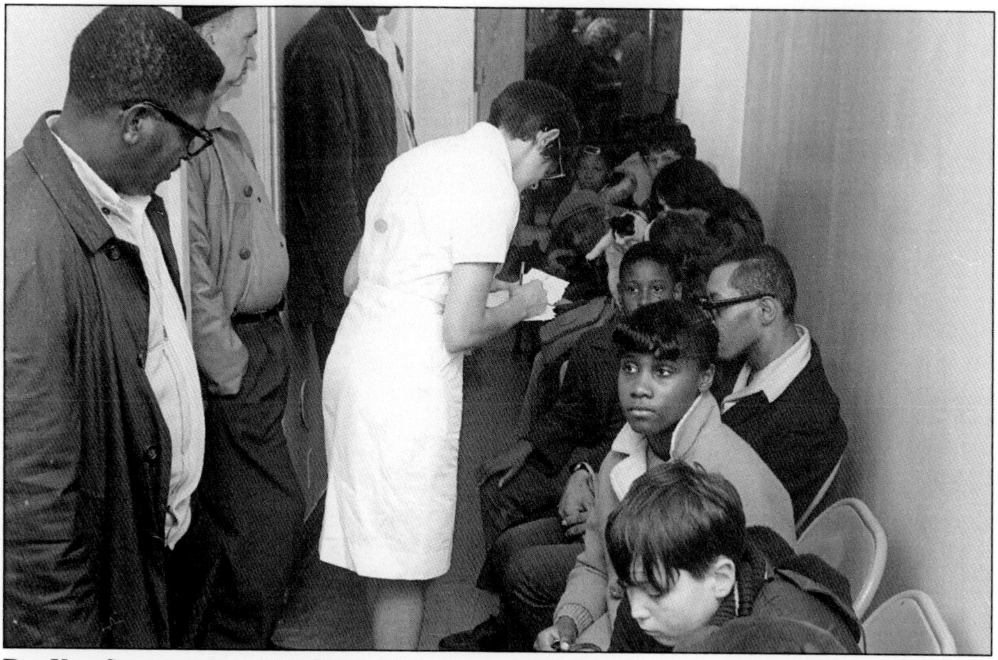

Did You See that Line? Michigan Humane Society Clinic Receptionist Dorothy Smith checks in people and their pets in 1968 at the Michigan Humane Society Detroit Memorial Veterinary Clinic. The shelter underwent renovations in the late 1950s to accommodate more veterinary clients, but the popularity of the Society's veterinary service outpaced its ability to add on again.

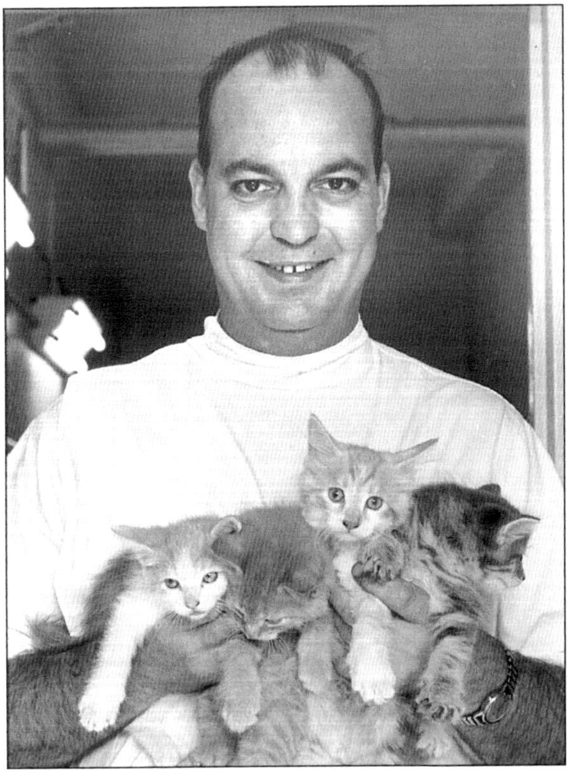

Quite a Handful. Michigan Humane Society Head Veterinarian William Bayley has his hands full of adorable kittens looking for a new home. Dr. Bayley wrote a column called "Veterinarian's Corner" for the Michigan Humane Review, a bi-monthly insert of the National Humane Review. His column centered on advice and veterinary care tips for pet owners.

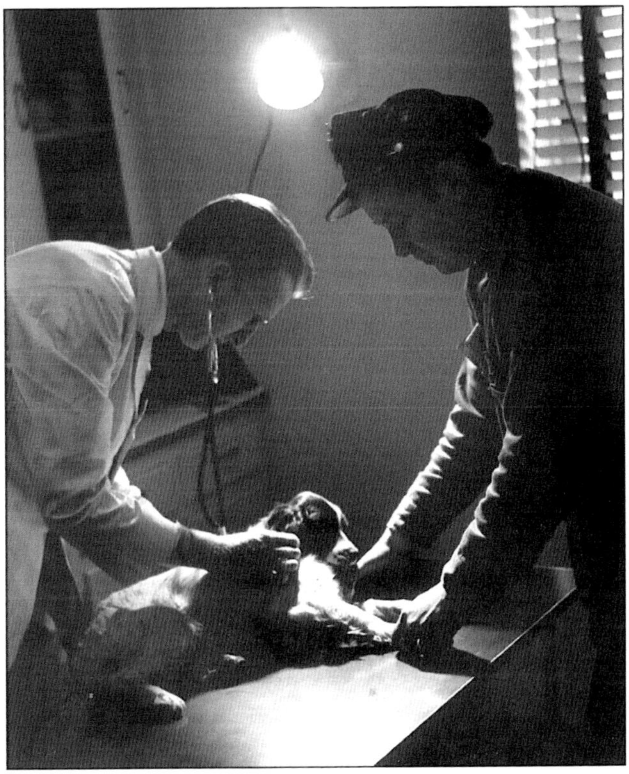

Adequate Medical Treatment. A Michigan Humane Society team comprised of rescue driver and veterinarian go to work making a proper and careful examination of this injured spaniel, trying to determine the best treatment action. Today's Michigan Humane Society operates 3 charitable animal hospitals and employs approximately 13 veterinarians.

Five

Education and Expansion

1960–1970

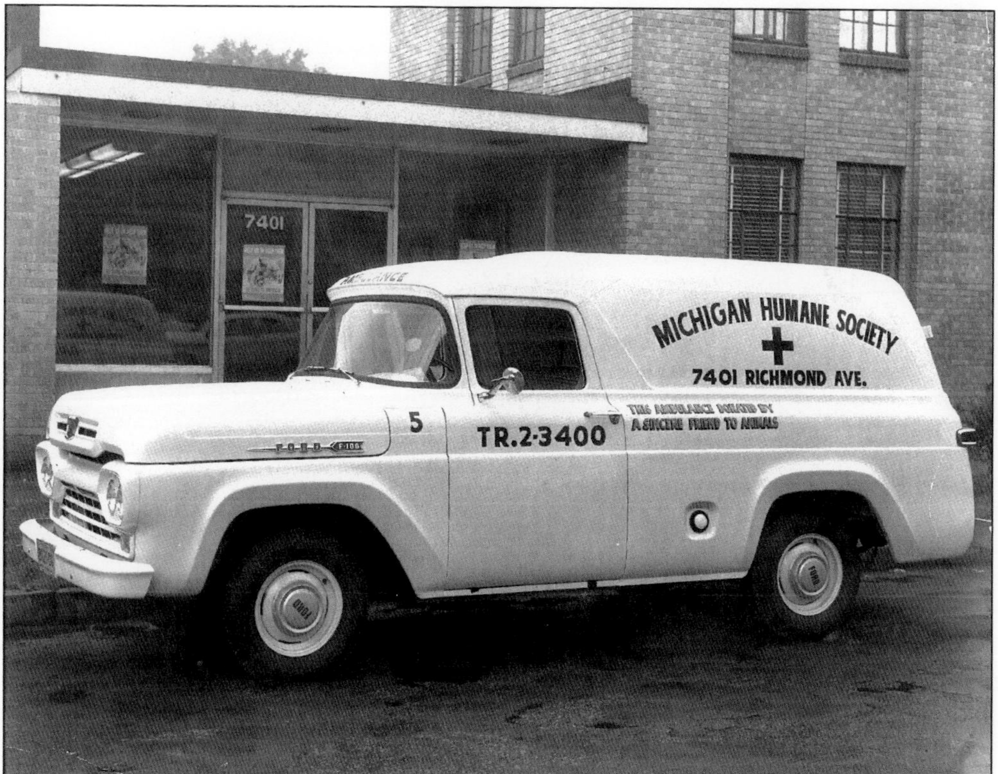

Helping Animals in Distress. The Michigan Humane Society has provided ambulance service to injured animals in the city of Detroit since before the automobile. The first ambulance was a horse ambulance to transport injured and ailing horses in need of treatment. Over the years, the society gained small animal ambulances and new horse ambulances, often through the generosity of people in the community. By 1960, its vehicles were vastly different from those first operated, but the service remained the same—seven-day-a-week rescue service for animals.

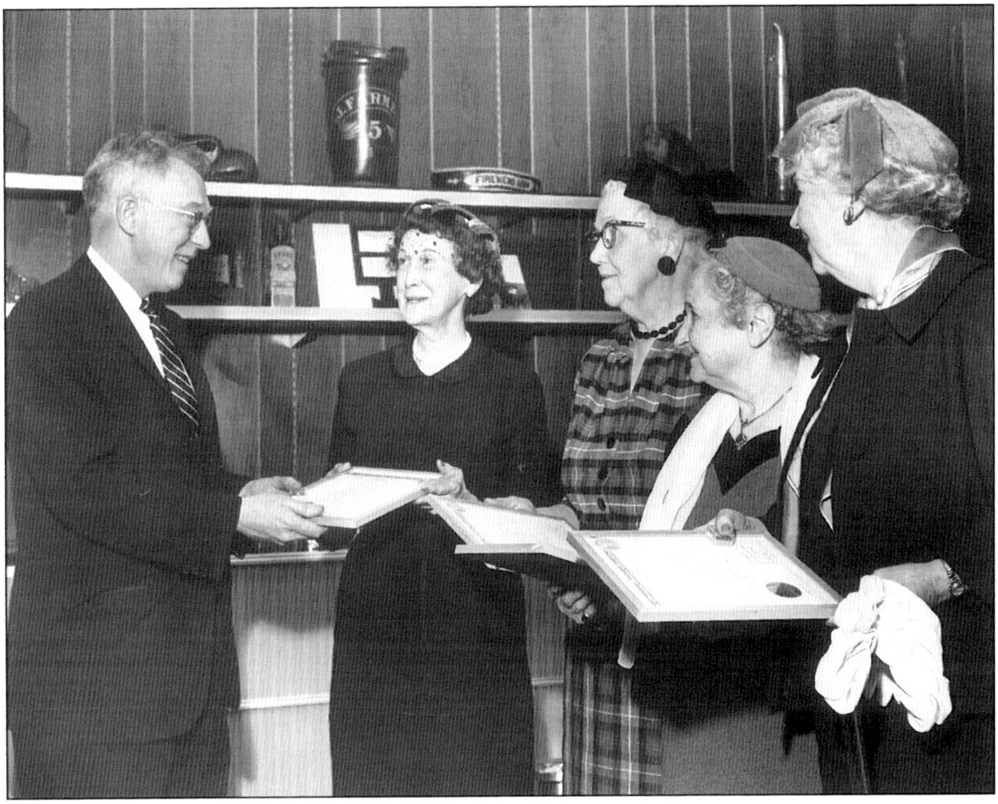

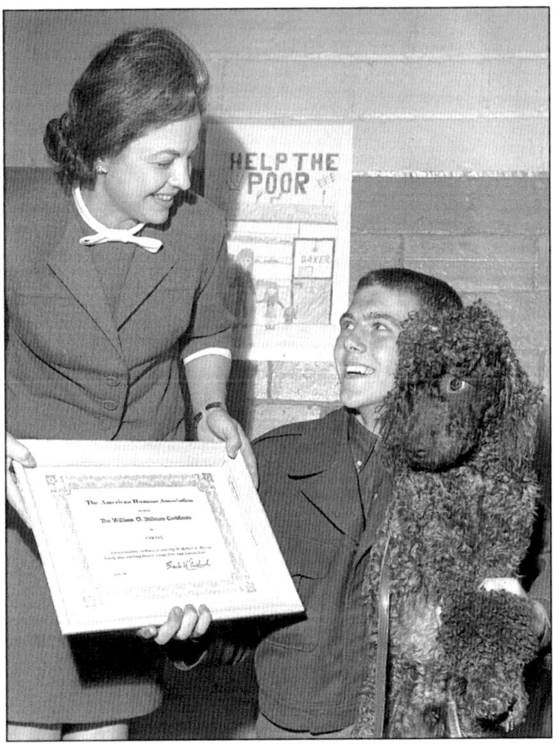

DEDICATION UNMATCHED. Michigan Humane Society officers and employees were, and today remain, dedicated to animal protection and welfare. The commitment of women in the humane movement is evident. In this 1962 photo, Michigan Humane Society Vice President John McNaughton awards service certificates and pins to Miss Edna Apel, Dr. Effie Arnold, Mrs. Ira Nash Evans, and Mrs. Wilson Mills for 35 years of service.

ANIMAL HERO SAVED THE DAY. Always ready to reinforce the bond between people and their pets, the Michigan Humane Society began to recognize acts of bravery on the part of animals and humans with the William O. Stillman Award (an early president of the American Humane Association). In 1963, Cocoa, a Poodle owned by Norman Maison of St. Clair Shores, alerted his family to a house fire and the family escaped the blaze.

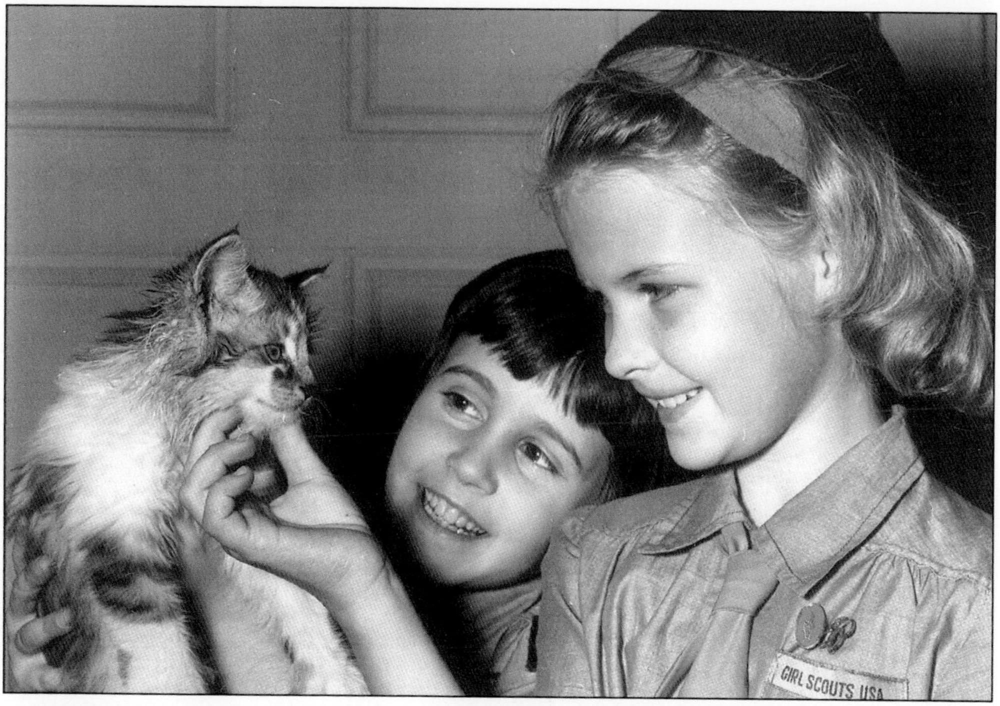

A Pup Called Scout and Smitten by a Kitten. Boy and Girl Scout groups were invited into the Michigan Humane Society shelter beginning in the 1950s to promote kindness to animals, and to teach them animal care and first aid classes. Scouting groups today often take tours of the shelters and clinic facilities and perform various charitable acts to earn badges such as building doghouses, collecting pet supplies, and landscaping Society grounds. Building alliances with the community was crucial in the early development of the Michigan Humane Society. Today, they work hard to nourish old alliances as well as nurture new ones.

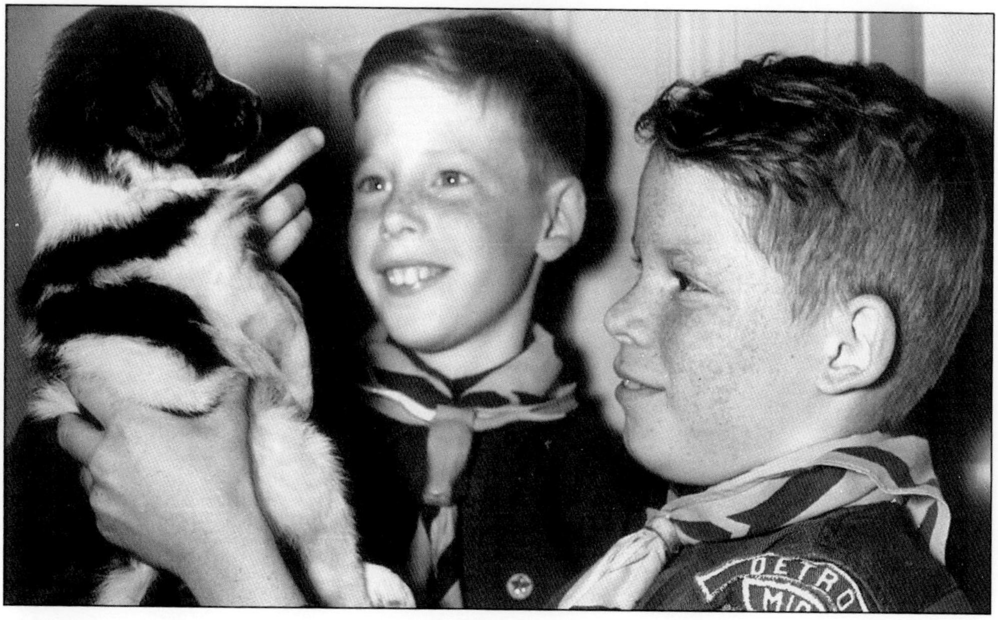

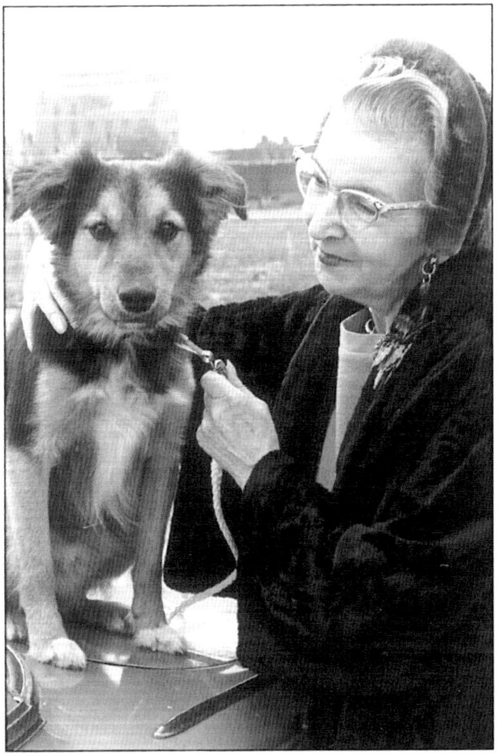

A Pup's Pal. Miss Olive Melba Walsh was a friend to the animals in the city of Detroit. Miss Walsh found this stray pup, Paddy, and brought him to the Michigan Humane Society shelter. While she was unable to take him home, Miss Walsh visited Paddy everyday during his stay at the Michigan Humane Society. Because of the special attention by Miss Walsh, he was a very social and friendly pup and soon found a permanent home with a new family.

Queenie, the Sightless Pup. A 6-week-old blind pup was found abandoned in a Detroit church in 1967. The Michigan Humane Society rescued the pup, dubbed Queenie, and was bombarded with letters and calls from people wanting to adopt her after hearing her story. The Swanks, a Northville, Michigan family, adopted Queenie, and soon found that her lack of sight was of no hindrance at all. Queenie turned out to be a spunky, exuberant pup and the family loved everything about her.

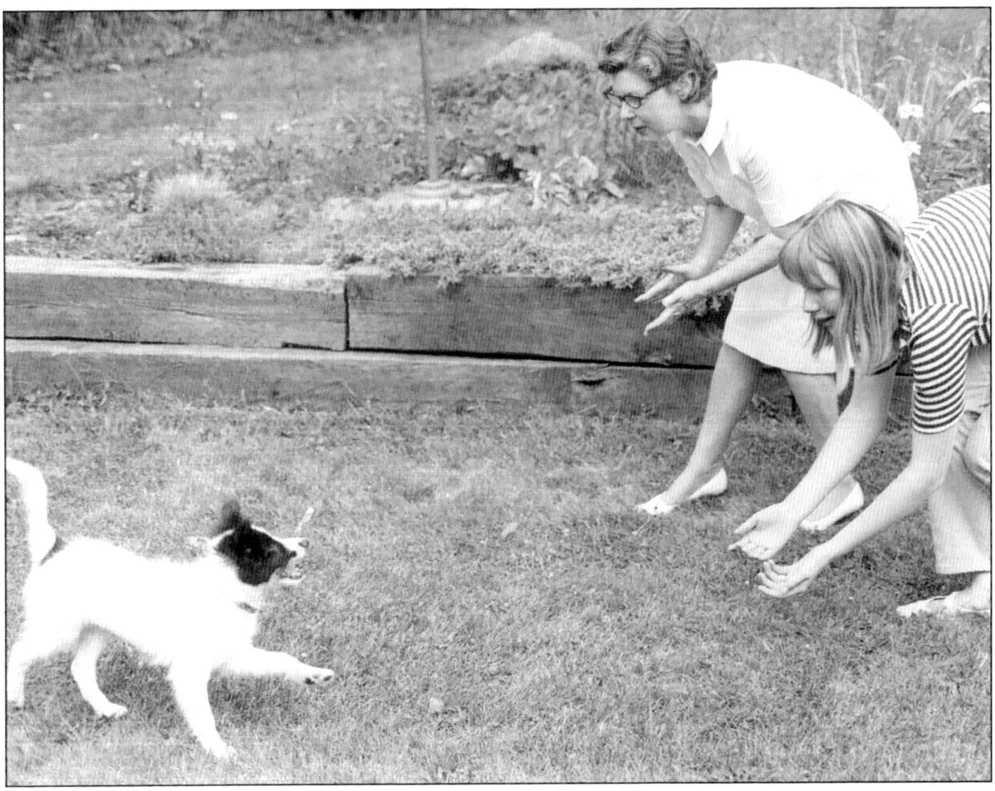

POLITICKING GONE TO THE DOGS. Michigan Humane Society humane education doggy safety demonstrator, Sport, is caught garnering support for "Be Kind to Animals Week" from Vice President Hubert H. Humphrey and Zoltan Ferency, Michigan Democratic Party chairman in 1967.

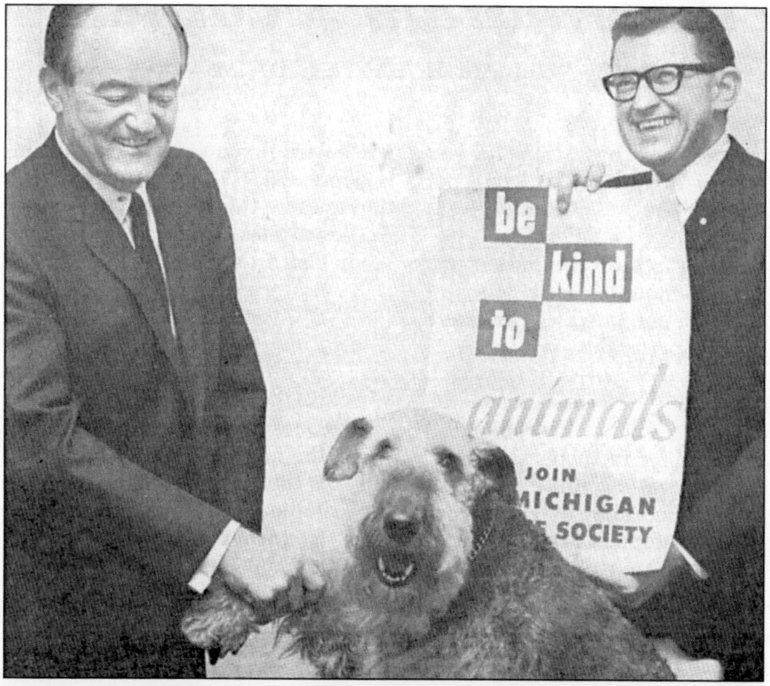

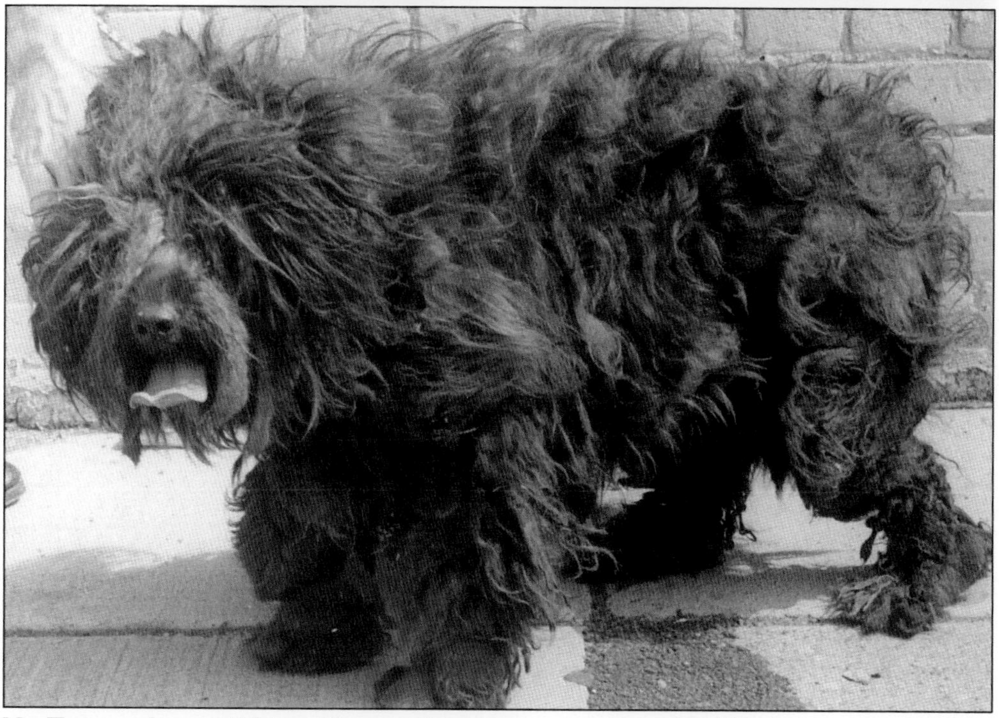

NO TIME TO CARE. Michigan Humane Society sees pets surrendered by their owners for many reasons. A family who said they didn't have time to care for him any more turned in this dog, a poodle mix, in 1969. He had been neglected for years. He had never been groomed and was fearful of being approached. He most likely had little socialization or interaction with the family. It took three hours to shave all the mats and tangles off this poor pooch.

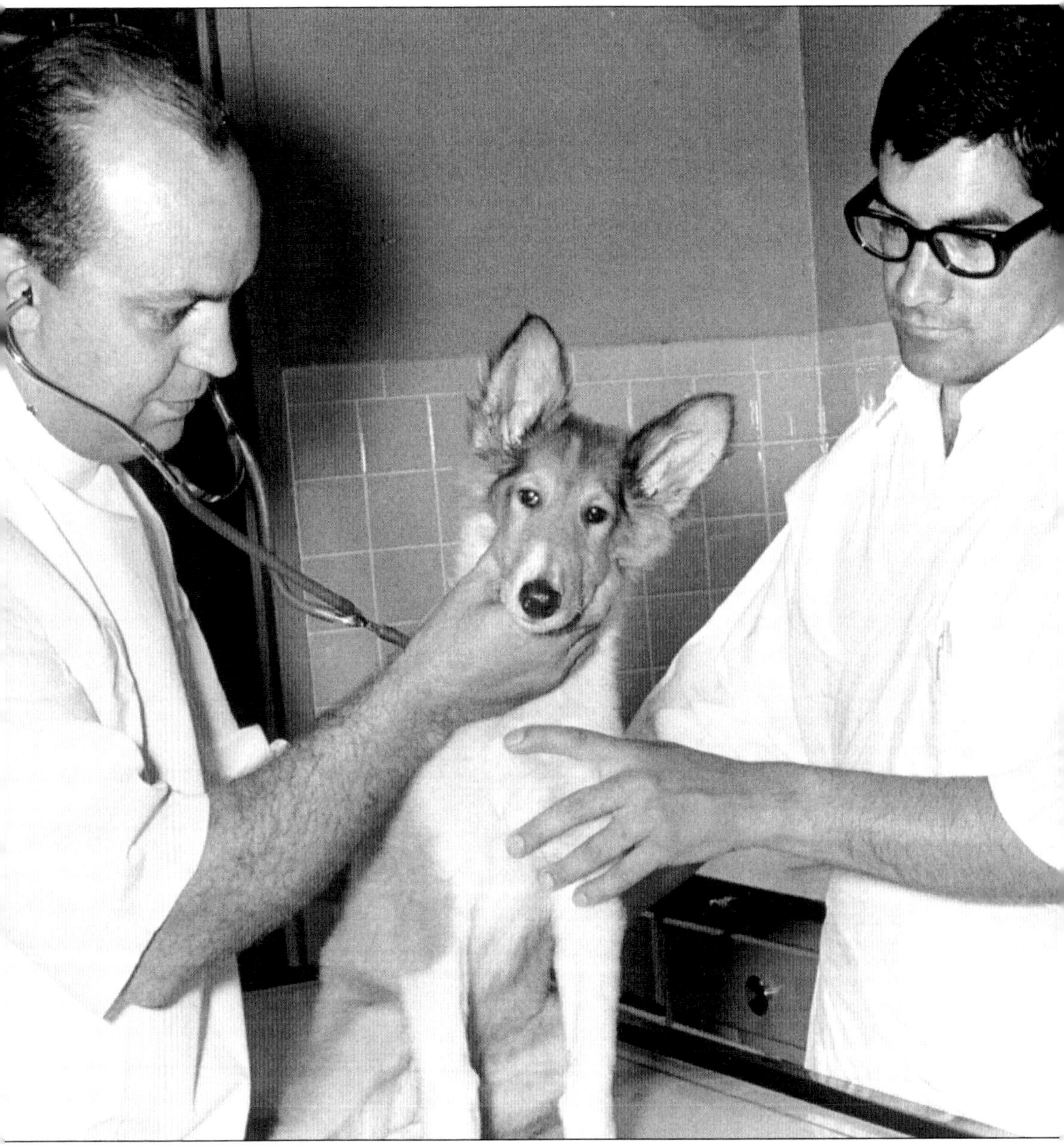

GETTING CHECKED OUT. Dr. William Bayley, head veterinarian at the Michigan Humane Society during the 1950s and 1960s, examines a stray dog brought to the shelter. The Society has provided veterinary care for the animals in their shelter since the early 1900s. In the 1930s, they established an elaborate placement bureau to provide veterinary care for pets in the city. By the 1950s, they employed a veterinarian and opened a veterinary clinic in the Detroit Shelter that was open to the pet-owning public. The Michigan Humane Society currently has three charitable animal hospitals in metro Detroit and recorded over 54,000 client visits in 2001. Their veterinary clinics provide on-site care for the animals in their shelters, as well as quality veterinary service for pet owners. Low-cost sterilizations are instrumental in curbing the tragedy of pet overpopulation, and in 2001, Michigan Humane Society clinics performed over 13,000 low-cost or no-cost sterilization surgeries.

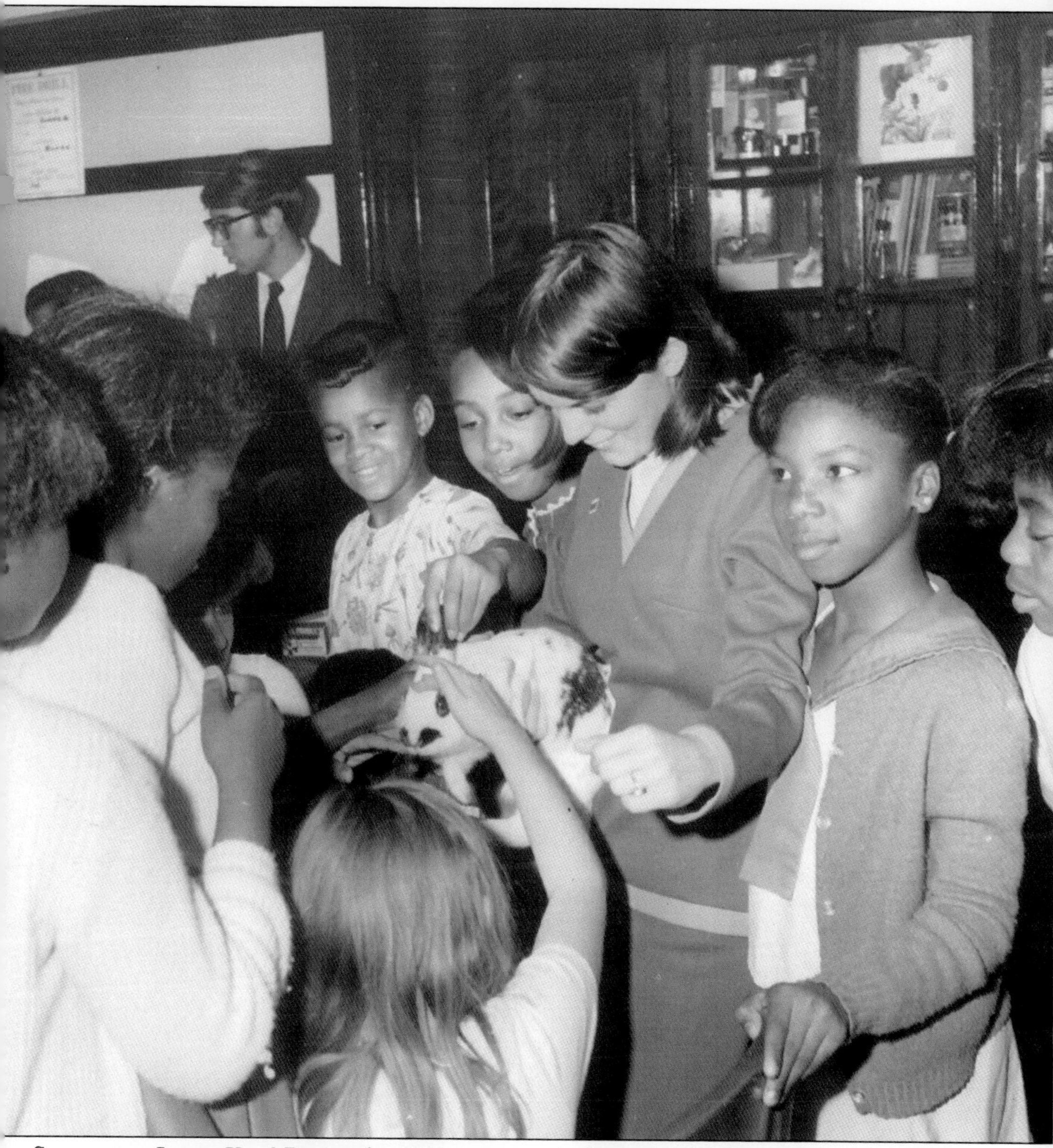

Somebunny Loves You! During the 1960s, requests for humane education visits skyrocketed. Here, Michigan Humane Society Humane Educator Fran Balcer is seen at one of many Detroit Public Schools. The presentations included teaching children how to care for a pet, how to approach an animal, how to handle a pet, and how to treat animals with kindness and respect. For some Detroit school children, it was the first time they were able to interact with animals such as dogs, cats, and rabbits.

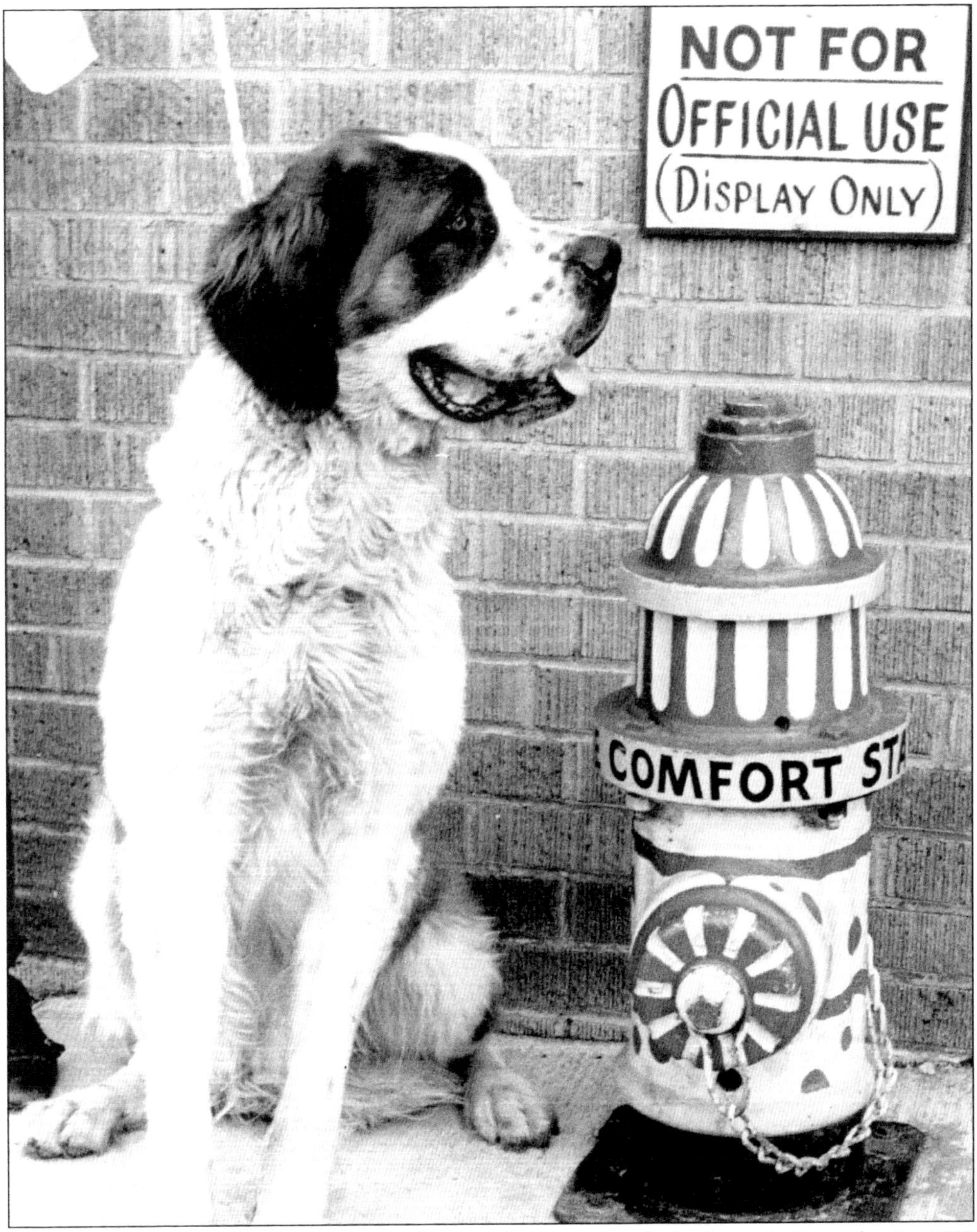

CAUSE FOR ALARM. Michigan Humane Society Manager Frank Andrews had an idea in 1968 that was cause for alarm. Every year for National Dog Week, Andrews did something special for our canine wards. A junkyard donated two scrap hydrants and Andrews decided to install two "comfort stations" in front of the shelter at 7401 Chrysler Drive. The Detroit News ran a front-page photo, failing to mention the hydrants were scrap pieces, and alarms sounded in the Detroit Fire Department. Officials of the fire department thought the Society had defaced real, working hydrants and sent an emissary to the Society. After learning the hydrants were scrap, the fire department was still concerned that firefighters would mistake them for real hydrants and try to use them. An agreement was reached allowing the Society to keep the comfort stations if a sign was mounted indicating they were display hydrants.

NEED SOME DOGGONED DIRECTIONS? Years of confusing road construction made finding the Michigan Humane Society shelter challenging during the 1960s. Signs were erected in the neighborhood directing people to the shelter. By 1969, the Chrysler Freeway was opened and made getting to the Society much easier. Perhaps this pooch felt the need to direct people personally.

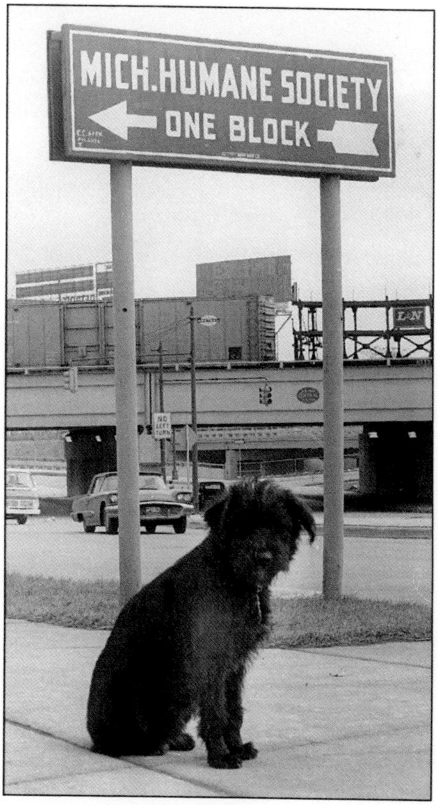

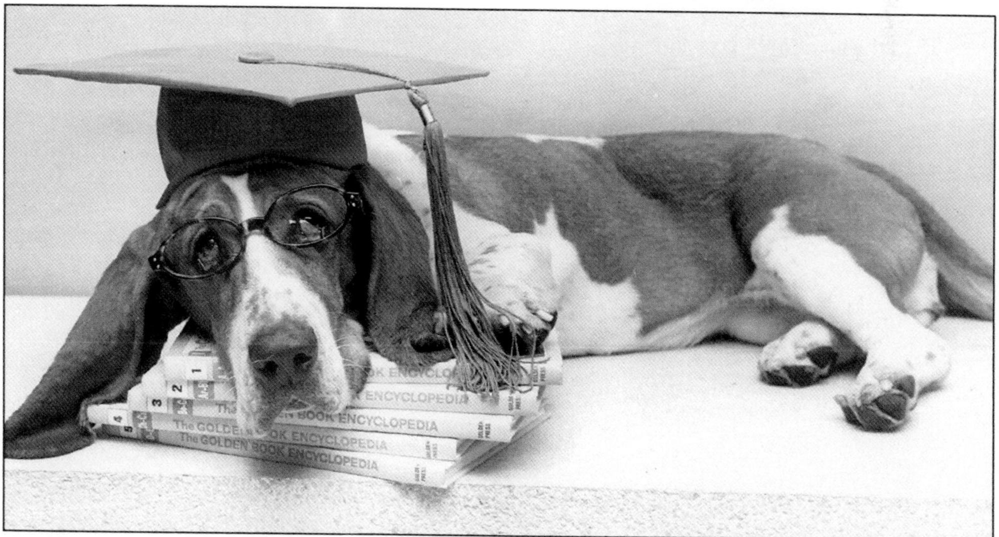

THE GRADUATE. The Southern Michigan Obedience Training Club classes held in the 1950s evolved into Michigan Humane Society Obedience classes in the 1960s. Free classes were held for pet owners at the Detroit Shelter facility, and in 1969, a record number of people signed up for the classes. Obedience classes are crucial in building a strong relationship for pet and owner, and the Michigan Humane Society today operates the Pet Education Center to help keep pets in homes.

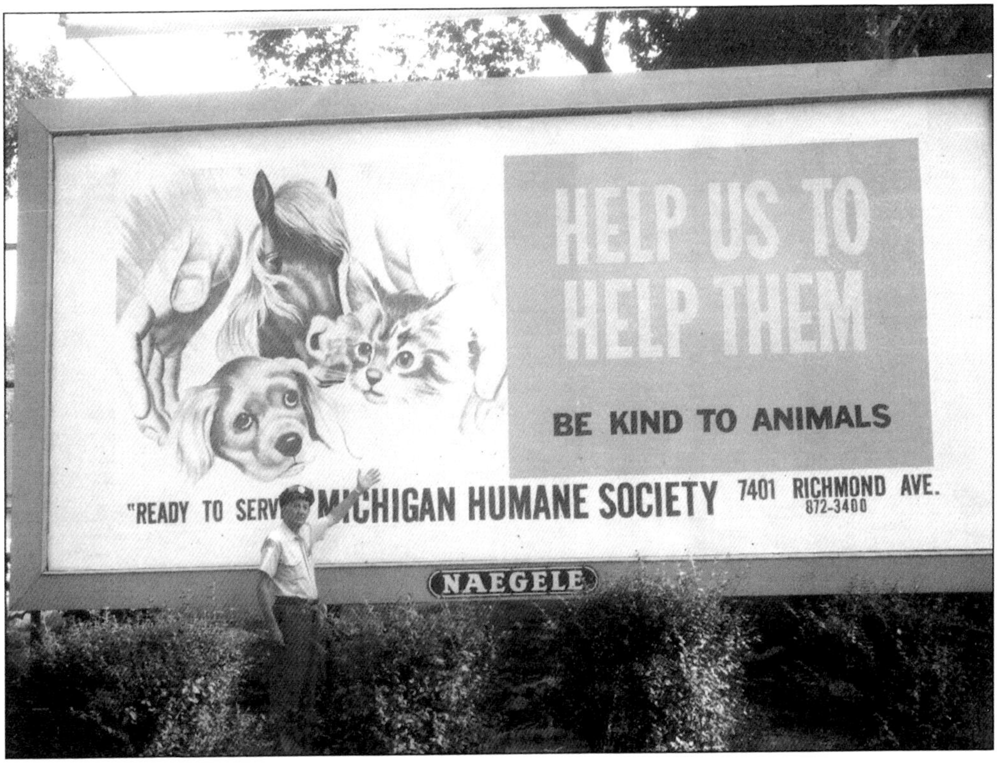

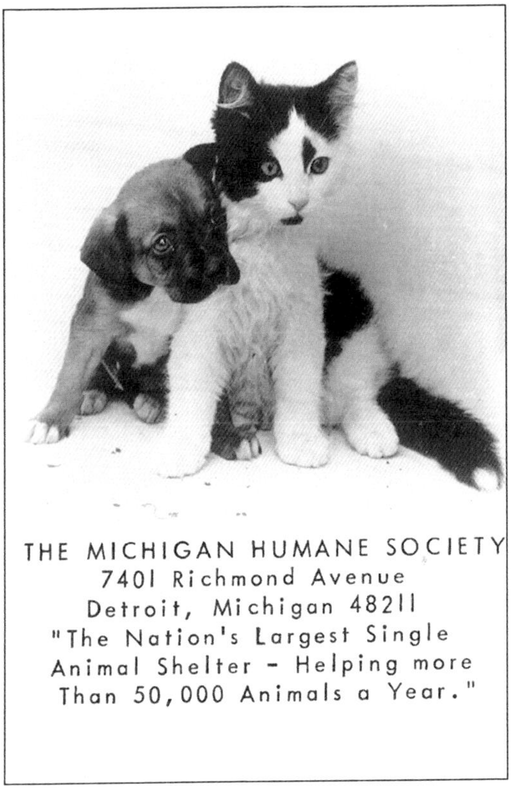

SIGN OF THE TIMES. Throughout the history of the Michigan Humane Society, "advertising" took on many forms. Window displays in the Hudson's Building, radio shows in the 1940s, mailed postcards, and this new outdoor advertising sign in 1965 were just a few of the ways the Michigan Humane Society communicated with the citizens of the Motor City and its suburbs.

PET POSTCARD. Postcards such as this were another way to spread the word of the good work of the Michigan Humane Society. They have been used for decades throughout the history of the organization. Cards like this were sent to new adopters, donors, supporters, and people new to the neighborhood.

Six

Lean Times, Mean Times

1970–1980

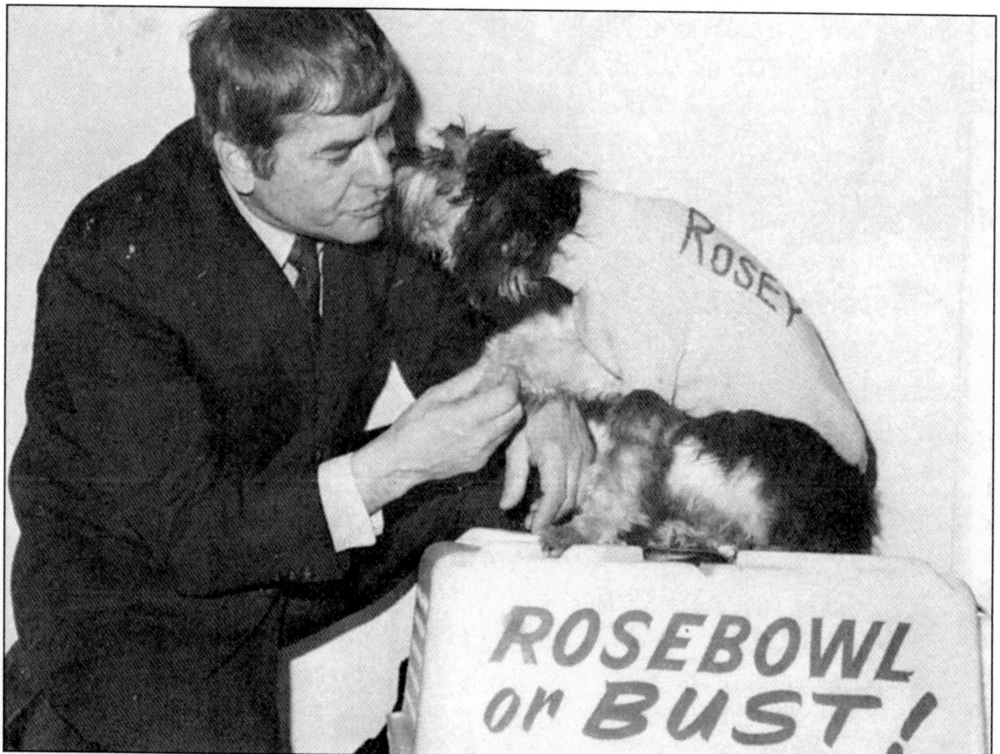

Rosebowl or Bust. Charley Manos, *Detroit News* feature writer, took Michigan Humane Society adoptable dog Rosey to the 1970 Rose Bowl and gained a companion for life. Their story hit Los Angeles before they landed, and the Rose Bowl queen and a member of the Los Angeles SPCA met them at the airport. Manos arrived in Los Angeles without tickets to the game, but Rosey charmed everyone and became a canine celebrity. Soon she and Manos were invited to parties, press conferences, and the game. Manos adopted Rosey and the two became a dynamic duo for the Michigan Humane Society.

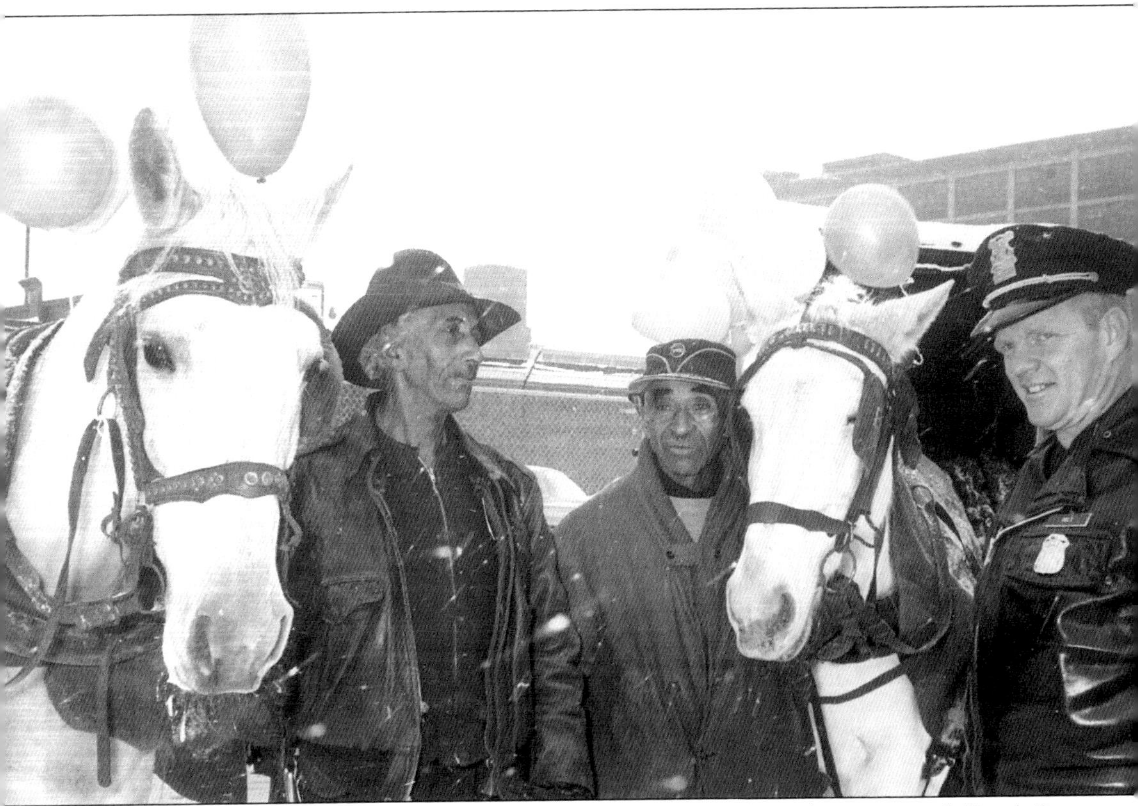

One Last Horse Holiday Party. Chicken, with John Clark, and Maggie, with Frank Berry, came out of semi-retirement in 1971 as the last two work horses in the city of Detroit to celebrate the end of an era. The last Michigan Humane Society Holiday Party for Horses was held in December of 1971. Begun in 1931 in an effort to encourage proper care and treatment of work horses, the Michigan Humane Society gave awards each year to the drivers of the best-kept horses in the city. These parties were also open to the public, and in 1947, the Holiday Party saw over 900 people and 63 horses come through the shelter. In this photo, Sgt. Jack Holt of the Detroit Police Mounted Unit presents the prizes to Chicken and Maggie. Maggie went on to live out her remaining years in comfort on a farm in Macomb County.

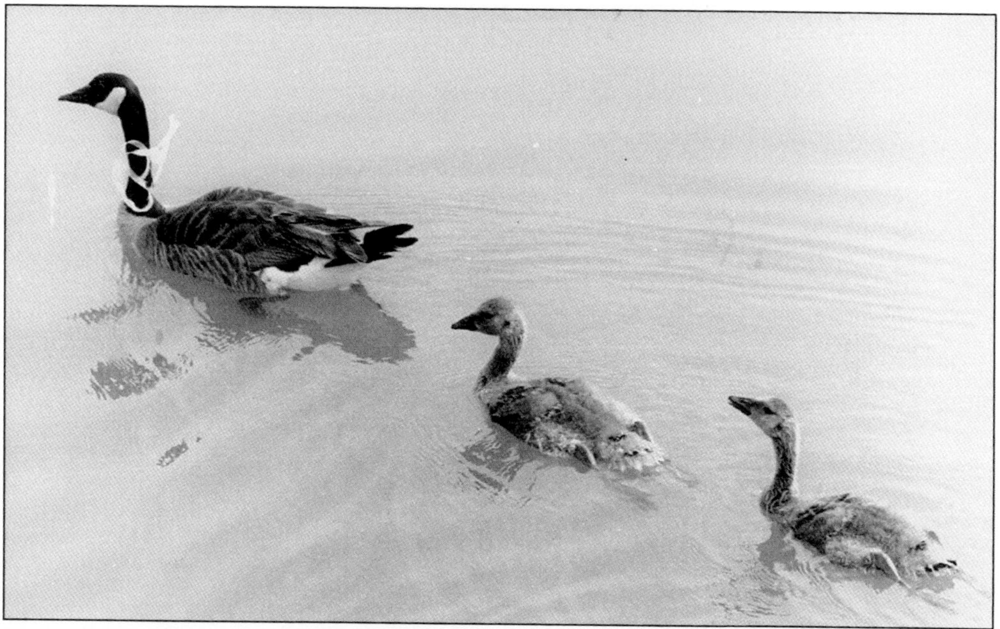

RING-NECKED GOOSE. As the city of Detroit grew and its boundaries were extended, conflicts with wildlife and wildlife endangerment became common. Litter, such as this plastic six-pack holder, presents a threat to many wild animals. In 1972, Michigan Humane Society employees captured this goose and removed the six-pack holder, saving her from certain death.

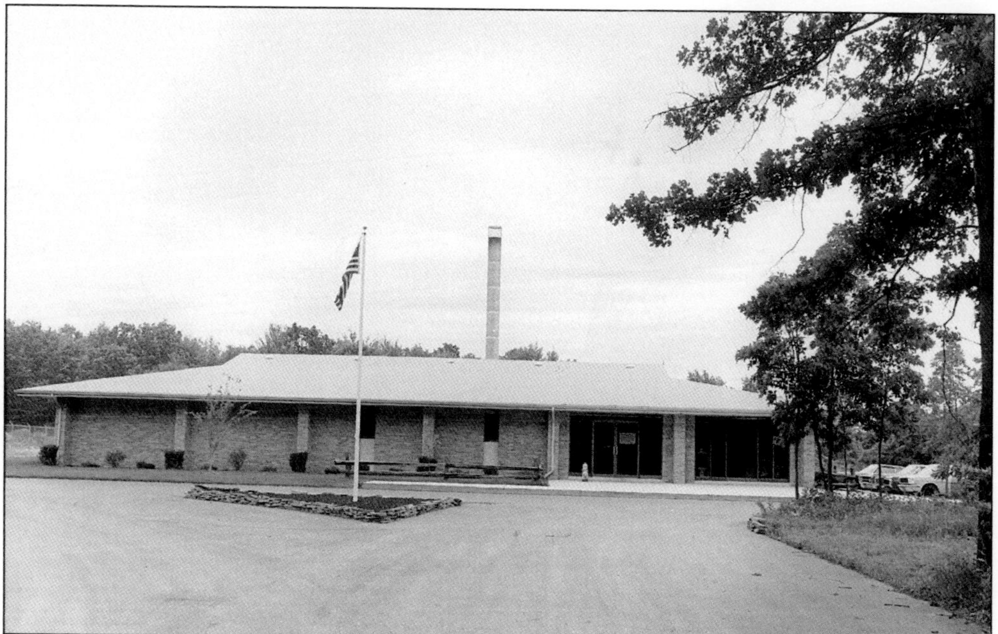

MEETING THE NEEDS OF OTHER COMMUNITIES. With the suburbs of Detroit expanding, the need for services dictated that the Michigan Humane Society expand for the sake of the animals. The Society began construction of a shelter facility in Westland in 1971 to serve the communities of Westland and Dearborn Heights. By 1975, Canton, Redford, and Sylvan Lake joined the growing list of communities in need of services provided by the Westland location.

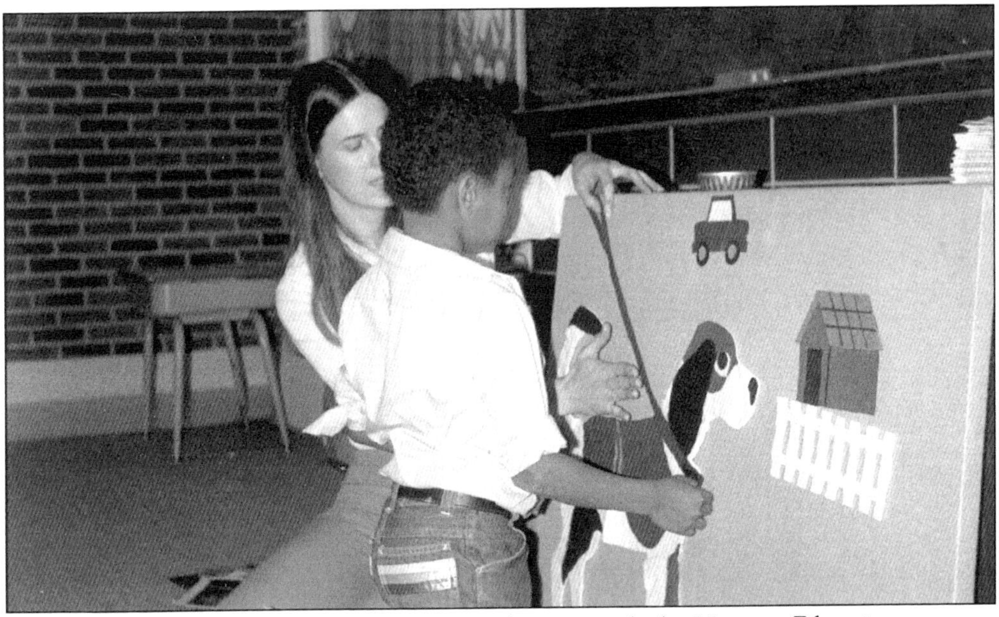

TEACHING KINDNESS AND HUMANE VALUES. In keeping with the Humane Education program, which started at the Michigan Humane Society in 1925, humane educators from the Society still visit Detroit public schools regularly to teach children proper care of and respect for all animals. Children take an active role in the presentations, and often the humane educator takes an animal along to allow for appropriate, supervised interaction between the children and the animal.

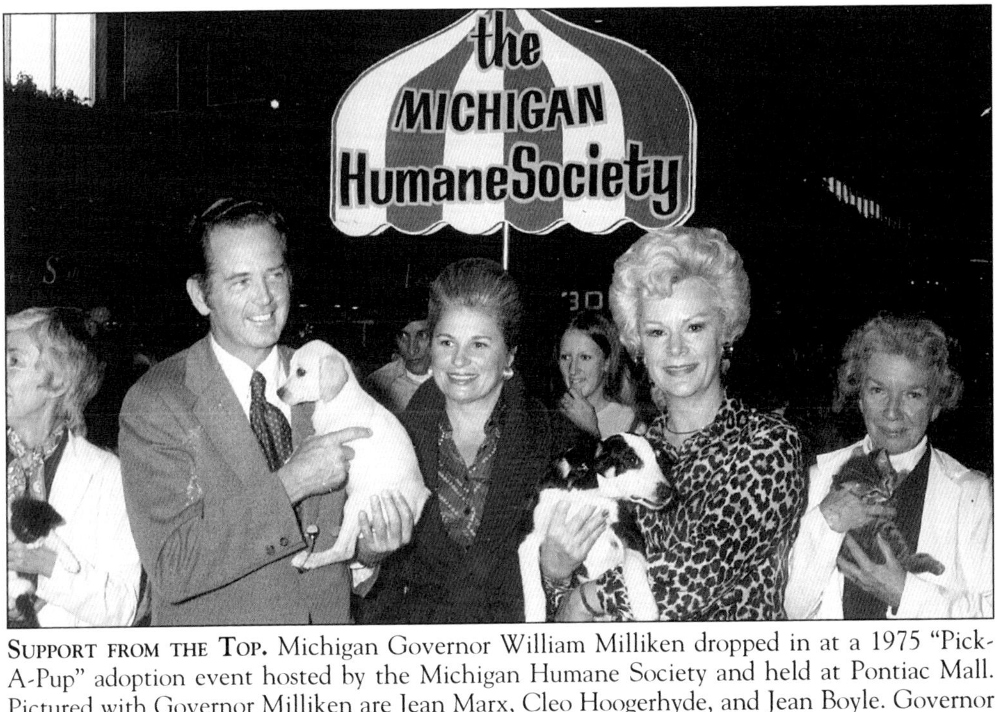

SUPPORT FROM THE TOP. Michigan Governor William Milliken dropped in at a 1975 "Pick-A-Pup" adoption event hosted by the Michigan Humane Society and held at Pontiac Mall. Pictured with Governor Milliken are Jean Marx, Cleo Hoogerhyde, and Jean Boyle. Governor Milliken was a friend to the Michigan Humane Society and provided much-needed legislative support during his time in office.

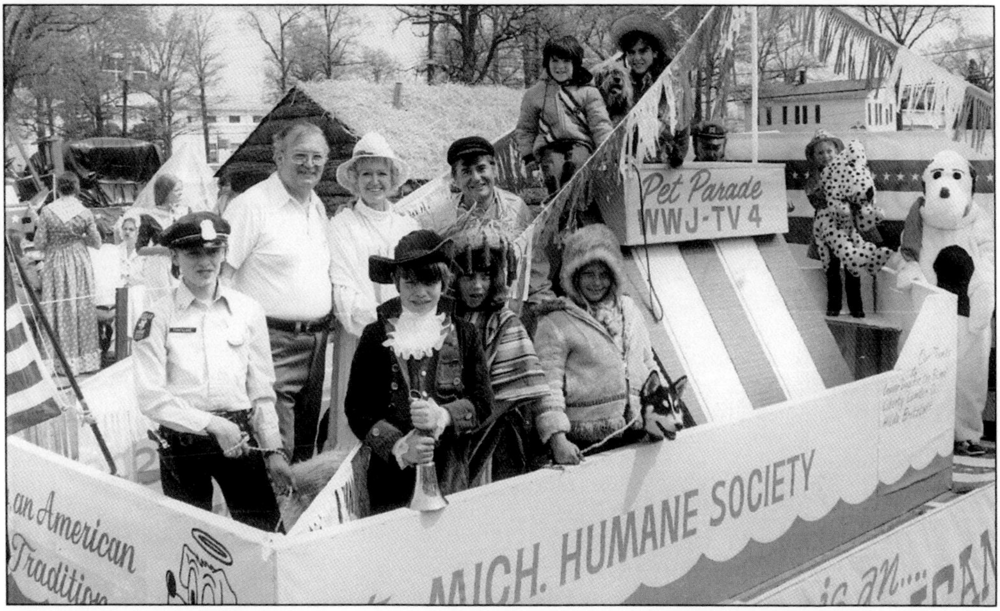

PETS ON PARADE! This Michigan Humane Society float, sponsored by WWJ-TV 4, appeared in the Wayne County Bicentennial Parade in 1976. Commissioner Irving Steiner and Charley Manos from the *Detroit News*, rode on the float to lend their support for the Michigan Humane Society.

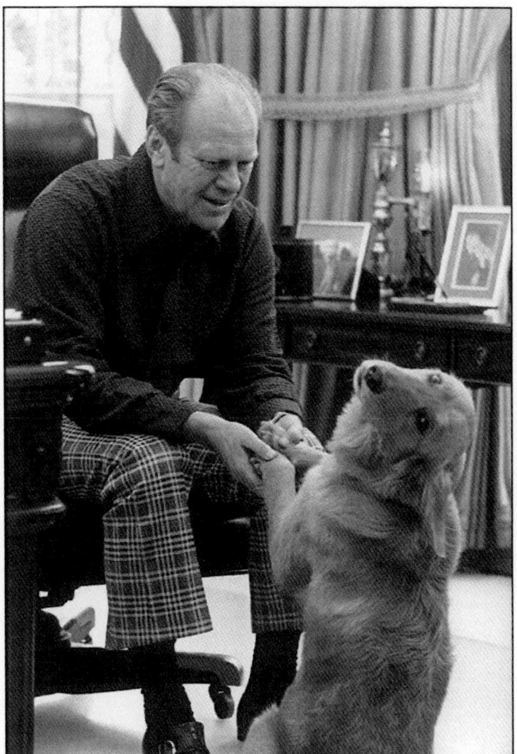

FOREVER PLAID! In 1977, the Michigan Humane Society celebrated 100 years of serving the animals of metro Detroit. Known around the country as one of the largest sheltering societies, the Michigan Humane Society garnered wishes from the very top. President Gerald Ford's trusted companion, Liberty, sent a personal thank you to the Michigan Humane Society in honor of its 100th anniversary.

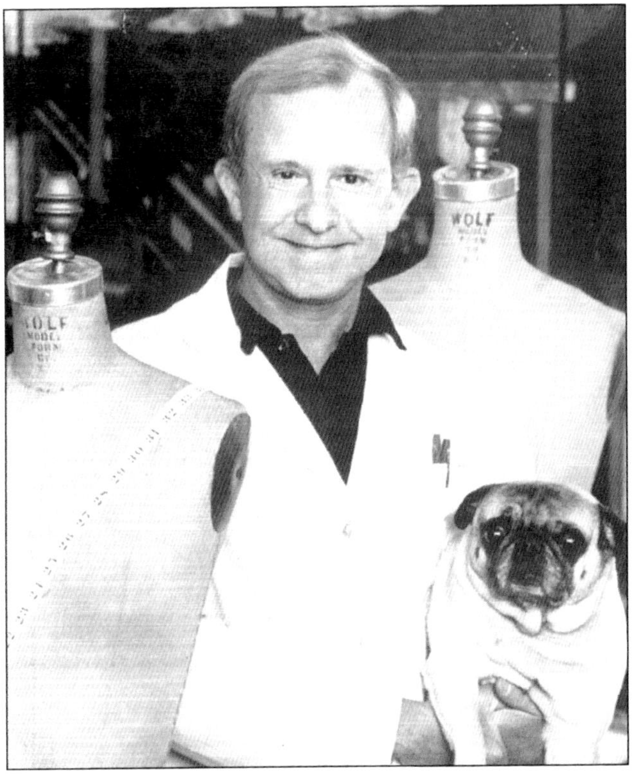

Fashion Gone to the Dogs. Adolfo of New York and Saks Fifth Avenue of Detroit hosted the first of many successful fashion show benefits for the Michigan Humane Society in 1975. The show was the first of its kind in Detroit, and through the efforts of Adolfo, Michigan Humane Society Board members, and Saks Fifth Avenue, the show remained a favorite for many years.

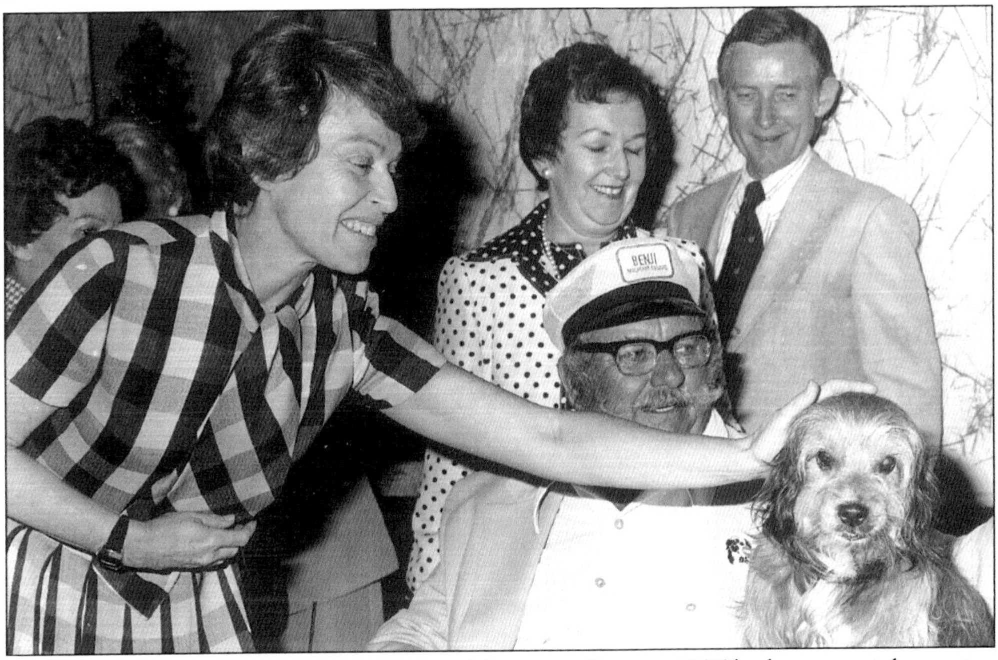

Benji, More than a Movie. The premiere of the movie Benji in 1975 had very special meaning for the Michigan Humane Society. Benji and trainer Frank Inn enjoyed a special lunch at the Ponchartrain in Detroit and attended a special movie premiere at a theater in Livonia to benefit the Michigan Humane Society.

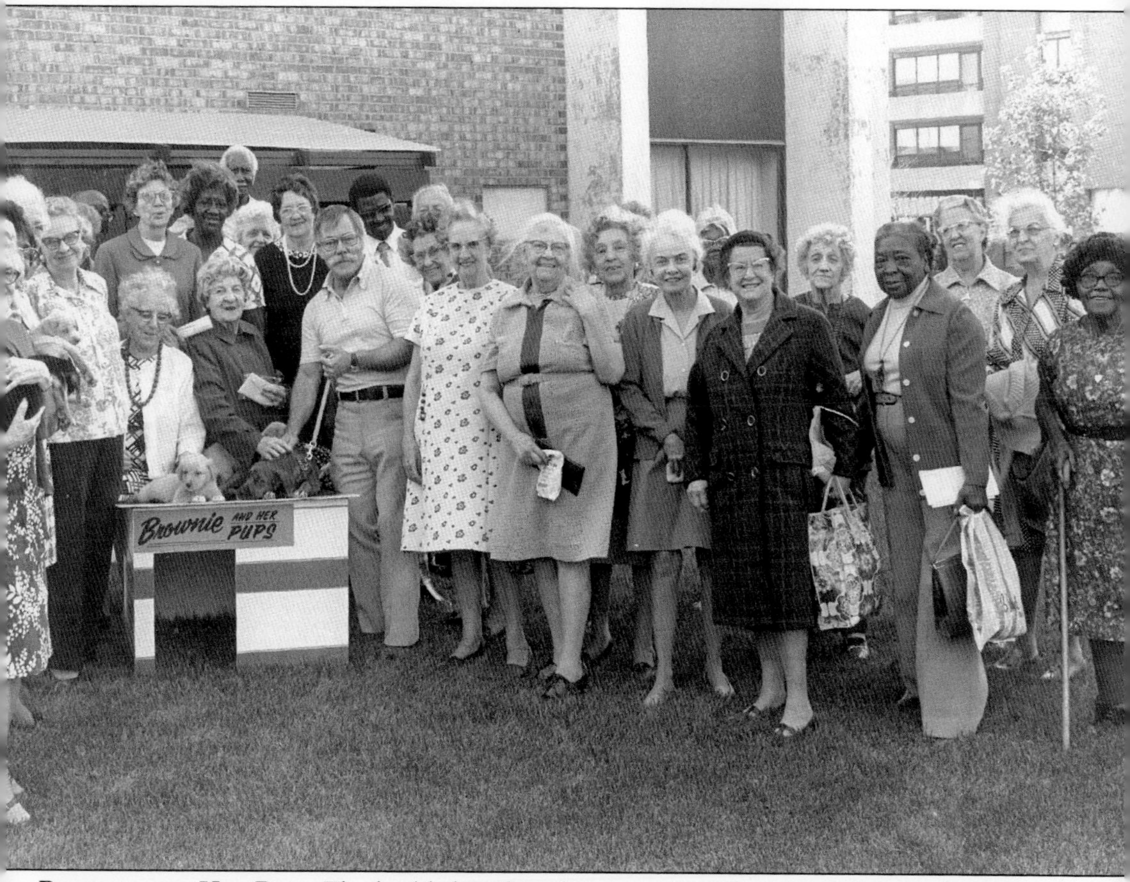

BROWNIE AND HER PUPS. The health benefits of interacting with companion animals were becoming more apparent in the 1970s. Before the days of organized Pet Visitation, Michigan Humane Society staffers Jim Yardley and Booker Bryant regularly visited nursing homes, senior activity centers, and senior residence housing in metro Detroit with shelter animals. Brownie and her pups were especially welcome in their many visits to seniors. Today, it is widely accepted that owning a pet is associated with cholesterol reduction, decreased blood pressure, and alleviation of stress. The Michigan Humane Society currently has a volunteer pet visitation group that makes regular visits to hospitals, nursing homes, assisted living centers, and other health care facilities using their own Therapy Dog International certified dogs. Pet visitation is highly rewarding to the volunteers and their pets, and it is very therapeutic to those visited.

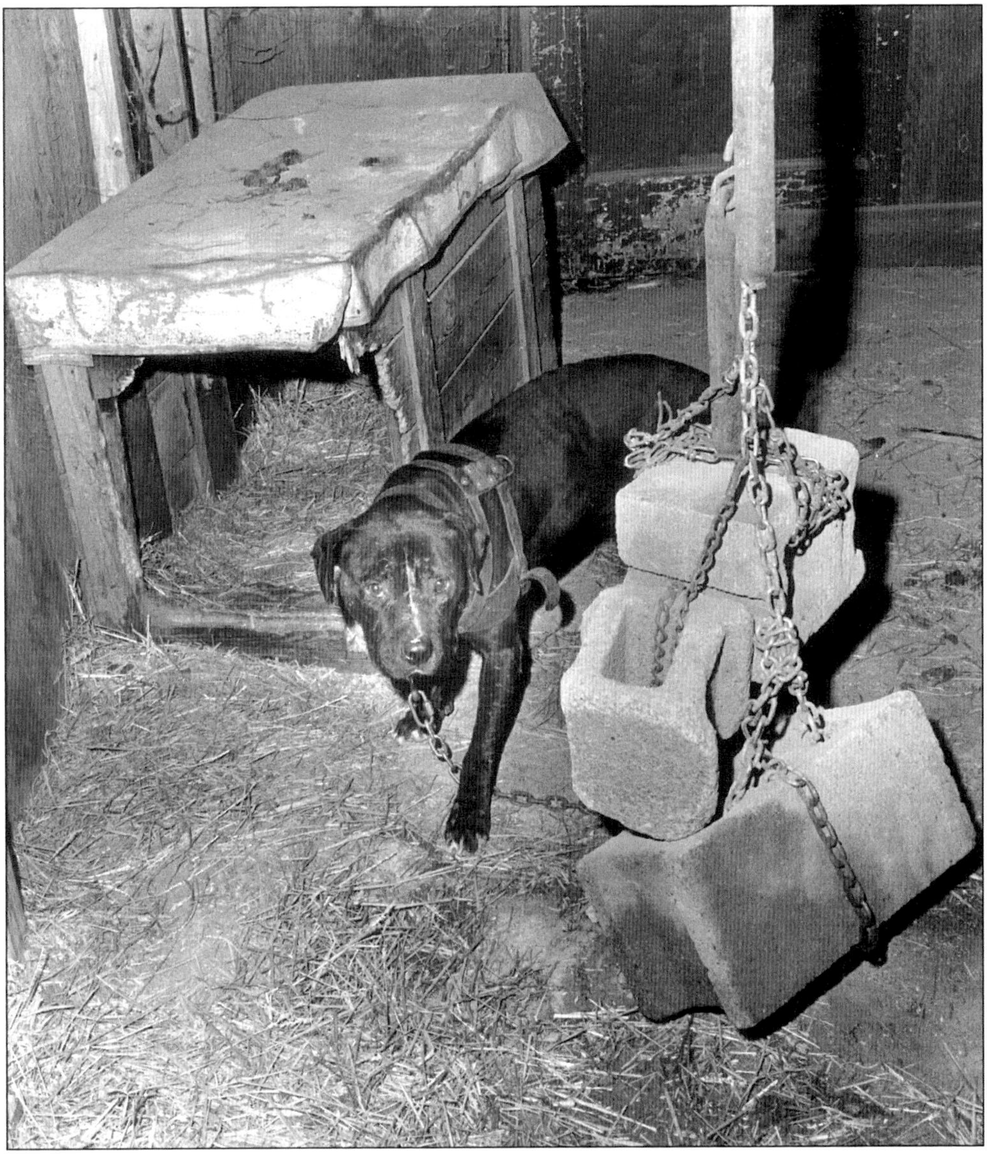

The Evils of Dog Fighting. Animal fighting has been around for centuries. Early in human civilization, the barbaric practice of pitting animal against animal was considered "sport" and matches were held publicly. In the early 1930s, cock fighting was popular in the city of Detroit. By the 1940s, dog fighting had replaced cock fighting as the "sport" of choice for animal fighters. In 1978, an eight-month undercover raid executed by the Michigan Humane Society and the Michigan State Police resulted in the confiscation of the dog in this photo and 64 others used in fights. Today's dog fighter operates in a seedy, underground climate, and dog fighting is difficult to prosecute even with an animal as scarred and cruelly tethered as the one in this photo. Dog fighting is a felony in all 50 states but is still common. The Michigan Humane Society Cruelty Investigation Department responds to complaints of dog fighting regularly. Frequently, other illegal activities can be associated with the fight. It is not uncommon for large amounts of money, guns, and drugs to be seized during a dog fight raid.

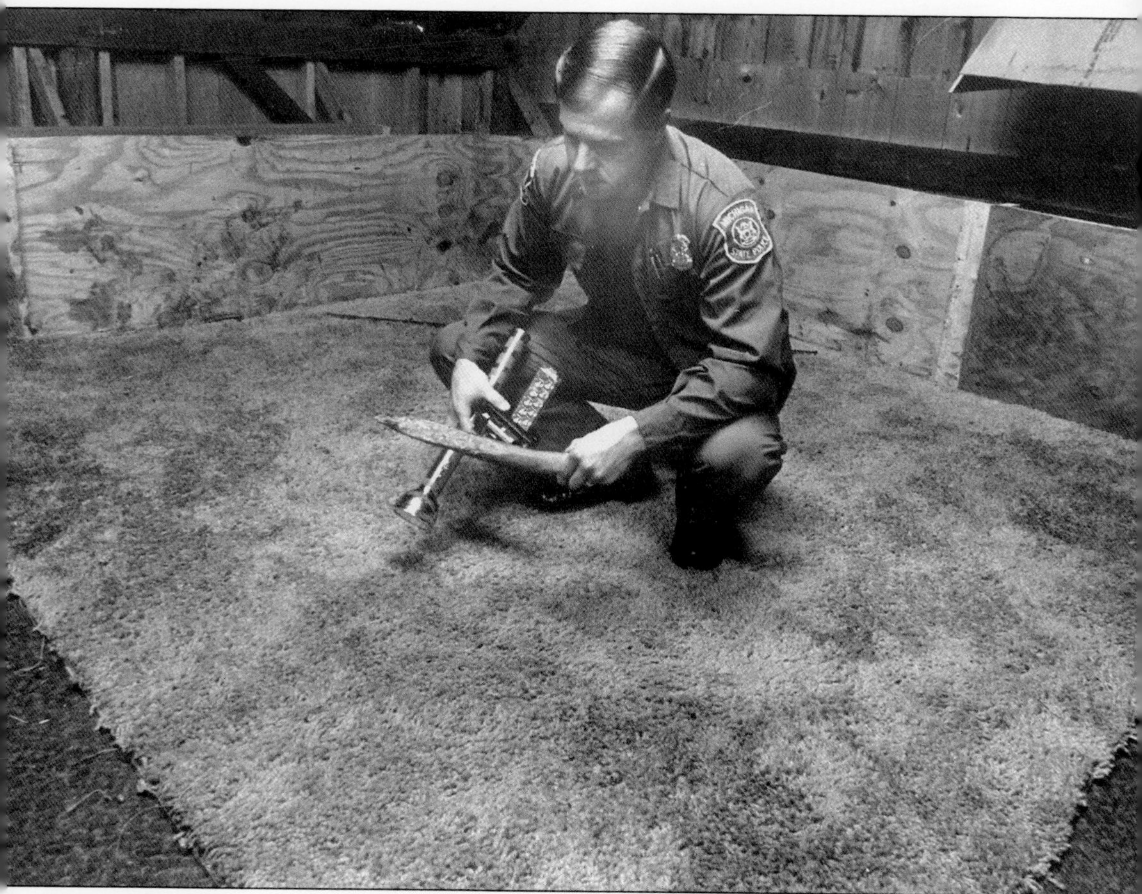

It's the Pits! Organized dog fights often take place in what is called a "pit." More often than not, these pits are simple plywood barriers surrounding a piece of carpet, like the one in this photo. The pit can be dismantled and set up with little effort. Dogs are forced to fight each other and the "pit" prohibits their ability to leave the fight. Paraphernalia collected at dog fight raids usually includes a "pry-stick" like the one seen here, used to pry the jaws of the dog open to make him let go of his opponent. Other items often collected are weights, scales, and treadmills. Dogs used in fighting follow rigorous training schedules set to build stamina, strength, and tenacity. Often fought to the death or until one dog is mortally injured, these fights are bloody and can be excruciatingly painful to the dogs.

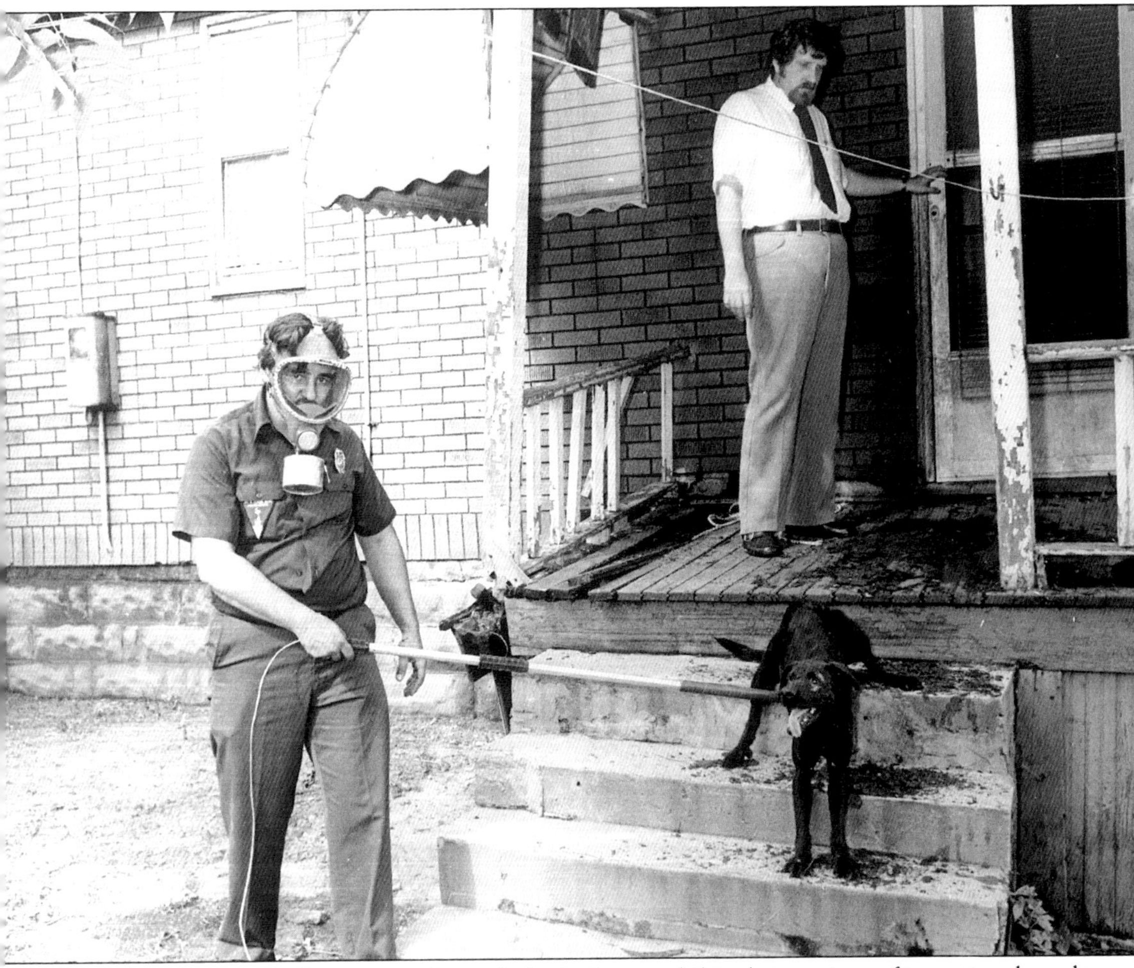

Abandoned and Neglected. Animals don't always exhibit obvious signs of intentional cruelty like physical scars. Some abuses result in poor temperament and poor health. Intentional abandonment and neglect at this house resulted in a call to the Michigan Humane Society Cruelty Investigation Department. According to neighbors, the owners of the home left for a 3-week vacation at the height of summer in Detroit and made no provisions for the care of the 14 to 16 animals inside. Conditions in the home were deplorable. There was no ventilation or air conditioning in the home, and the smell was so overpowering that investigators could not enter the home without gas masks. The dogs were fearful of humans, were not properly socialized, and had received no veterinary care.

STRIKE A POSE! Julie was the first Michigan Humane Society adoptable pet to be featured on WWJ-TV 4. Dave Kelly, then WWJ news director, broadcast this photo of Julie one day, and the resulting 300 phone calls prompted Kelly to bring in Michigan Humane Society adoptable pets regularly. In November 1972, the weekly WWJ "Pet Parade" feature began on the noon and 7 p.m. newscasts.

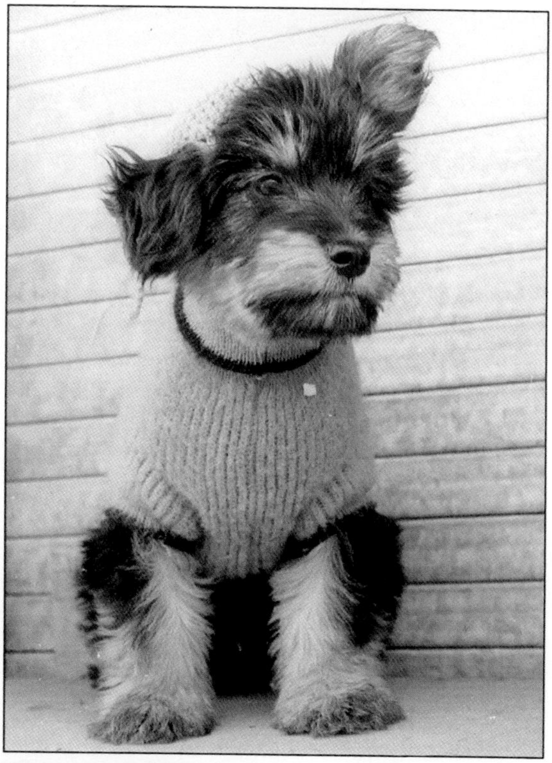

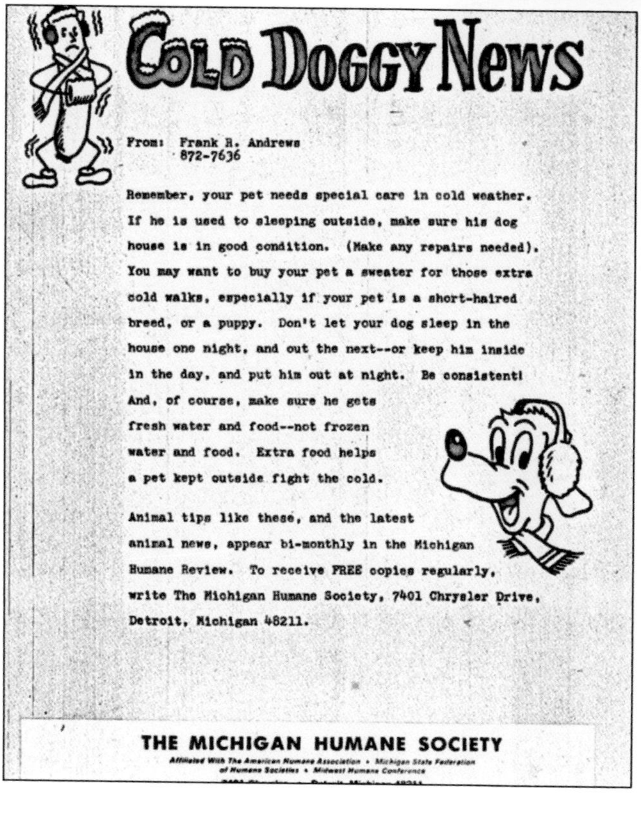

COLD DOGGY NEWS

From: Frank R. Andrews
872-7636

Remember, your pet needs special care in cold weather. If he is used to sleeping outside, make sure his dog house is in good condition. (Make any repairs needed). You may want to buy your pet a sweater for those extra cold walks, especially if your pet is a short-haired breed, or a puppy. Don't let your dog sleep in the house one night, and out the next--or keep him inside in the day, and put him out at night. Be consistent! And, of course, make sure he gets fresh water and food--not frozen water and food. Extra food helps a pet kept outside fight the cold.

Animal tips like these, and the latest animal news, appear bi-monthly in the Michigan Humane Review. To receive FREE copies regularly, write The Michigan Humane Society, 7401 Chrysler Drive, Detroit, Michigan 48211.

THE MICHIGAN HUMANE SOCIETY

COLD DOGGY NEWS. Executive Director Frank Andrews sent this special bulletin to pet owners during the frigid Detroit winter of 1970. It seems rescue calls during the winter never decrease as pet owners continue to leave pets outside during severe weather. The Michigan Humane Society sends thousands of information and educational pieces every year in an effort to educate pet owners and the general public on appropriate animal care.

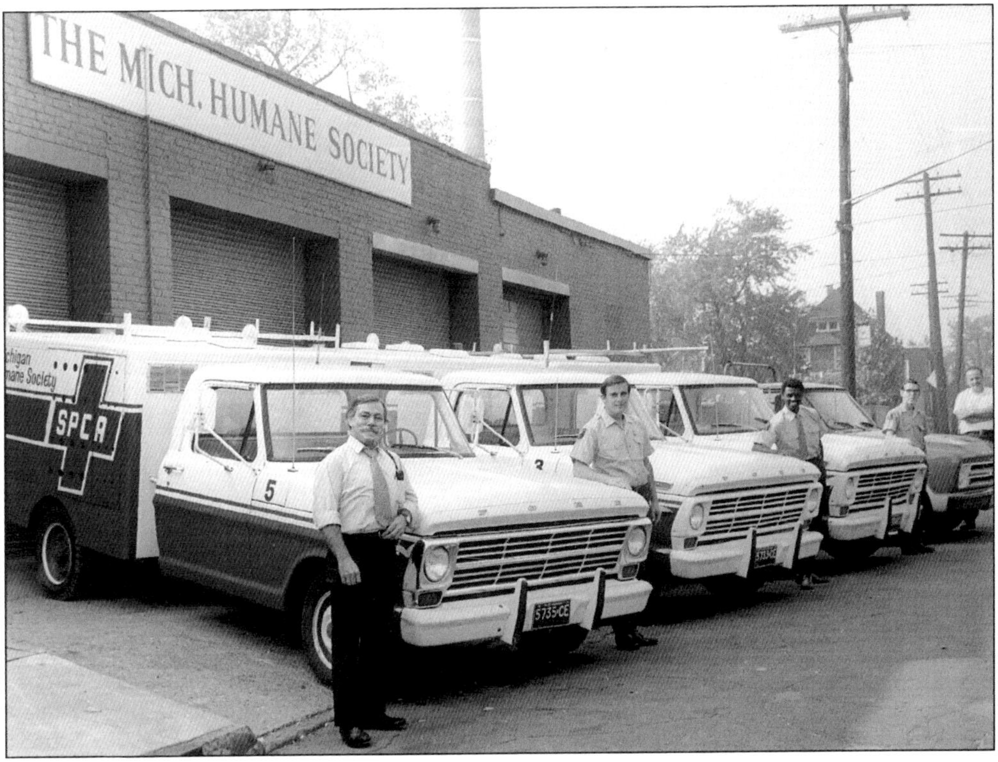

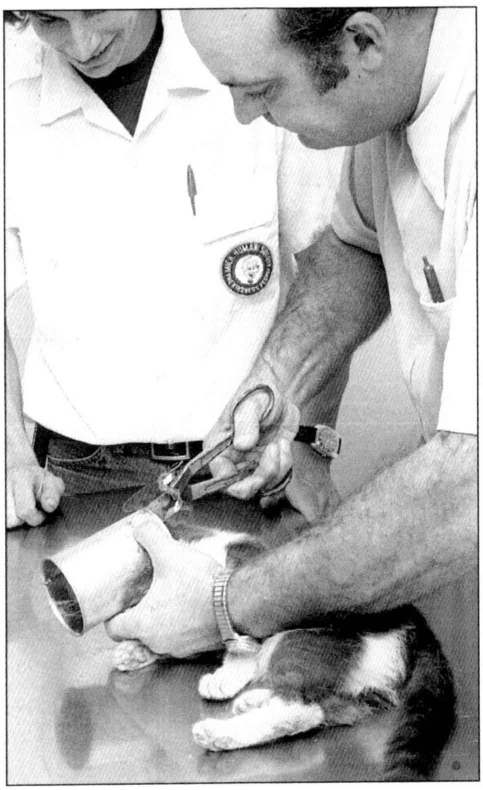

READY AND ABLE. The Michigan Humane Society has operated a fleet of ambulance and rescue wagons and vehicles since its beginning in 1877. The first vehicle was a horse ambulance. By the 1920s, the society operated a fleet of horse ambulances and small animal ambulances. The ambulances used in 1975 reflect the changing times and no longer accommodate a horse or large animal, but rather the smaller companion animals that abound in the city.

CANNED CAT. This poor feline stuck his head where it didn't belong. Rescue driver James Edwards was dispatched to the East Side, and the cat somehow managed to get himself and his can up a tree. Edwards captured the cat and returned to the shelter. Dr. William Bayley, Chief Veterinarian at the Michigan Humane Society, sedated the little kitty and delicately cut the tin can off his head.

Seven

Innovation and Development

1980–1990

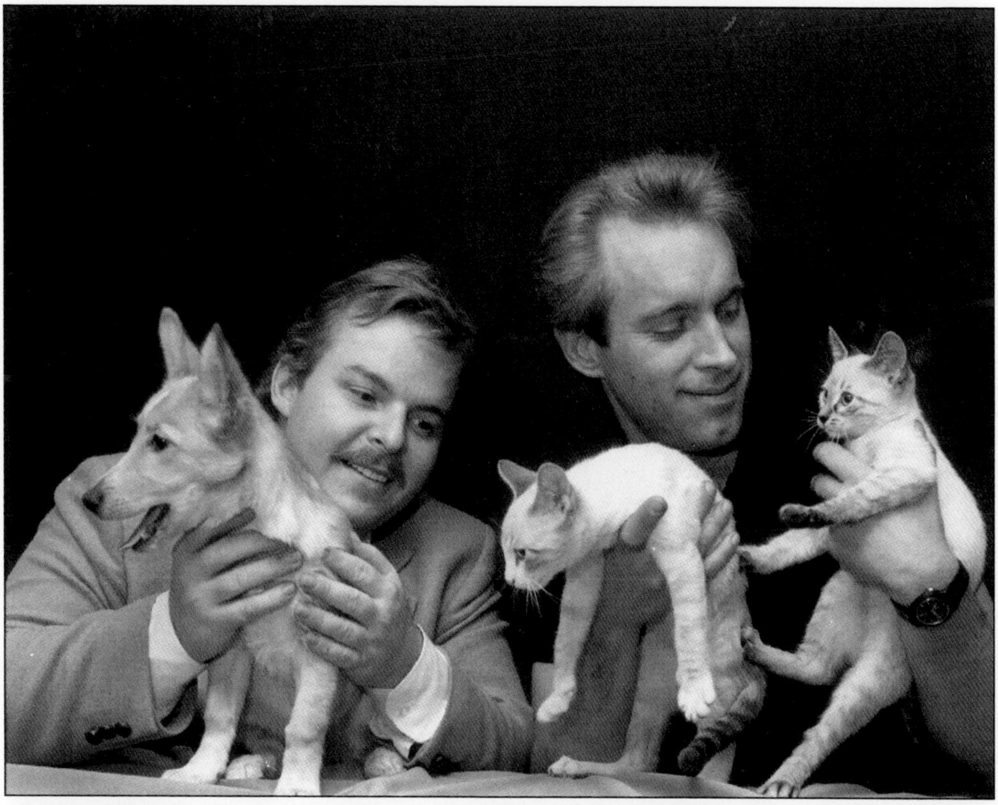

Ambassadors of Good Will. Popular Detroit radio personalities Jim Harper and Steve Gannon lend their support to "Be Kind to Animals Week" in this 1984 photo. "Be Kind to Animals Week" is the oldest recognized event on behalf of animals. Jim Harper is still a popular radio host in the Motor City, and his relationship with Michigan Humane Society is stronger than ever.

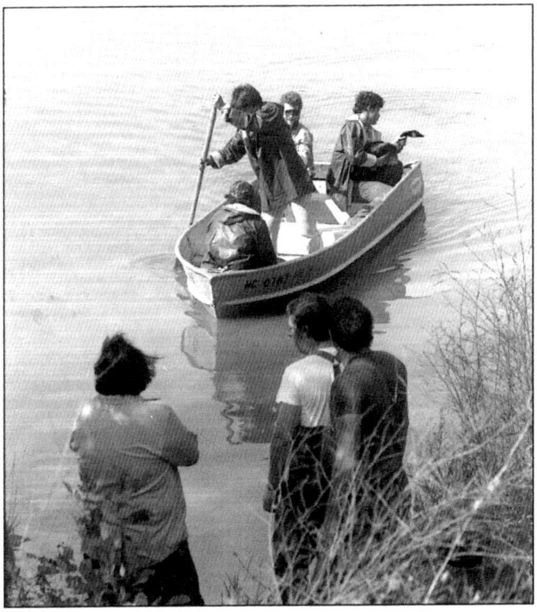

Rescue on the Water. In October 1980, Waterford Lake in Northville was the scene of a dreadful oil spill. The Department of Natural Resources called the Michigan Humane Society for help in rescuing almost 100 geese and ducks covered in oil. The first load of oil-laden geese arrived at the Michigan Humane Society shelter at 4:30 p.m. Dr. Richard Wojciechowski organized a team of staff and volunteers to begin clean up of the birds. Each bird was given a solution of dextrose and water to combat the dehydrating effects of the oil and then washed three times in a detergent solution. The birds were kept at the Michigan Humane Society shelter for one week to allow natural oils removed during washing to return to their feathers. The birds were then banded by U.S. Fish and Wildlife personnel, taken to the Michigan State Game Farm in Mason, Michigan, and released.

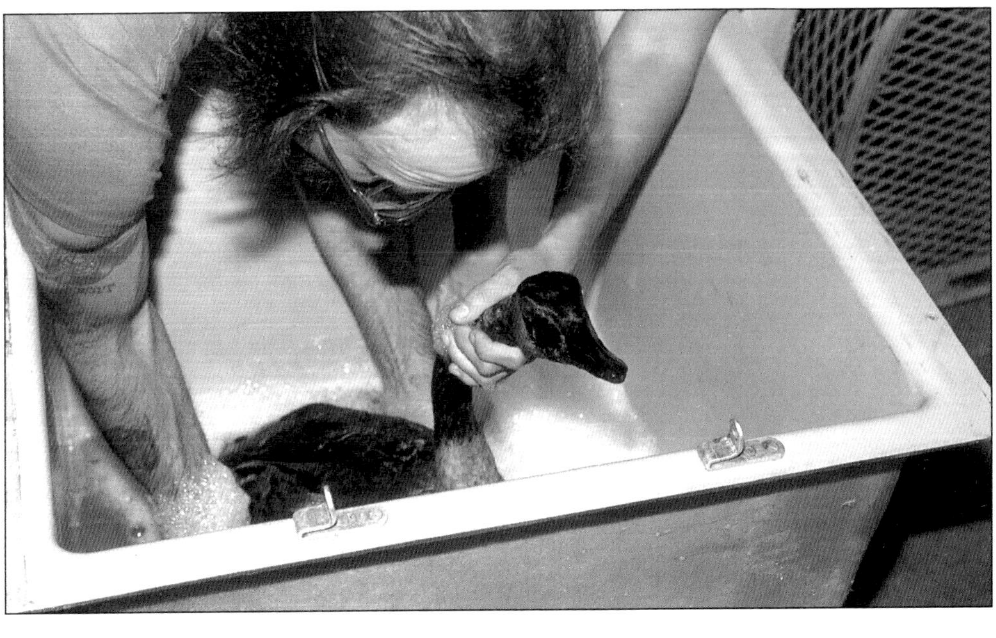

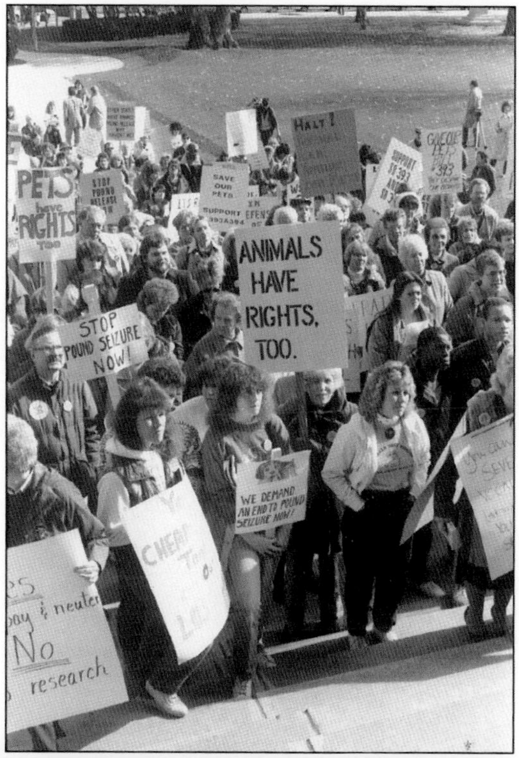

RALLY THE TROOPS! The Michigan Humane Society publicly opposed the use of animals in experimentation as early as 1928. Ever vigilant, the Michigan Humane Society organized a public rally in Lansing in 1984 to oppose pound seizure, or the practice of selling shelter animals to research facilities. A number of these facilities operate in Michigan and the Society's attempts to abolish pound seizure at the state level have been unsuccessful. However, with information provided by the Michigan Humane Society, many citizens have stopped pound seizure in their local animal control agencies.

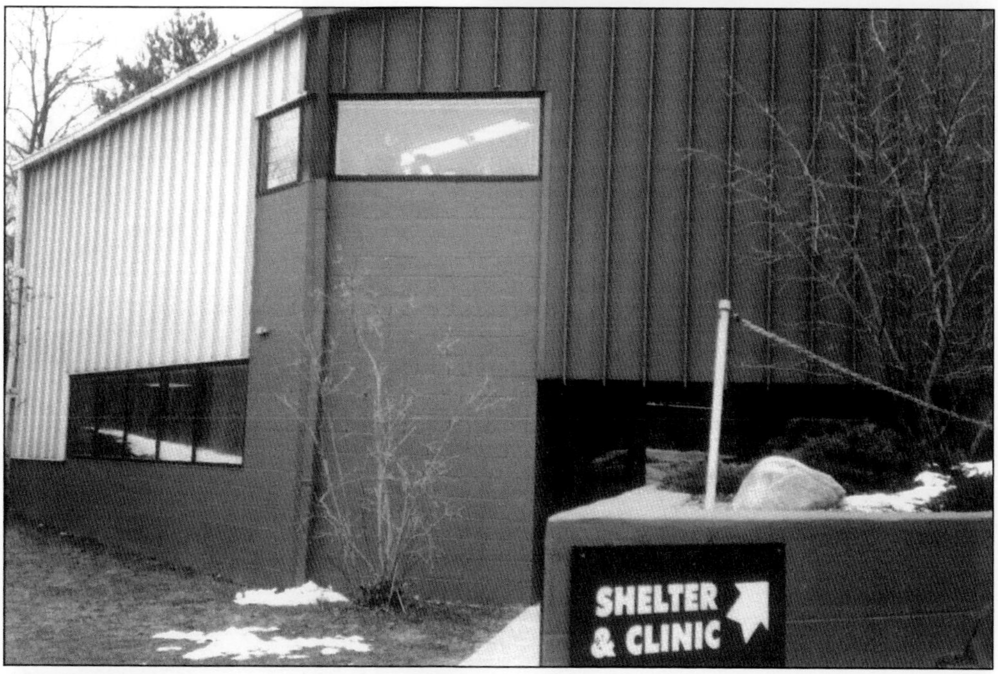

ANOTHER ADDITION TO THE MICHIGAN HUMANE SOCIETY. In 1982, Michigan Humane Society again expanded to serve the needs of communities north of the city. Through a grant from the Kresge Foundation, the Michigan Humane Society began construction of a shelter and clinic facility on Auburn Road in Rochester Hills, Michigan.

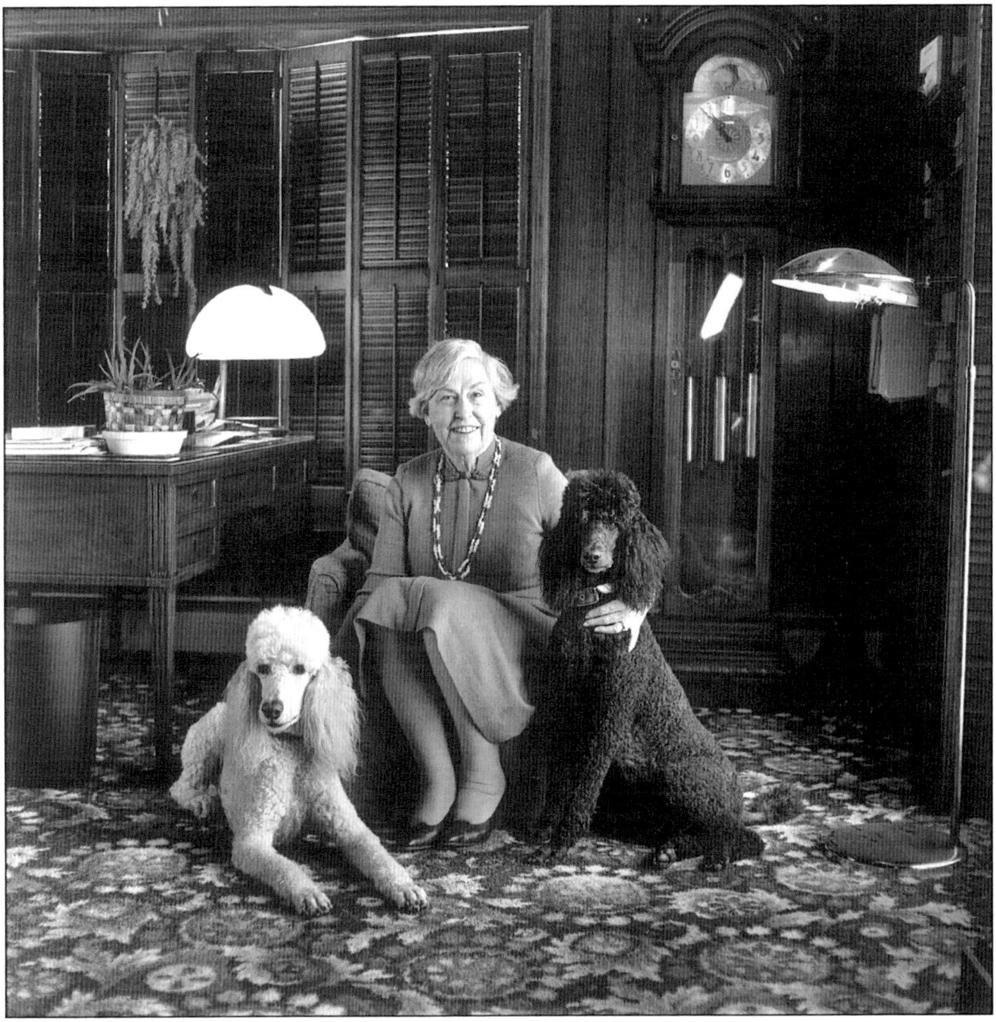

THE POLITICS OF HUMANE LEGISLATION. Michigan's Lieutenant Governor Martha Griffiths, pictured here with pets Sam and Cleo, was a staunch supporter of animals and fought tirelessly against the exploitation of any living being. In the 1950s, she introduced the first federal humane slaughter legislation. In a 1984 Michigan Humane Society interview, from which this photo came, Griffiths offers this perspective: "The right of all life to be free from torture is, in fact, a human right that should be extended to all life forms. Any one that is cruel to life in one form is capable of cruelty to life in any form." Griffiths stressed the importance of community involvement with the legislature. "People need to know what bills are under consideration in Congress or in their state legislatures that affect their pets and other animals."

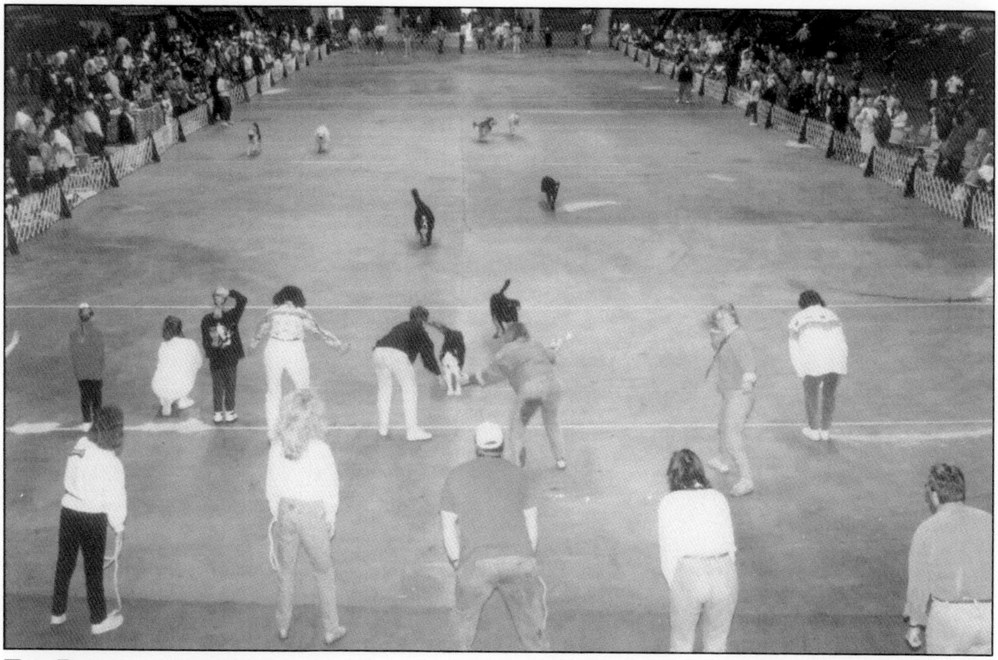

THE RUNNING OF THE MUTTS! After their trip to the Rose Bowl, Charley Manos and Rosey became unstoppable in supporting the Michigan Humane Society. In 1984, the first "Rosey Mutt Derby" was held to benefit the "Rosey Rescue League"— the Michigan Humane Society Rescue Department that operated seven days a week.

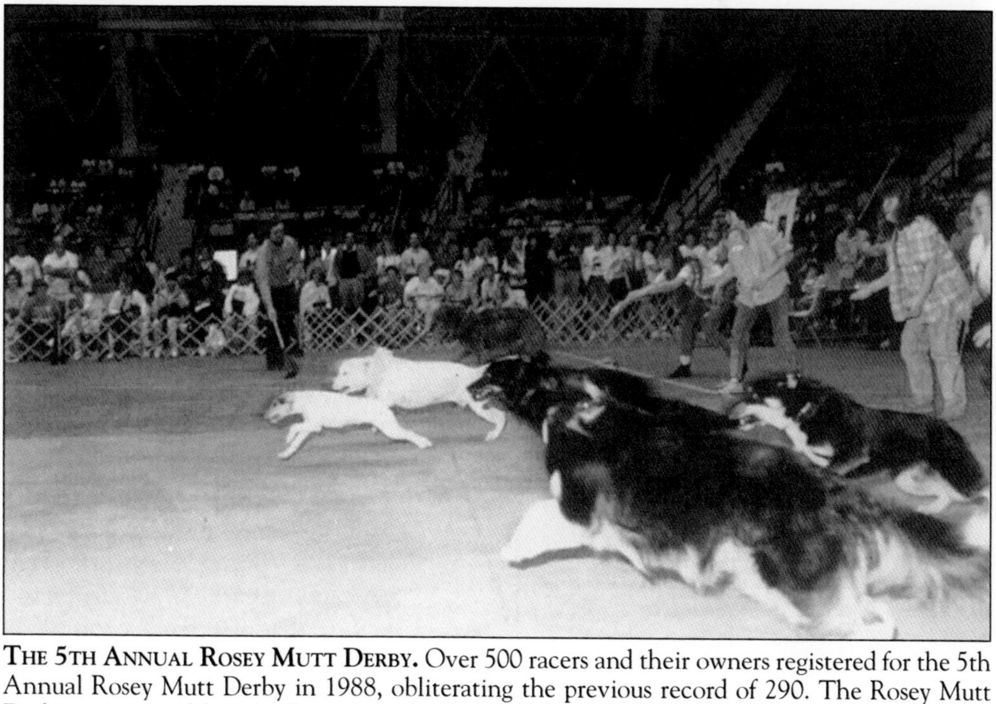

THE 5TH ANNUAL ROSEY MUTT DERBY. Over 500 racers and their owners registered for the 5th Annual Rosey Mutt Derby in 1988, obliterating the previous record of 290. The Rosey Mutt Derby was a crowd favorite for years and resulted in much needed funds for the operating budget of the Michigan Humane Society.

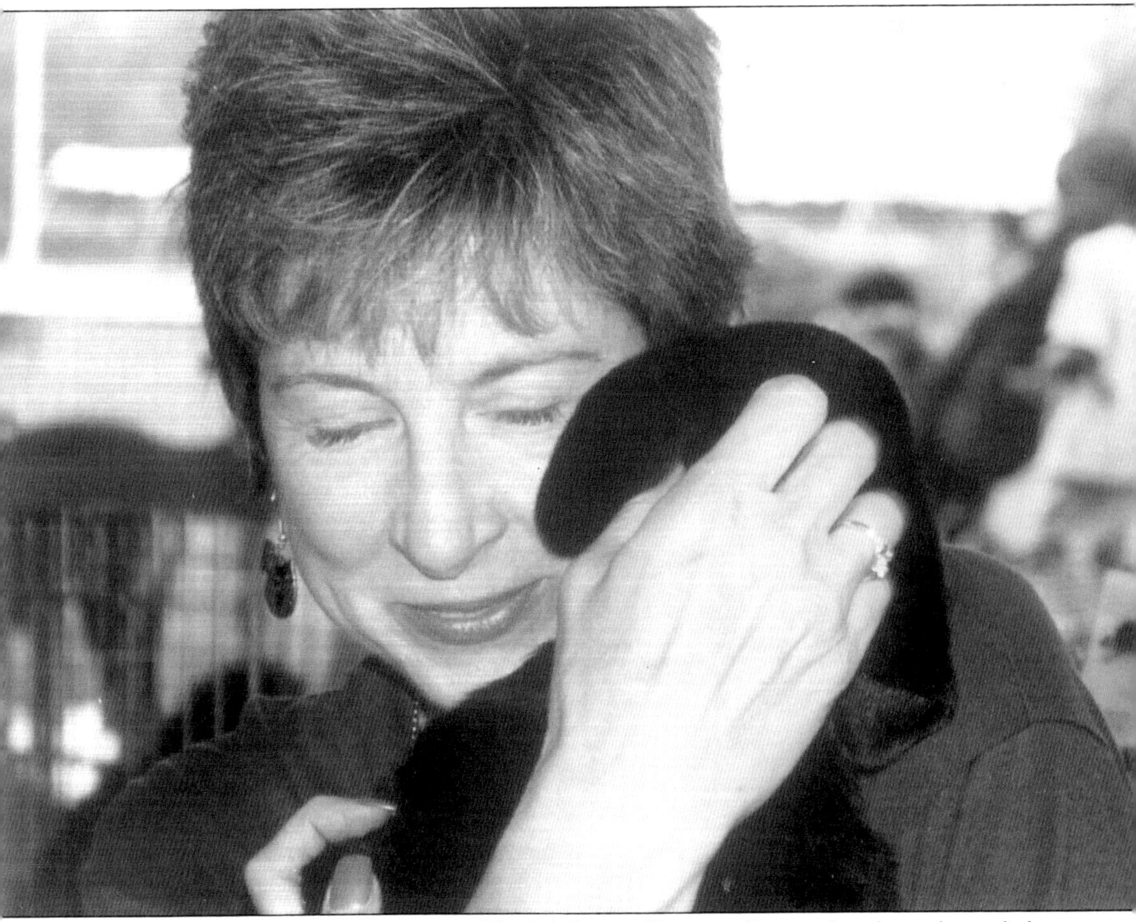

THE REWARDS OF VOLUNTEERING. The Michigan Humane Society has long depended upon volunteers for the success of its many programs and services. It hosts several off-site adoption events each year that require numerous volunteer animal handlers and transporters. It utilizes foster homes for animals that are ill or too young to be adopted, and volunteers are crucial to the foster program. Volunteers assist in their shelters by walking the adoptable dogs, and socializing the more timid animals. Volunteers pack the surgery packs used in their clinics and help to keep the facility clean. Even our Pet Education Center relies on volunteers to visit adoptable dogs in the shelters and perform what is called Level One training. Adoptable dogs are taught basic commands such as "sit" and "down" to provide them with a basic understanding of obedience. Today, the Michigan Humane Society boasts over 800 active volunteers. This volunteer provides, and receives, comfort from a pup awaiting adoption.

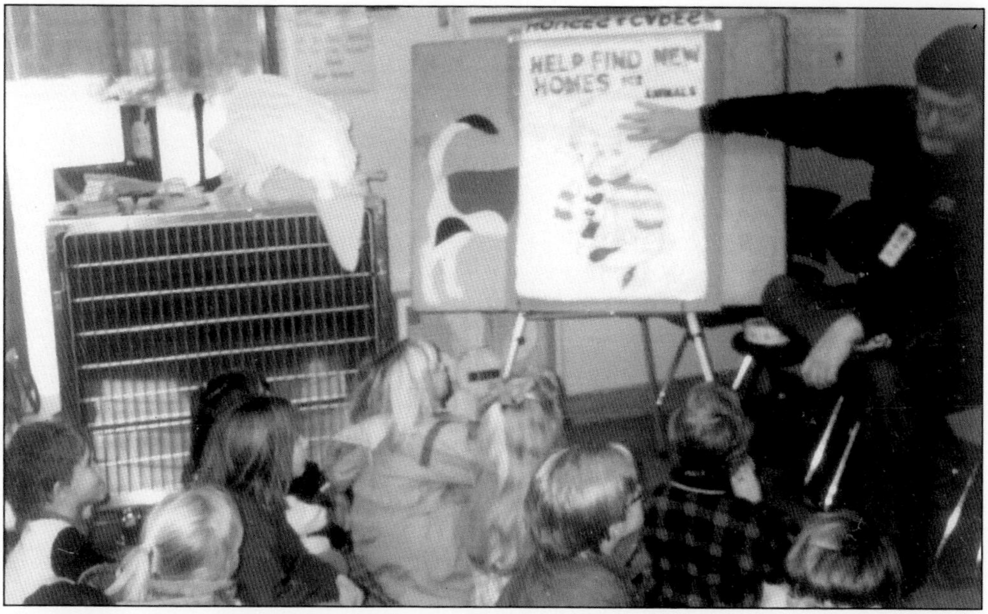

CONTINUING EDUCATION. The Michigan Humane Society began a program of Humane Education in 1925. That program has carried on throughout the years and is still a mainstay. Humane Educator Ron Blauet visits hundreds of schools each year, in addition to conducting shelter and clinic tours for groups ranging from pre-kindergarten to high school.

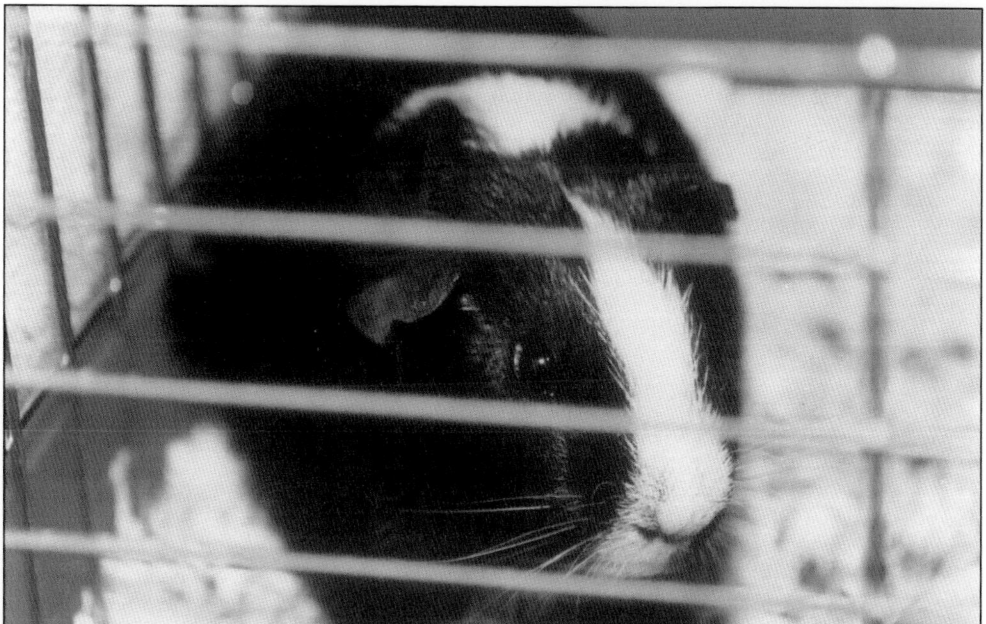

ANIMALS OF ALL SHAPES AND SIZES. The Michigan Humane Society started out focused primarily on the treatment of workhorses in the city in the late 1800s. Through the years, the Society has opened its doors to all other animals, both wild and domestic. It is not uncommon for the Michigan Humane Society to have Guinea pigs, rabbits, hamsters, rats, chinchillas, birds, turtles, and ferrets, in addition to cats and dogs.

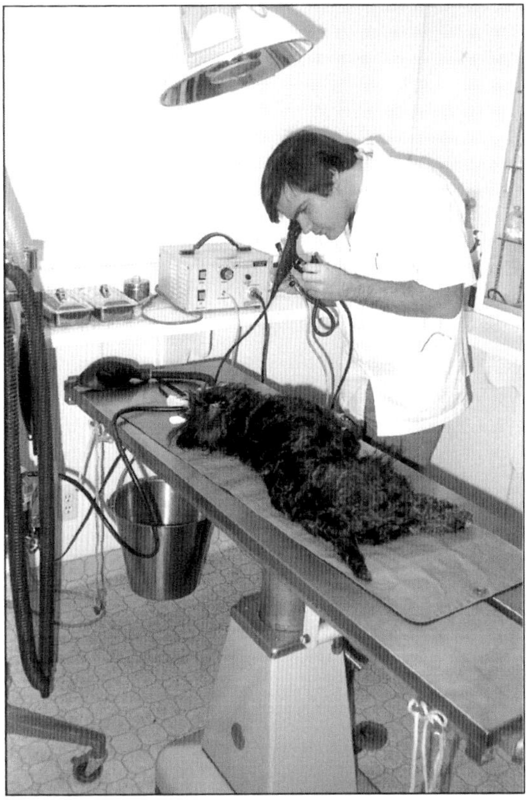

IRS Rules in Favor. In the summer of 1984, the IRS met to decide whether the Michigan Humane Society could continue the operation of its full service veterinary hospitals as part of its nonprofit corporate structure. Their ruling was as follows: "It is evident that providing veterinary services is related to this organization's exempt purposes." This ruling confirmed what the Michigan Humane Society knew for years: full service veterinary hospitals are an integral part of the Society's programs to measurably reduce companion animal overpopulation as well as prevent cruelty to animals.

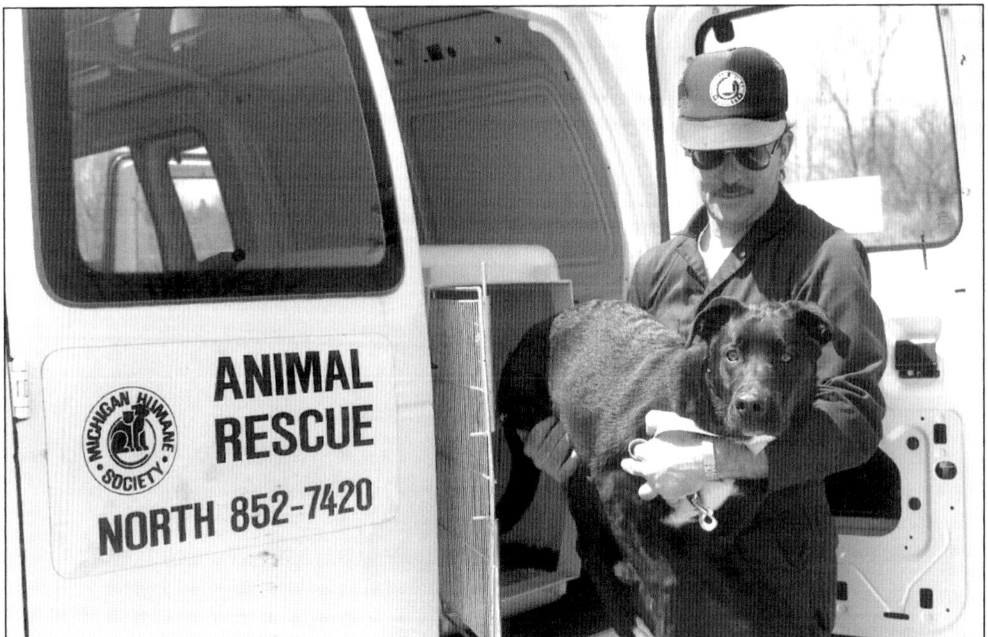

Another Rescue. When the shelter and clinic north of Detroit in Rochester Hills was built, the Society was able to expand its outreach and provide services to communities that had previously been without.

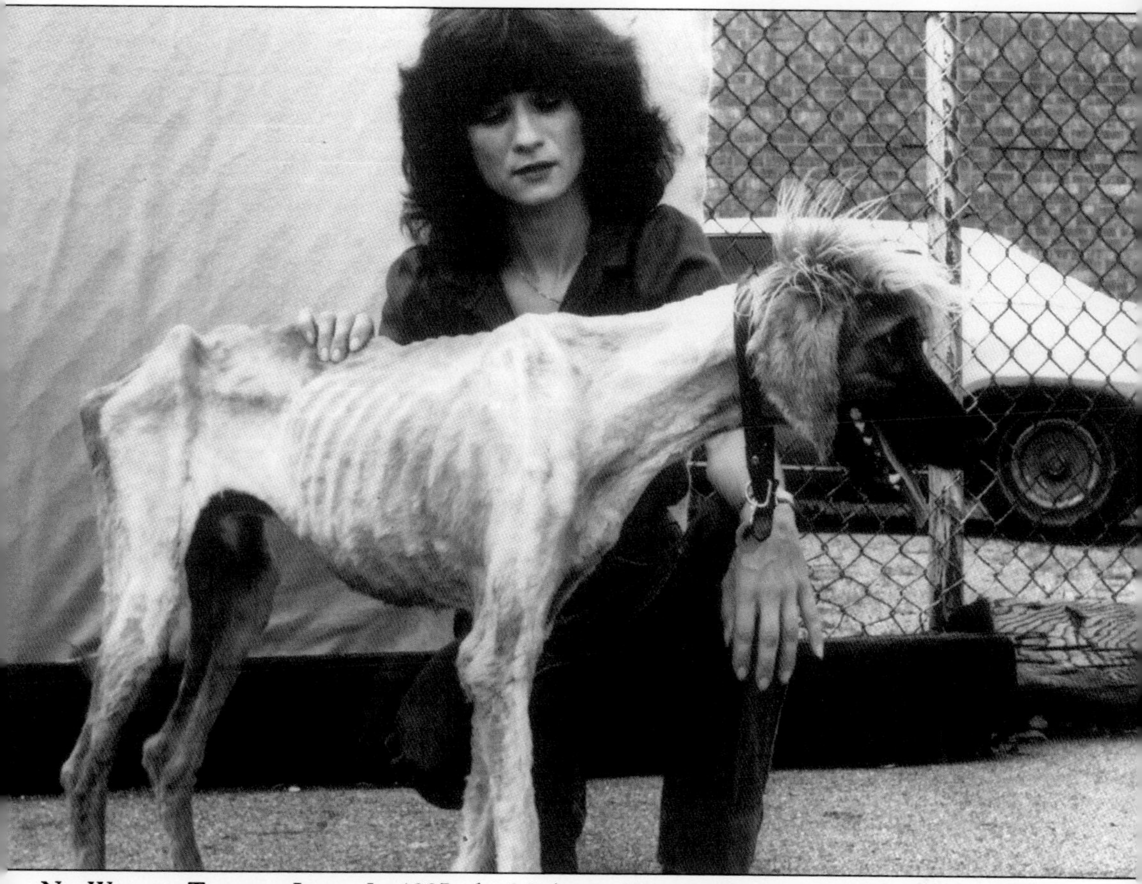

No Way to Treat a Lady. In 1987, the Michigan Humane Society Cruelty Investigators were dispatched to a home in Detroit to pick up a neglected dog. What investigators saw when they got there shook them to the core. A six-year-old Afghan was in desperate need. She could not get up or stand on her own. After 3.5 pounds of matted hair was shaved from her body, she weighed a mere 19 pounds. She had the heart of a lion and her spirit touched all who came to know her or heard of her story. Dubbed "Lady" by the Michigan Humane Society staff, she made a remarkable recovery and was adopted into a wonderful new home and finally lived the good life. Lady's previous owner was charged with animal cruelty and ordered to pay restitution to the Michigan Humane Society in the amount of $750.

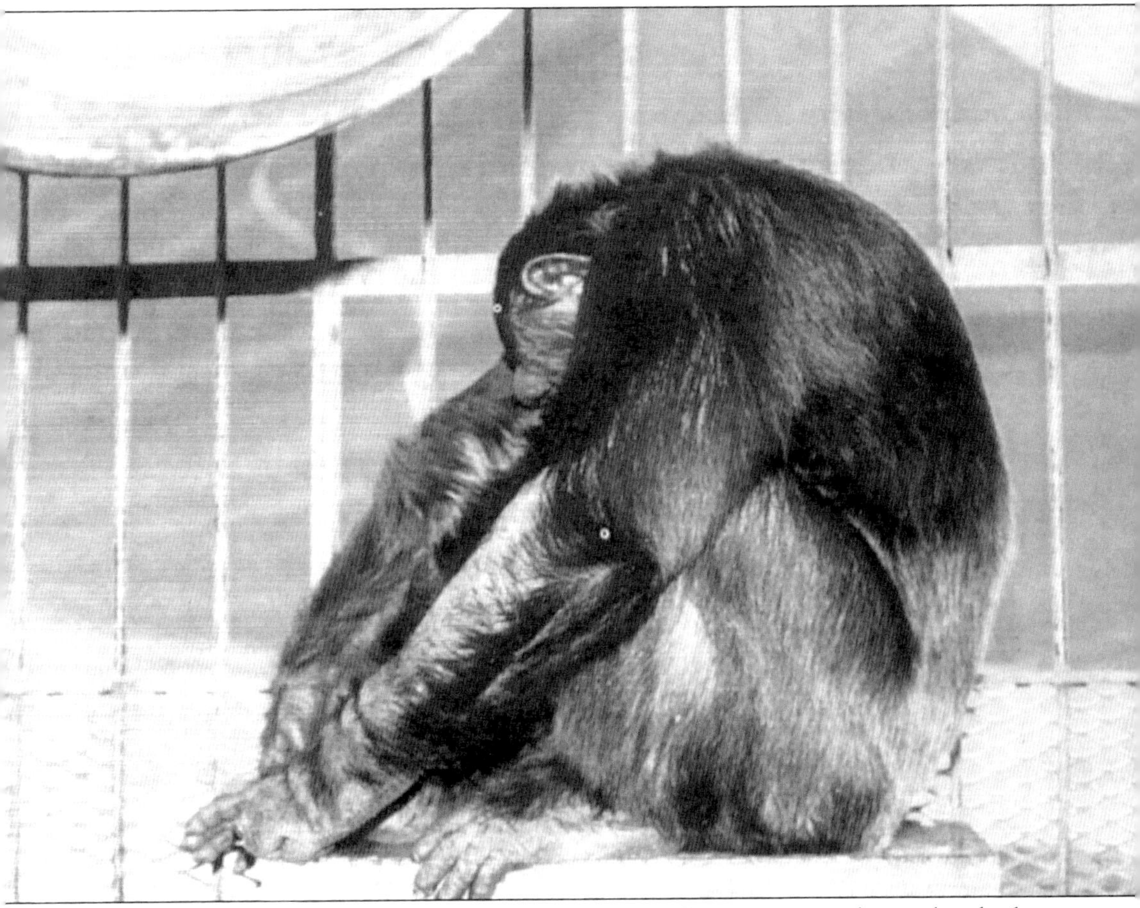

THE LIFE OF TYRONE. In 1987, the Michigan Humane Society witnessed a cruel and inhumane existence endured by a primate called "Tyrone the Terrible." For three years, Tyrone traveled from town to town in a 10-by-16-by-8-foot cage as part of a carnival. For $1, carnival goers could watch Tyrone be subjected to maltreatment by carnival hands until he flew into a rage and provided "entertainment" for the crowd. The Michigan Humane Society video taped this "performance" and was able to confiscate Tyrone and his cage with the help of Sterling Heights police. Tyrone was temporarily housed at the Michigan Humane Society Rochester Hills Shelter. It was not enough to have taken him from this abusive life. The Michigan Humane Society embarked on a journey to find a permanent home and a guarantee that his life would be far better than it had been before. Special funds were collected and the Michigan Humane Society was able to secure placement for Tyrone at Primarily Primates in San Antonio, Texas. Tyrone lived out his days in comfort and with other primates until his death in 2001.

Eight

Moving Forward

1990–2002

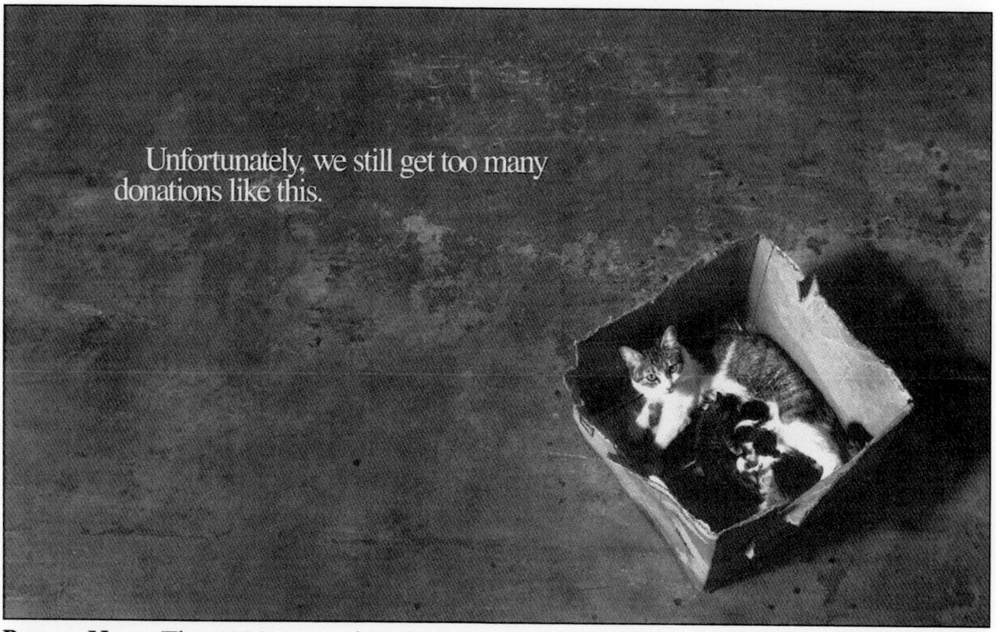

Please Help. The 1990s proved to be a decade of growth and change for the Michigan Humane Society. Mass appeal and education pieces like this one were designed with the help of advertising agencies in an effort to reach as many people as possible and to drive home the reality of the Society's work.

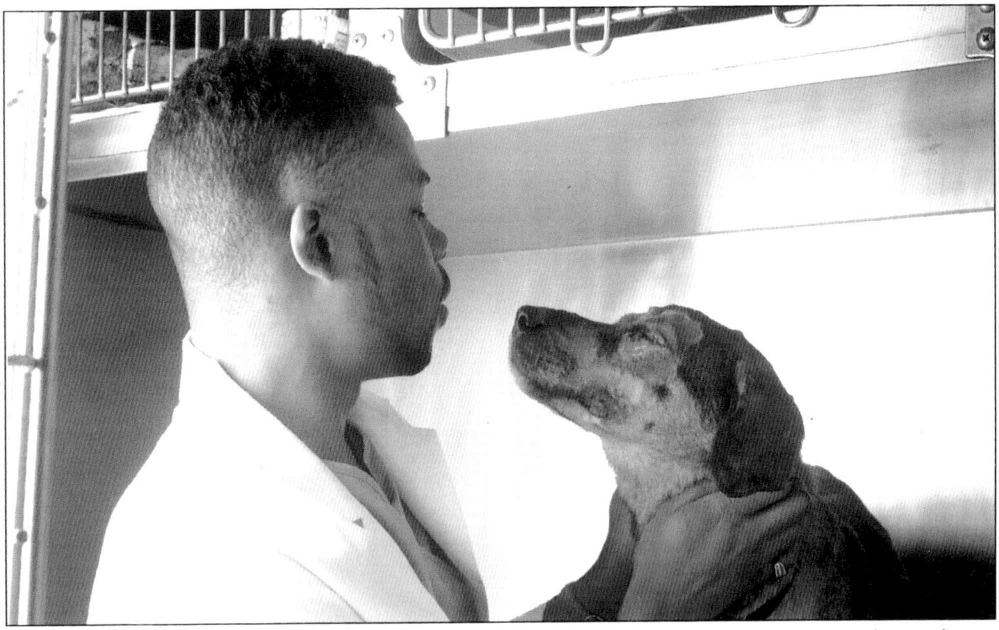

Hard Reality of Cruelty. The Michigan Humane Society has seen far too much cruelty in its 125 years of service. One can only be amazed and impressed by an animal's ability to trust and love again after suffering horrible cruelty at the hands of man. This dog suffered burns over most of his face and body but was still receptive to and comforted by the words and touch of this Michigan Humane Society employee.

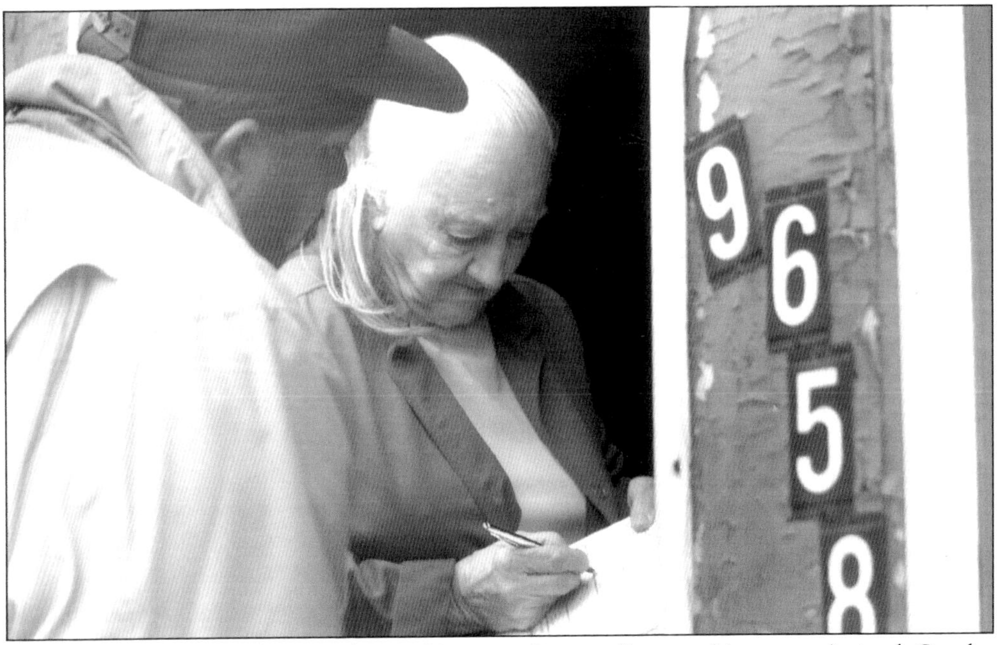

Signed Surrender. When Michigan Humane Society Rescue drivers or Animal Cruelty investigators arrive on the scene, they often will ask the owner of the animal for a written surrender. If the animal is in immediate danger or peril, the animal can be removed from the premise without an owner signature.

FREE SHOT CLINICS. Since 1991, the Michigan Humane Society has provided free shot clinics for pet owners in inner city neighborhoods. These clinics also provide an opportunity to authorize free sterilizations by giving out certificates for free surgeries to those most in need. It is not uncommon to see animals held by electrical cords, tow chains, or rope. To date, these clinics have provided vaccinations to over 28,000 animals.

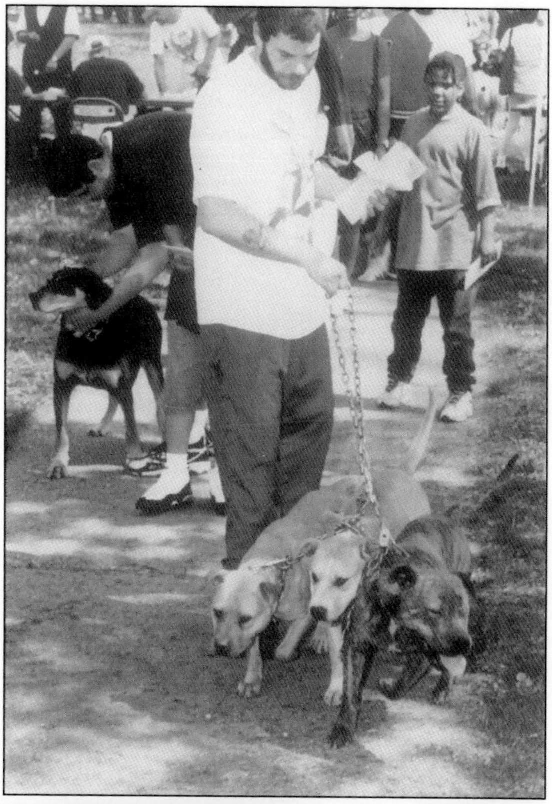

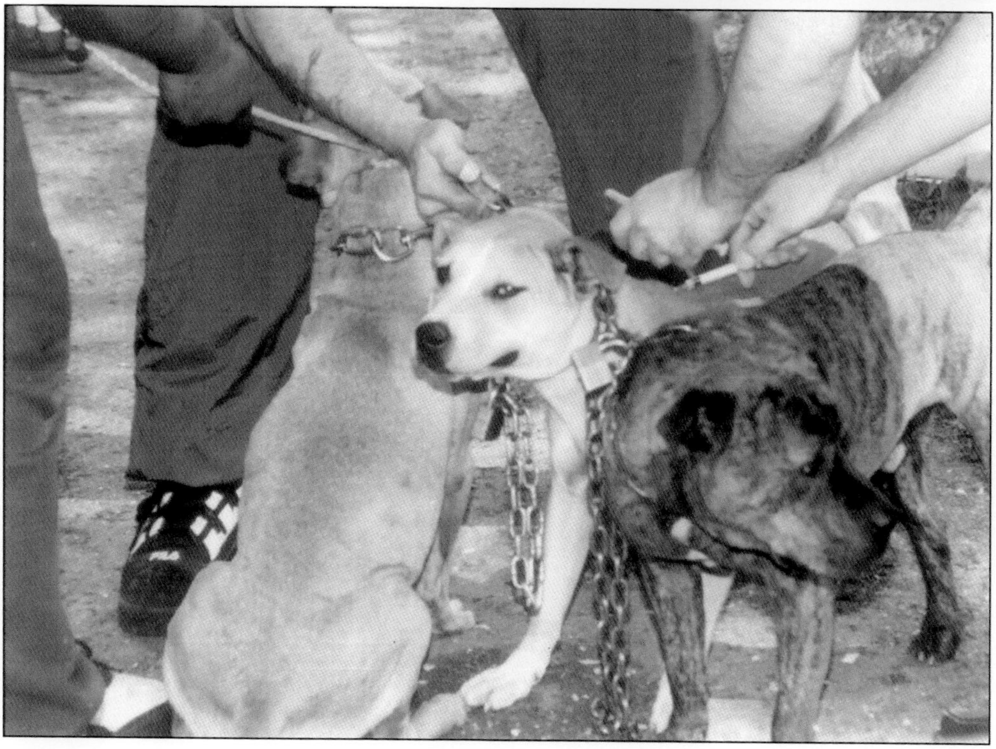

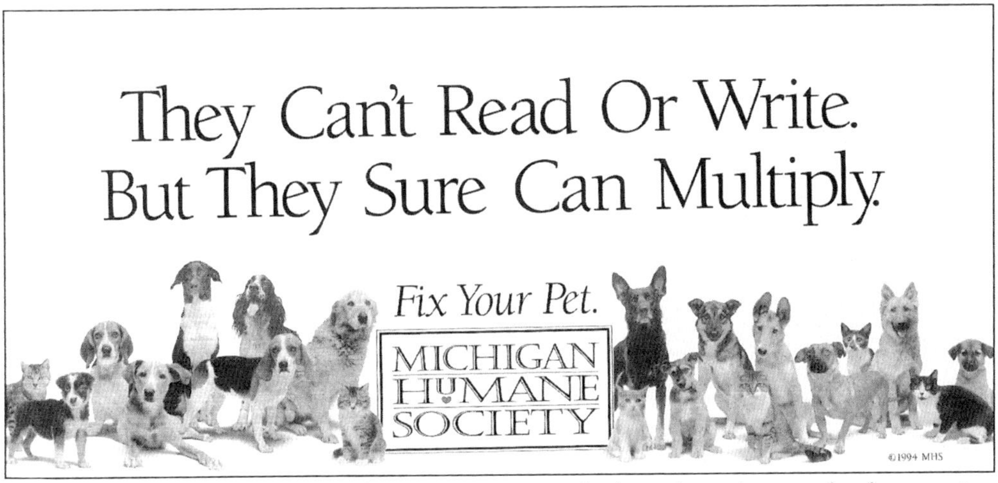

OVERPOPULATION. In an effort to educate pet owners and others about the tragedy of companion animal overpopulation, the Michigan Humane Society developed a series of printed materials. Images such as this one were used on billboards, signs, and brochures.

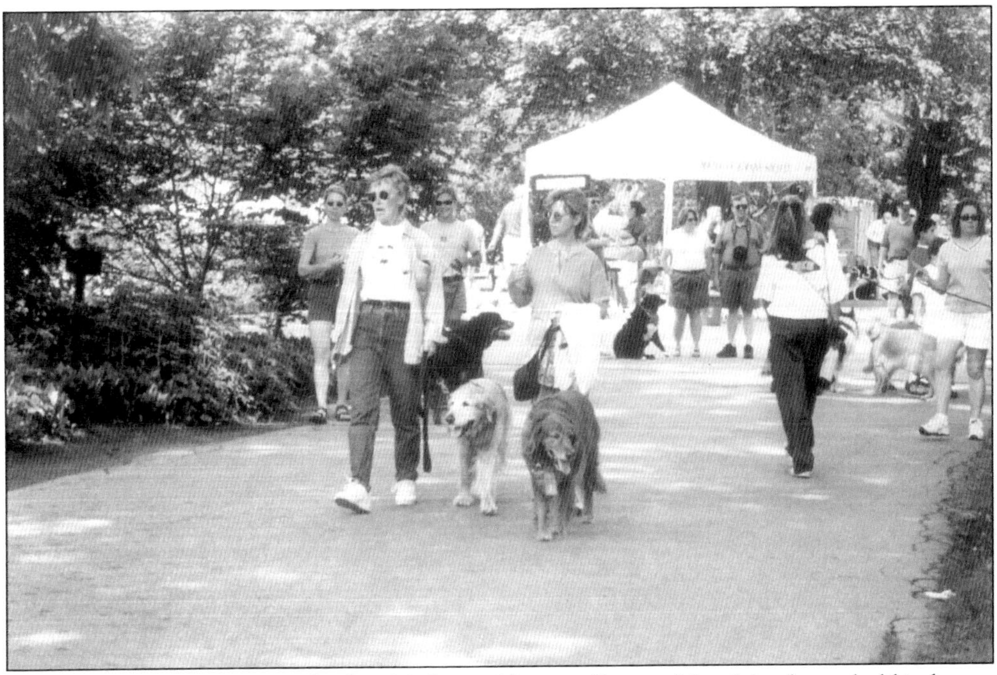

MARCHING MUTTS! In 1989, the first Michigan Humane Society Mutt March was held in honor of longtime friend and Board member, Laura Lee Greer. The Mutt Marches continue today and bring in thousands of dollars. Walkers gather donations from friends and family and then enjoy a five-mile stroll in scenic surroundings with their best four-footed friends.

PRACTICE! PRACTICE! PRACTICE! Early in 1950, the Michigan Humane Society recognized the role that training and obedience play in keeping pets and families together. Classes were organized on Saturday mornings outside the Detroit Shelter through the 1960s. The opening of the Michigan Humane Society Pet Education Center in 1997 was the result of hard work by dedicated employees. Today, the Pet Education Center offers obedience and training classes, private consultations, and classes for children and pets.

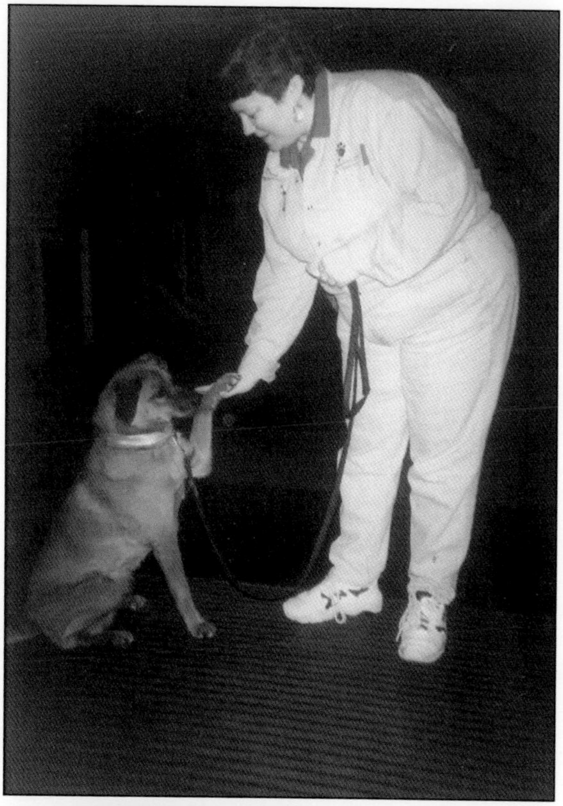

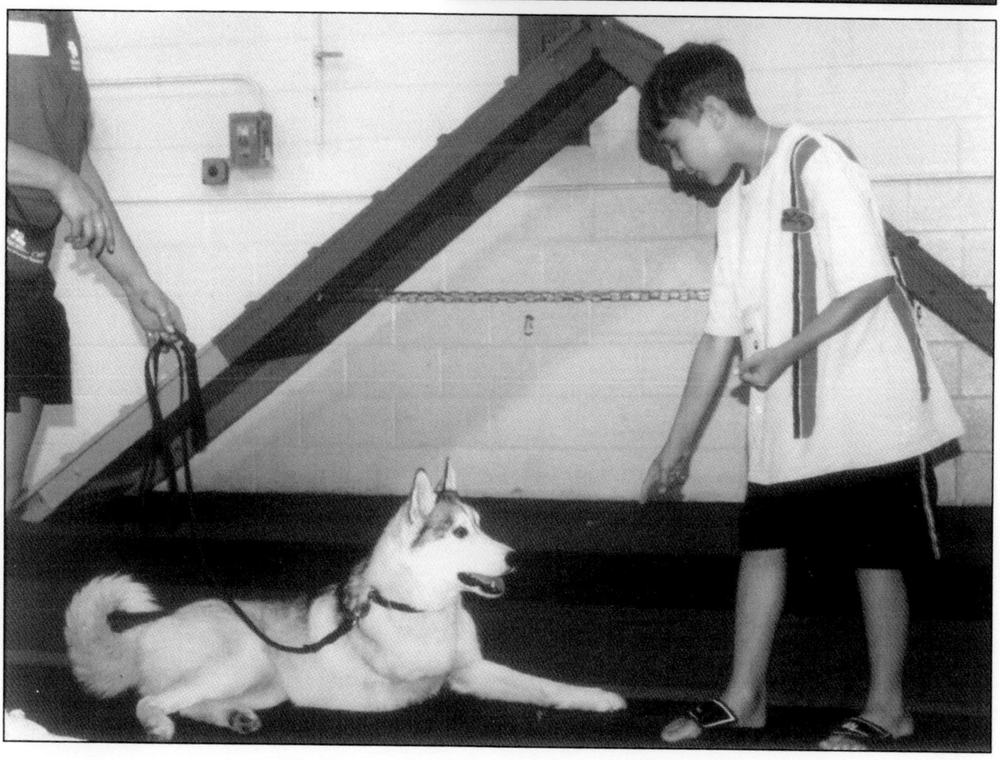

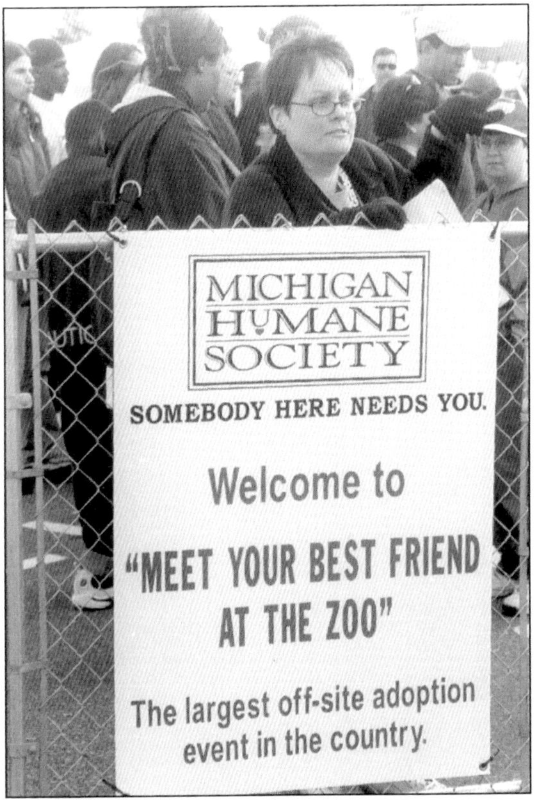

MEET YOUR BEST FRIEND AT THE ZOO! The first annual "Meet Your Best Friend at the Zoo" was held in 1993 on the grounds of the Detroit Zoo. This off-site adoption event brings hundreds of animals from several animal welfare groups to the Detroit Zoo in Royal Oak, Michigan. This partnership between the Detroit Zoo and the Michigan Humane Society has been instrumental in finding homes for over 6,000 homeless animals.

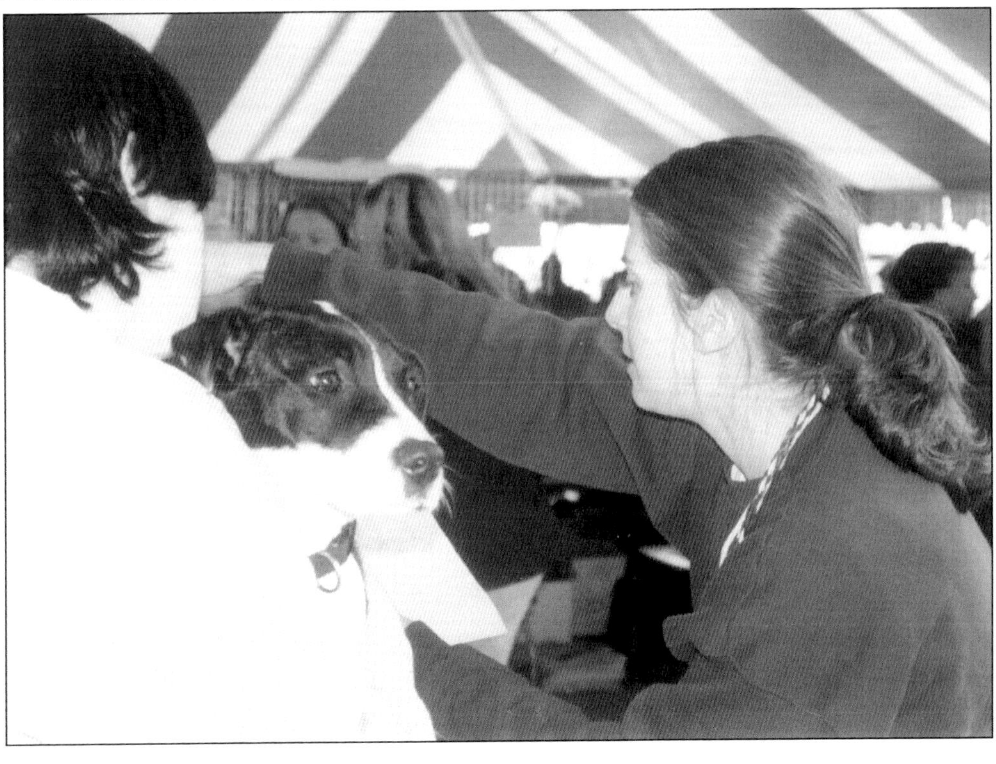

Paw Paw Pourri! Opened in 1990 in Royal Oak, Michigan, the Michigan Humane Society retail store, Paw Pourri, was well received. A wide selection of gift items was available. Paw Pourri also provided an opportunity to educate and inform people in a community with no Michigan Humane Society facility.

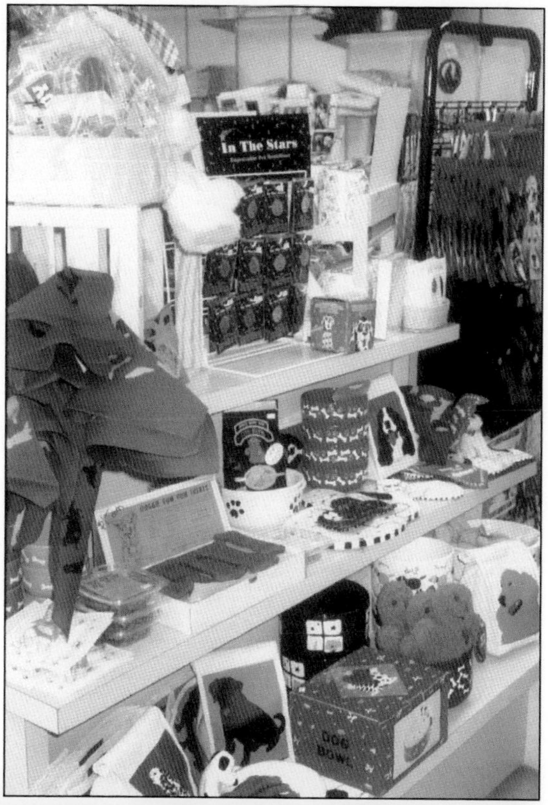

Wow, A Bow Wow Brunch! Since 1990, the Michigan Humane Society has held an annual "Bow Wow Brunch" champagne fundraiser to benefit the animals in their care. The elegant afternoon includes a champagne reception, a silent auction with wonderful items on which to bid, special guest appearances by some adorable adoptable animals, and a fabulous meal. In this photo, Michigan Humane Society employee Lin Gardiner takes the "runway" with one of the adoptable dogs for the afternoon.

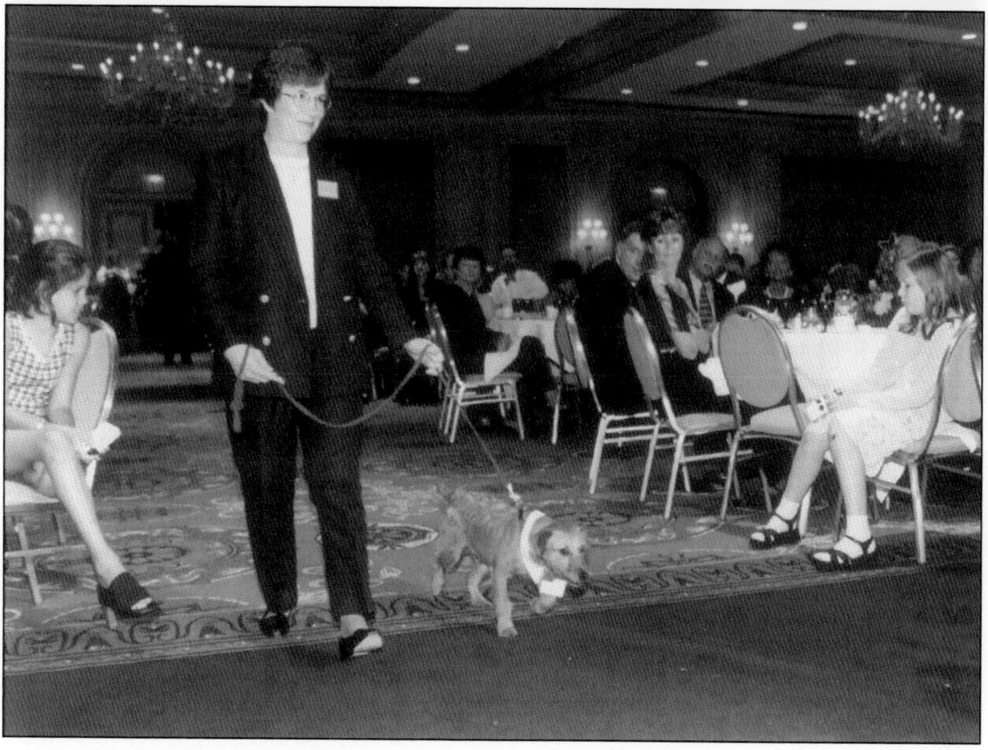

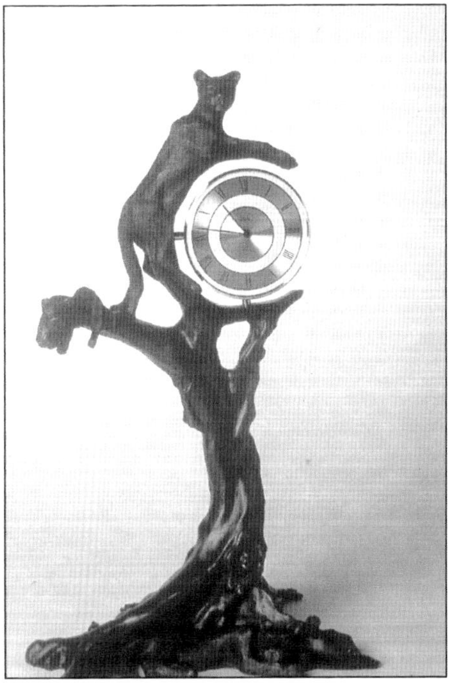

Paws for Celebration. In honor of the 120th anniversary of the Michigan Humane Society in 1997, a celebration featuring Ed McMahon, Frankie Valli, and the Four Seasons, dinner, dancing, and a live auction was held at Neiman Marcus Somerset Collection. Works of art created exclusively for the Michigan Humane Society by students at the Center for Creative Studies, like the one seen in this photograph, rounded out the evening.

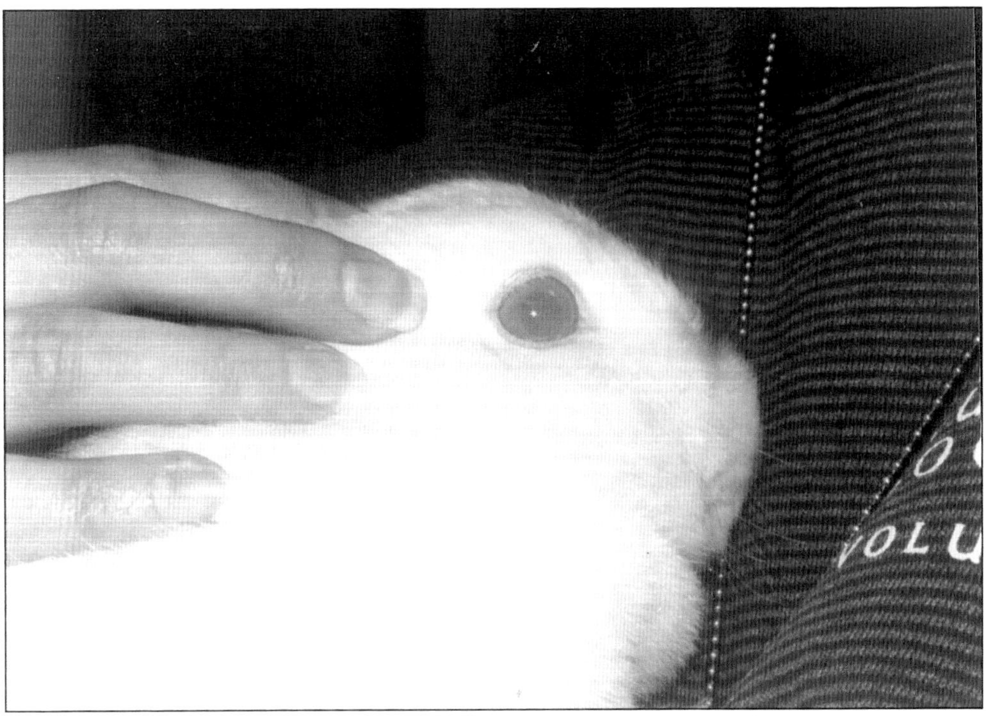

Somebunny Here Needs You! The Michigan Humane Society provides shelter and care to over 48,000 animals each year. Over 56 percent of the animals cared for are turned in by their owners. Animals given as gifts, like rabbits at Easter or puppies at Christmas, often are brought to shelters after only a few months. Most often, the new pet owner has a lifestyle that simply is not conducive to pet ownership. Think twice before giving a pet as a gift.

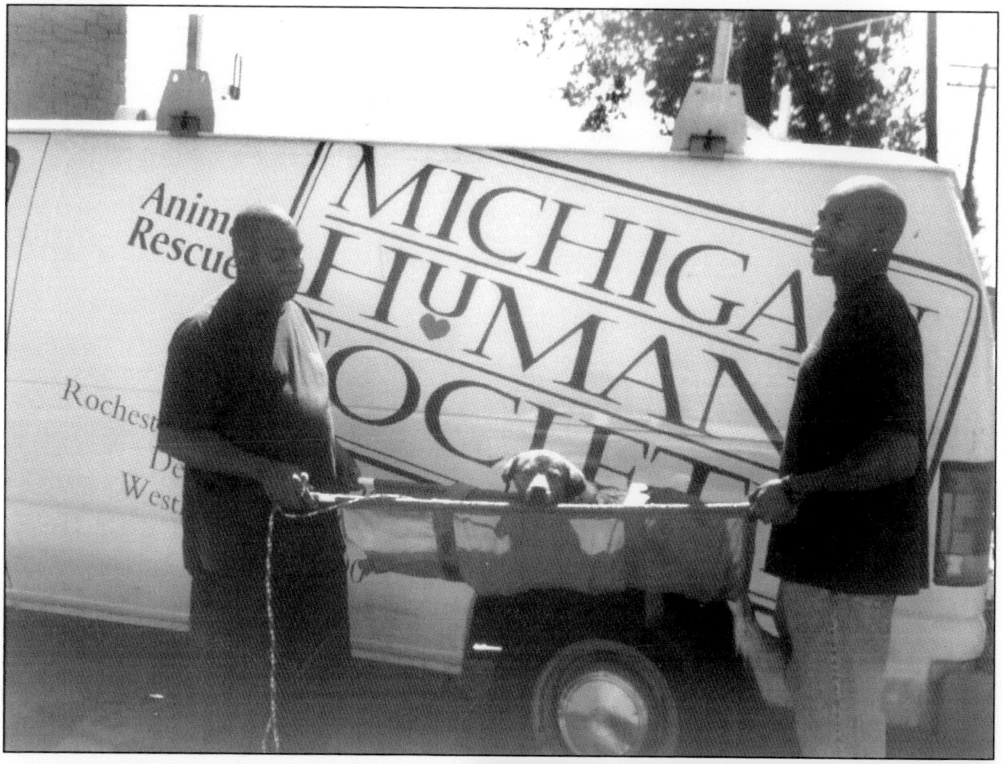

Only the Vehicles Have Changed. The rescue vehicles have certainly changed since the early horse ambulance of the 1900s. Today, the Michigan Humane Society operates a rescue fleet of five vehicles, each equipped with stretchers, like the one seen here, and other emergency response and animal handling equipment. The Michigan Humane Society Rescue Department responds to calls 365 days a year, and in 2001, responded to over 4,800 calls concerning animals in distress.

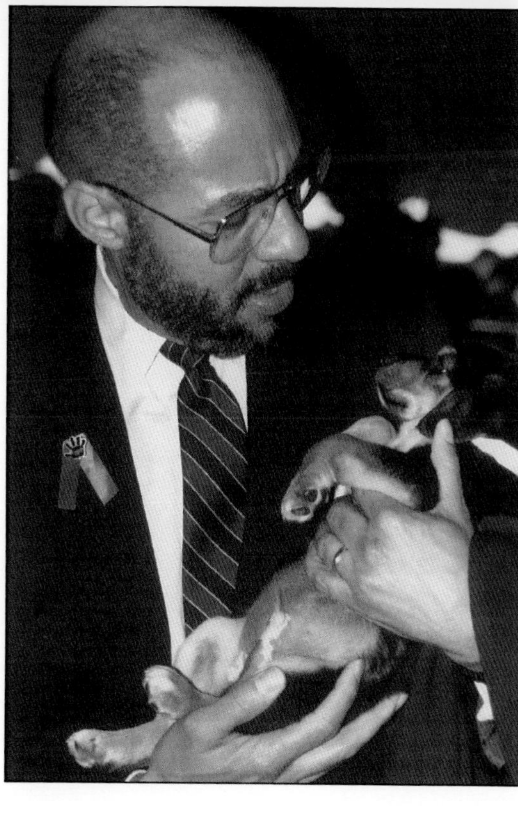

Bundle of Joy. Detroit Mayor Dennis Archer was a supporter of the Michigan Humane Society and attended a number of Society functions including their Bow Wow Brunch and the off-site adoption event, "Meet Your Best Friend at the Zoo." Here, Mayor Archer cuddles a pup at the 1997 Bow Wow Brunch celebration.

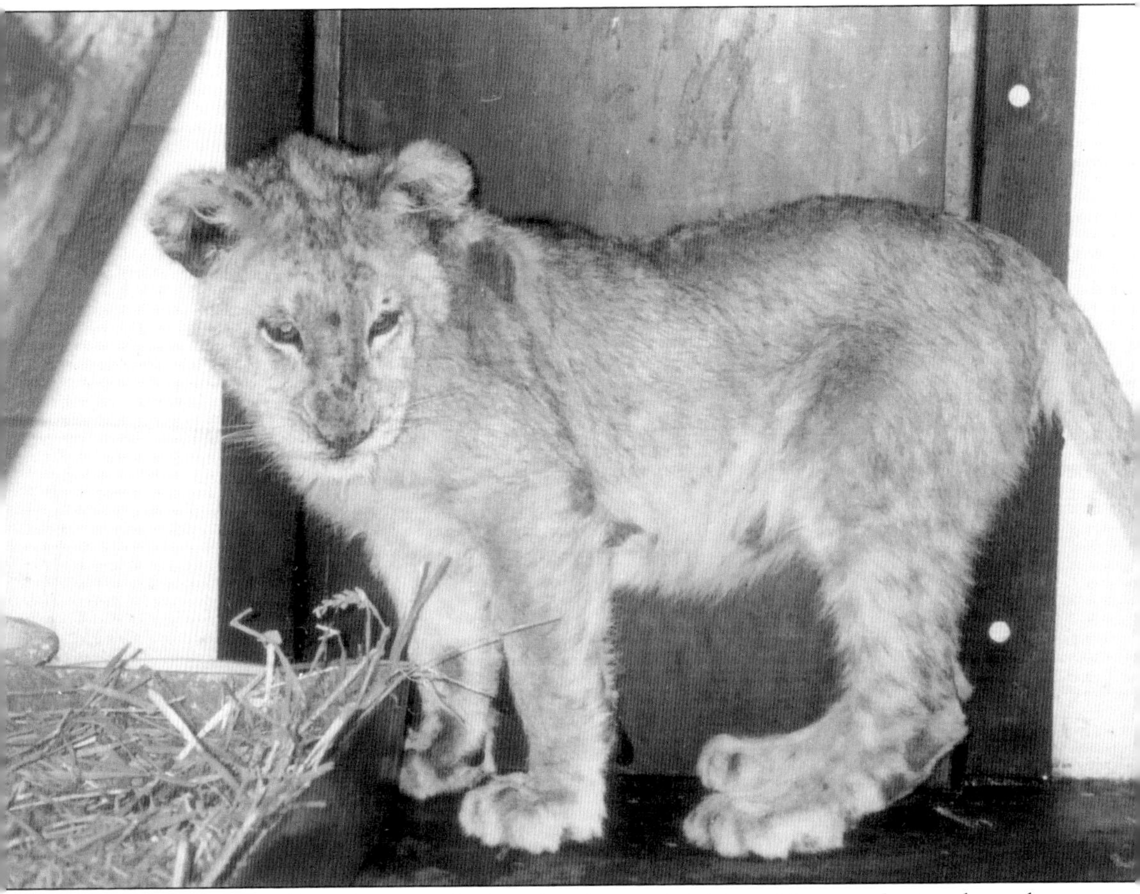

Wild Animals, Not Pets. In the last decade, the Michigan Humane Society has taken in over 35 large cats and countless reptiles from people who either could not provide a suitable environment or figured out that a wild animal is not a pet. Animals such as lions, cougars, tigers, panthers, alligators, and pythons have all found themselves at the Michigan Humane Society after being confiscated by police or turned loose in the city to fend for themselves. The Michigan Humane Society provides temporary shelter for these animals and makes every effort to place them in accredited sanctuaries or zoos. Unfortunately, there are more and more exotic animals ending up in shelters, and space in sanctuaries and zoos is very limited. In 2000, through the efforts of the Michigan Humane Society, it became illegal in Michigan for a private individual to own, possess, sell, or breed large carnivores, such as the big cats.

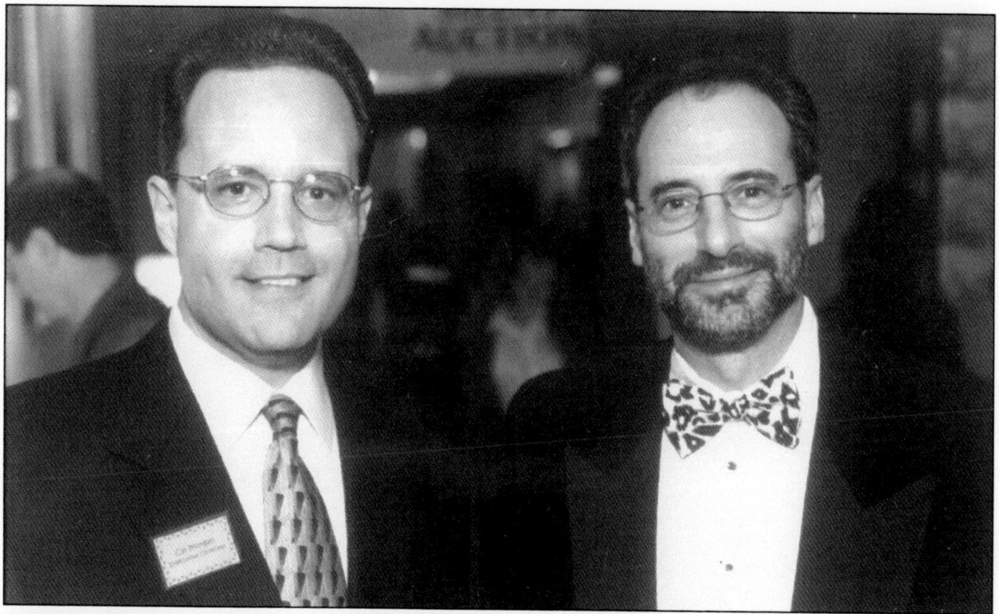

BUILDING RELATIONSHIPS. As the Michigan Humane Society celebrates its 125th Anniversary in 2002 and begins another year of serving the needs of animals, it is driven to nourish old alliances as well as nurture new relationships. Under the leadership of Cal Morgan, pictured at left, with Ron Kagan, Director of the Detroit Zoo, the Michigan Humane Society has ambitious strategic goals on its horizon.

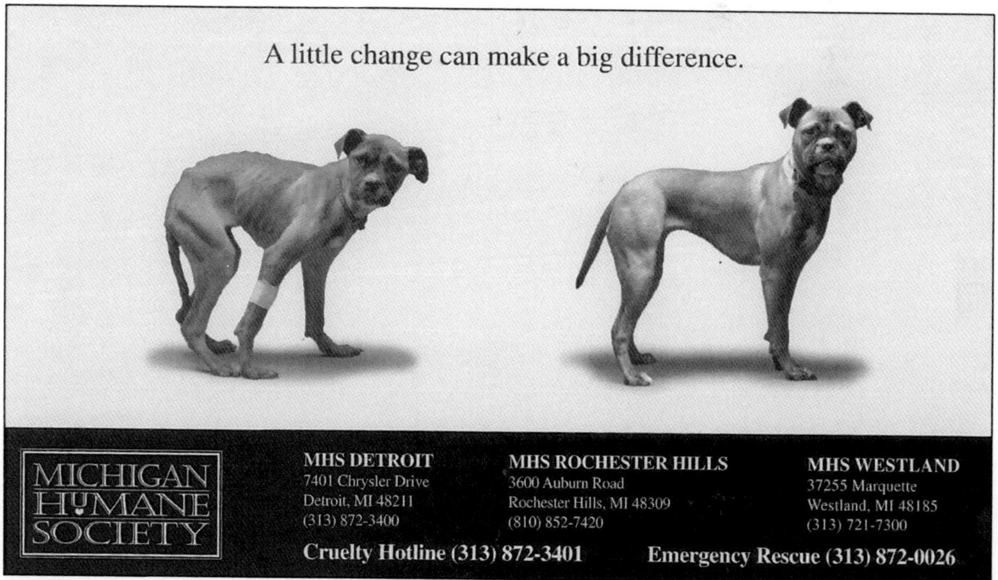

BIG DIFFERENCE. Pebbles, pictured here, became a poster child after she was found by a Michigan Humane Society Cruelty Investigator on a cold November day. She was chained up in her own backyard, emaciated, dehydrated, and suffered from hypothermia. The man that owned Pebbles wanted her enough to pay $300 for her but didn't care enough to feed and shelter her. There are thousands of abused, abandoned, and neglected animals in the city. The Michigan Humane Society works toward the day that no animal will be mistreated.

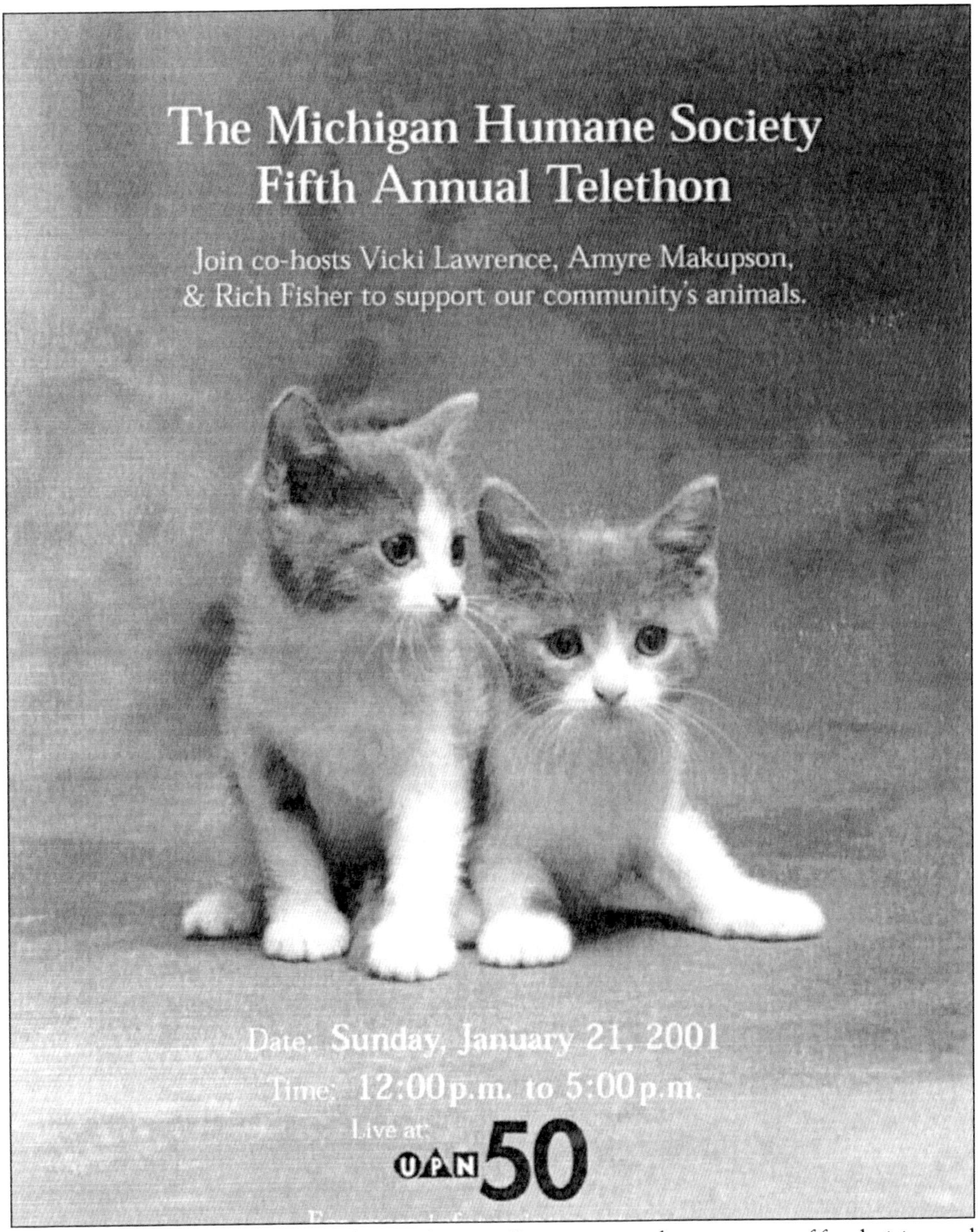

TELETHON TIME! In 1997, the Michigan Humane Society entered a new arena of fundraising and adoption advocacy by hosting a live Telethon. The Telethon is the Society's most prominent fundraising event of the year, as well as an all around entertaining afternoon. Viewers are charmed by the adoptable animals, warmed by the touching happy ending stories, educated by veterinary and pet behavior tips, and thrilled by some special guests. Guests in the past have included Tim Allen and Vicki Lawrence. Local television and radio personalities lend their talents for the live, five-hour show. Thanks to corporate sponsors and thousands of dollars in pledges from dedicated viewers, the Michigan Humane Society Telethon has topped $500,000 for the past two years, making it the most successful pet telethon in the country. The Telethon has also resulted finding new homes for over 400 animals.

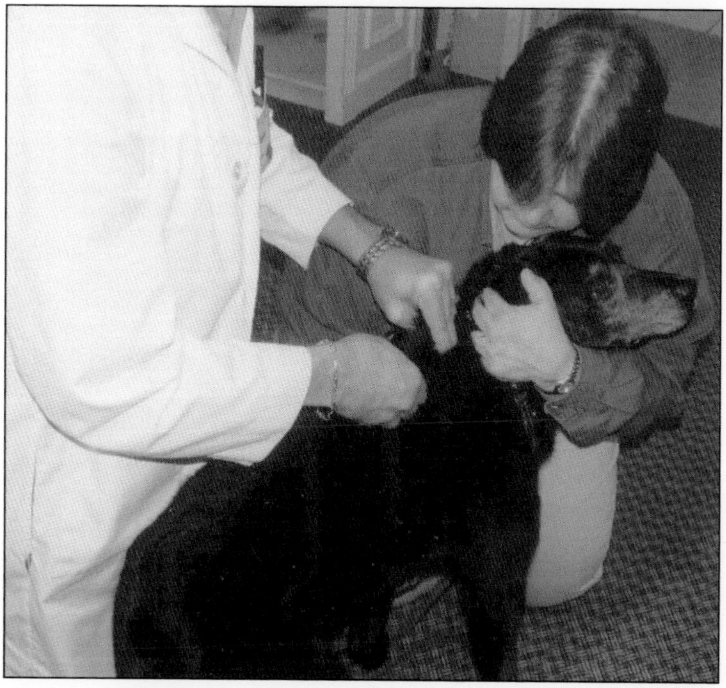

MICROCHIPPING. Estimates indicate over four million pets are lost each year. Most of these animals have no identification. The Michigan Humane Society has long advocated putting an ID tag on your pet. In the Spring of 2001, the Michigan Humane Society began offering microchipping to pet owners, and has since implanted over 2,000 pets with this unalterable form of identification. The chip is no bigger than a grain of rice and the procedure no more painful than a routine vaccination.

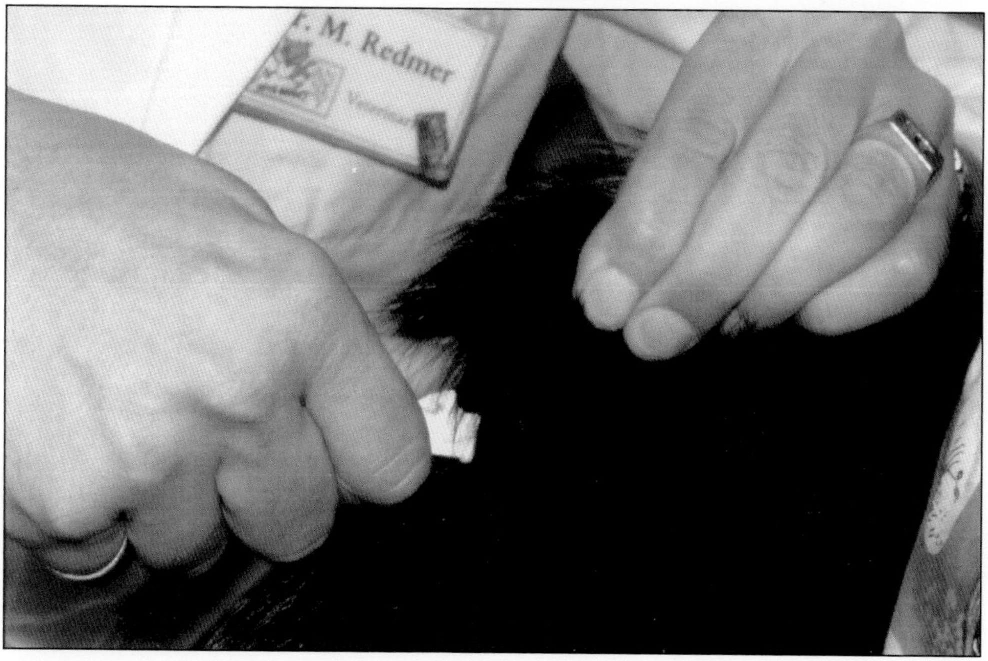

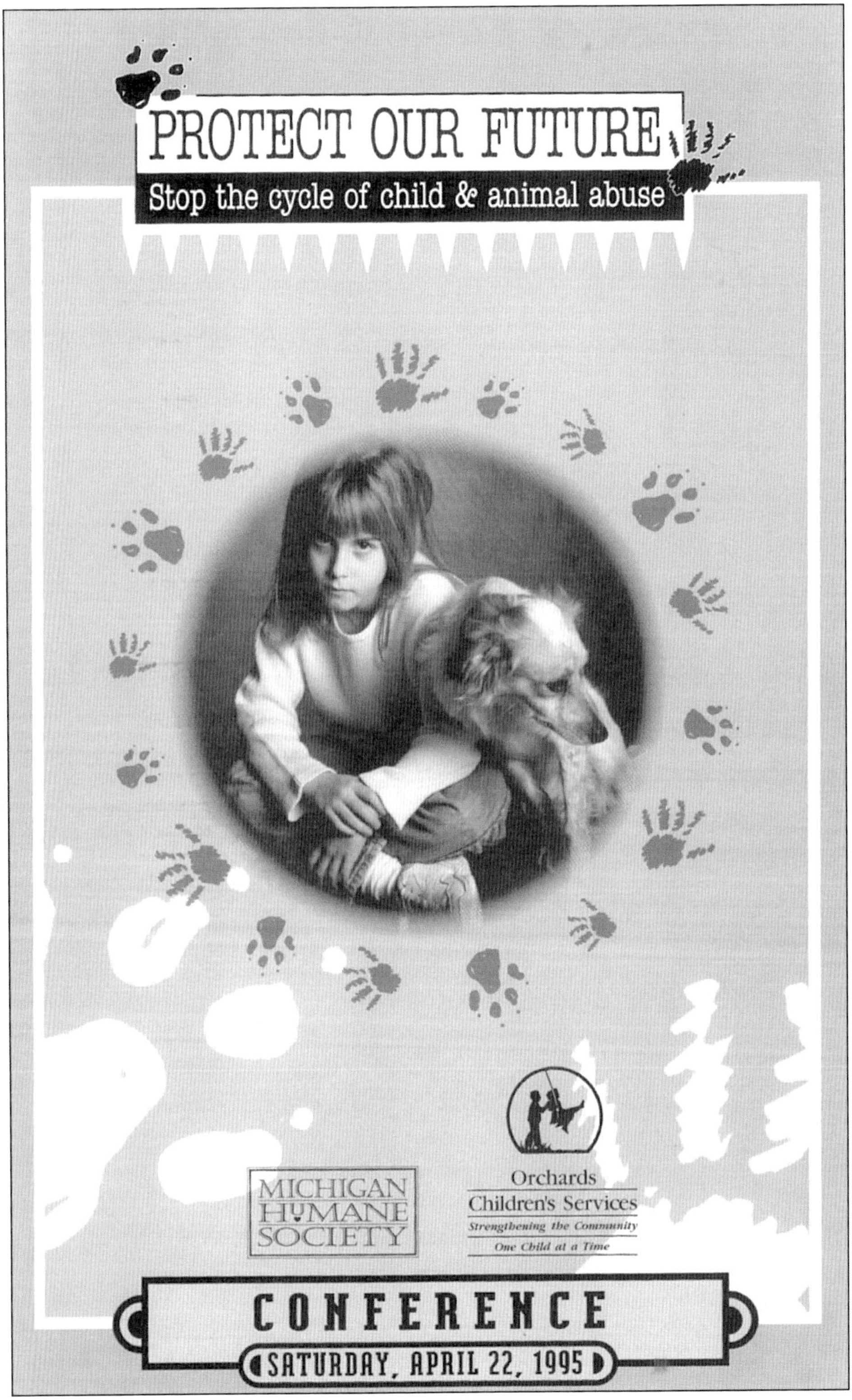
PROTECT OUR FUTURE
Stop the cycle of child & animal abuse
MICHIGAN HUMANE SOCIETY
Orchards
Children's Services
Strengthening the Community
One Child at a Time
CONFERENCE
SATURDAY, APRIL 22, 1995

Working with Other Agencies. A number of government and city agencies have a need for canine assistance. Dogs are used for detection of things such as bombs, illegal drugs, and even illegal agriculture products. The Michigan Humane Society has worked for a number of years with agencies such as U.S. Customs, sheriff's departments, and local police departments in an effort to help place some dogs that pass through our doors. The agency in need of a canine typically provides a short list of characteristics in which they are interested. The Michigan Humane Society shelter staff and managers determine if an animal meets the needs of the agency and places a call to that agency informing them of a possible candidate for placement. In some instances, the officers visit regularly. The Michigan Humane Society is proud to have several dogs that have successfully been placed with federal and local agencies. Carlie, shown here, graduated from the U.S. Customs Canine Enforcement Training Center in Front Royal, Virginia, in 2000.

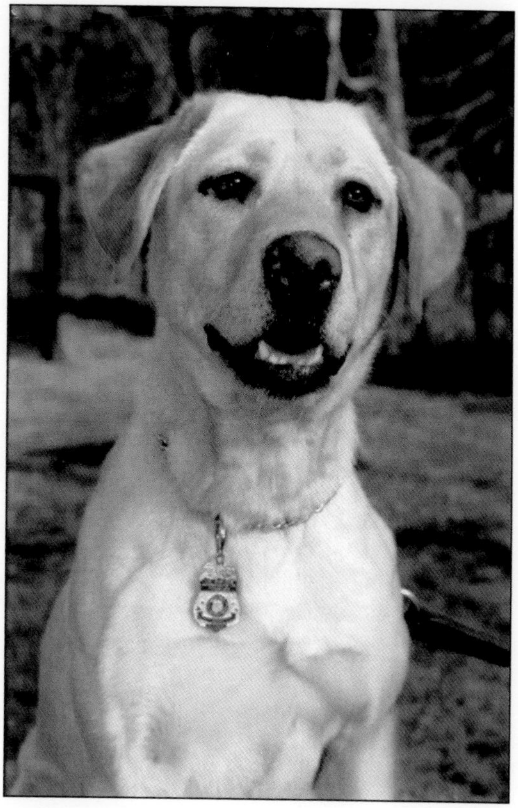

Opposite: **Breaking the Cycle.** Evidence is mounting that children and animals are often the shared victims of abuse and neglect. Victims of domestic violence frequently report abuses to children and/or animals in the home. More often than not, victims of domestic violence refuse to leave their situation if there is also an animal being threatened, because most victims' shelters won't allow animals. In 1995, the Michigan Humane Society co-sponsored an unprecedented conference to explore the link between child abuse and animal abuse that included Michigan's leading children's services organization. The goal of the conference was to inform and create a better understanding among professionals of how cruelty to animals is related to the more general world of human interpersonal violence. Often, children who abuse animals grow up to become adults who abuse humans. Due to the tireless efforts of the Michigan Humane Society, it is now Michigan law that juveniles charged with animal cruelty be given mental evaluation.

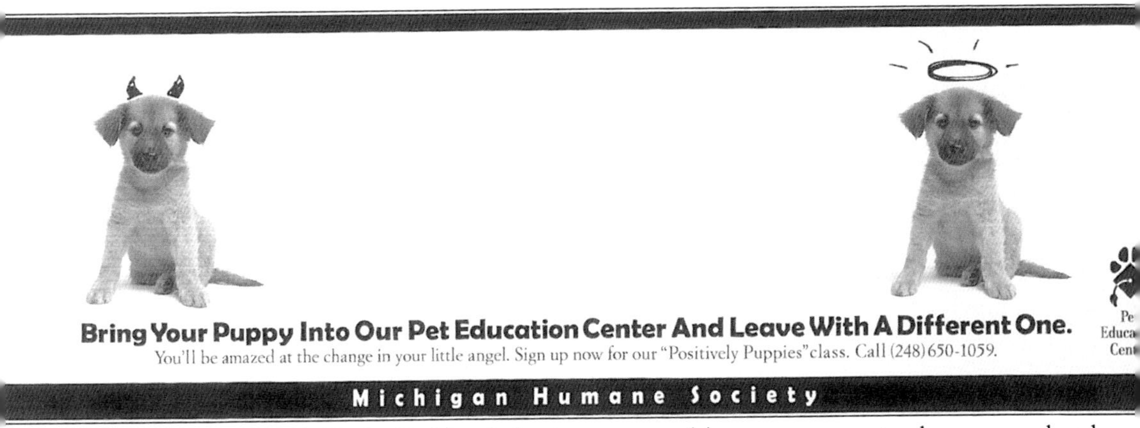

THE DEVIL MADE ME DO IT. Problem behaviors are one of the top reasons animals are surrendered to animal shelters across the country. As early as 1953, the Michigan Humane Society offered obedience classes for pets and their owners in an effort to reduce the number of pets coming to the shelter for behavior problems. The Michigan Humane Society's Pet Education Center, established in 1997, offers a variety of classes, seminars, and individual consultations designed to teach dogs manners, resolve problem behaviors, strengthen the bond between companion and pet, and ultimately ensure a lasting and joyful relationship. Clever advertisements like this one were launched in 1999. Today, the Michigan Humane Society Pet Education Center is an integral part of the Society's operations.

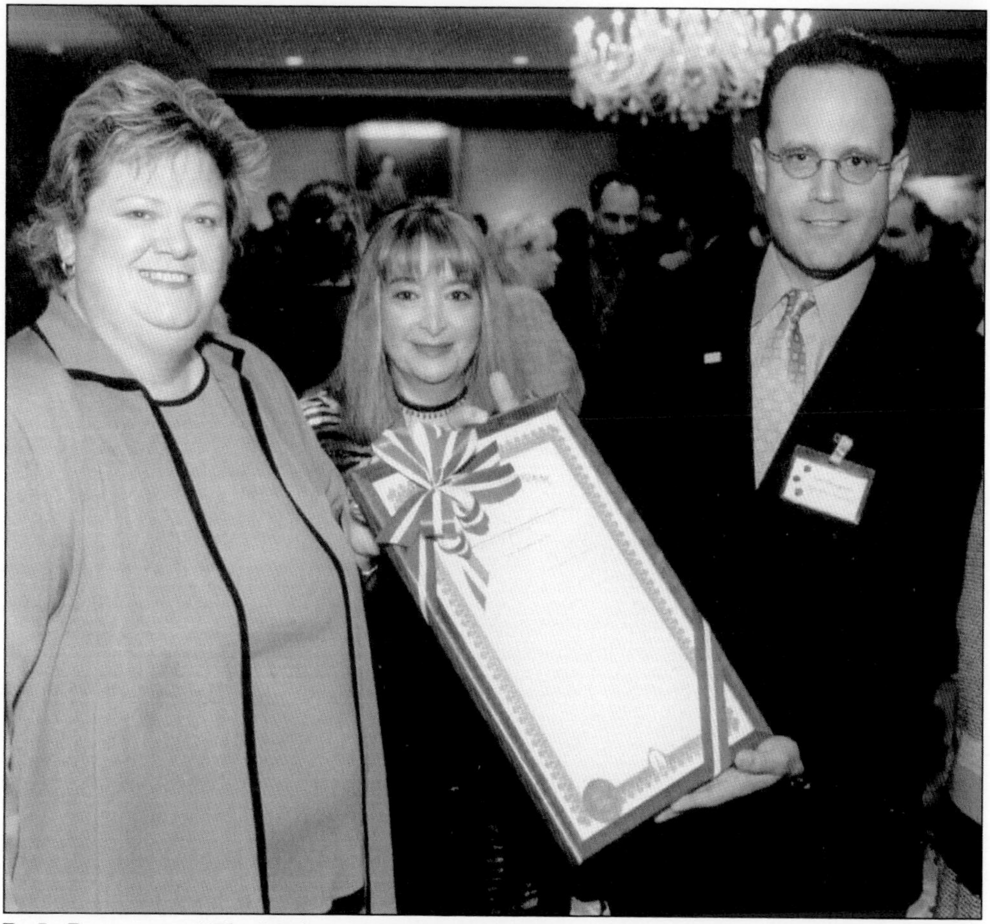

Be It Proclaimed! The Michigan Humane Society enjoys a long history of a strong legislative presence and is proud to speak on behalf of animals. In honor of the 125th Anniversary of the Society, State Representative Laura Toy presents Michigan Humane Society Legislative Advocate Eileen Liska and Michigan Humane Society Executive Director Cal Morgan with House Resolution Number 374, which commemorates the anniversary of the Society and its 125th year of service to animals. The resolution applauds the Michigan Humane Society's efforts to investigate animal cruelty, find homes for thousands of homeless and unwanted animals, provide low-cost or no-cost sterilization surgeries, provide no-cost pet vaccinations, assist injured wildlife through the Wildlife Rehabilitation Center, affect legislation involving animal welfare in the state, and teach humane values for the benefit of all animals.

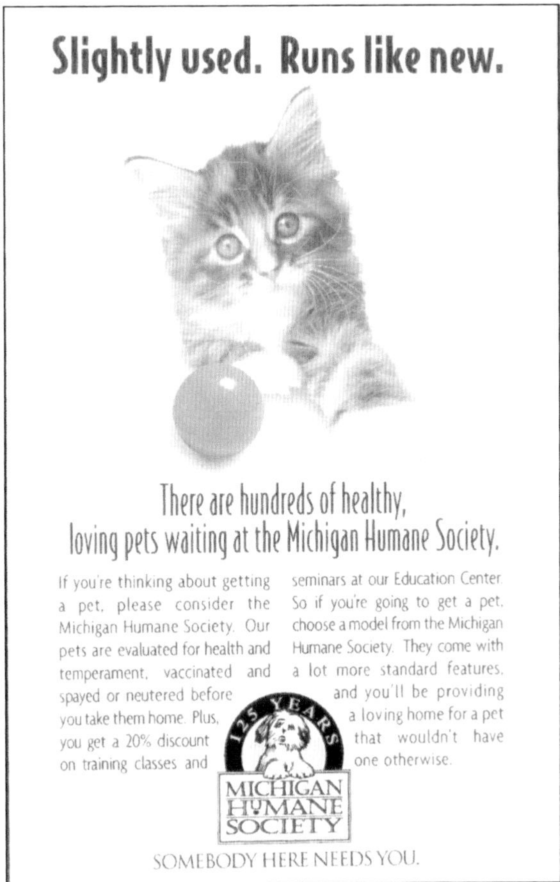

THE COMPLETE PACKAGE. The Michigan Humane Society has been very fortunate through the years and has enjoyed working with a number of agencies to produce award-winning advertisements and educational pieces. The ads seen here were designed by Michael Flora and Associates of Troy, Michigan, and received the distinguished Mobius Award for Public Service Announcement. Moving forward, the Michigan Humane Society strives to end animal suffering and works toward securing a home for every animal.

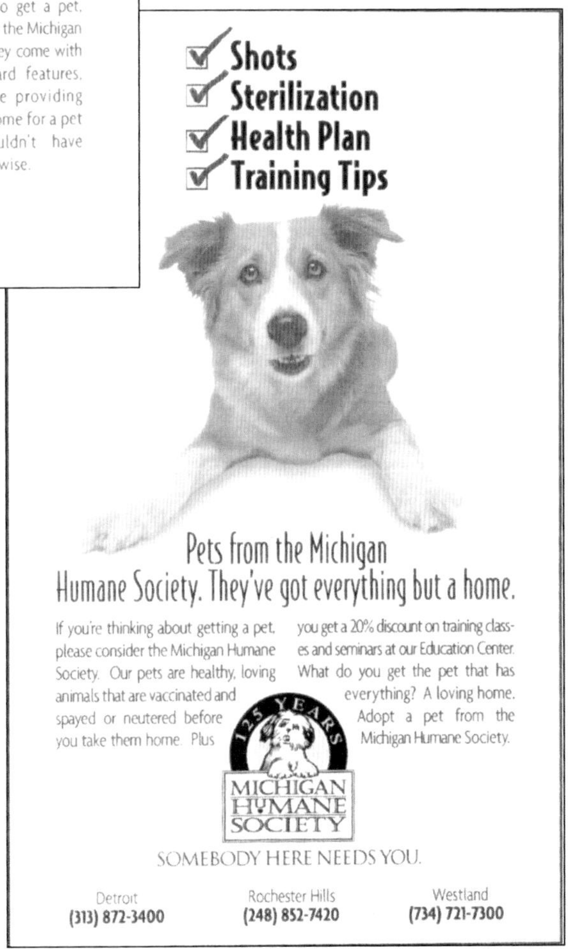